REASON
in BALANCE
the

The Case Against
NATURALISM
in Science,
Law & Education

PHILLIP E. JOHNSON

InterVarsity Press
Downers Grove, Illinois

InterVarsity Press
P.O. Box 1400, Downers Grove, Illinois 60515
World Wide Web: www.ivpress.com
E-mail: mail@ivpress.com

InterVarsity Press® is the book-publishing division of InterVarsity Christian Fellowship/USA®, a student movement active on campus at hundreds of universities, colleges and schools of nursing in the United States of America, and a member movement of the International Fellowship of Evangelical Students. For information about local and regional activities, write Public Relations Dept., InterVarsity Christian Fellowship/USA, 6400 Schroeder Rd., P.O. Box 7895, Madison, WI 53707-7895.

All Scripture quotations, unless otherwise indicated, are from the New Revised Standard Version of the Bible, *copyright 1989 by the Division of Christian Education of the National Council of the Churches of Christ in the U.S.A., and are used by permission.*

The Los Angeles Times *excerpt on pages 222-24 is copyright, 1993,* Los Angeles Times. *Reprinted by permission.*

Published in association with the Literary Agency of Yates and Yates, Orange, CA

ISBN 0-8308-1929-0

Printed in the United States of America ♾

Library of Congress Cataloging-in-Publication Data

Johnson, Phillip E., 1940-
    Reason in the balance: the case against naturalism in science.
    law, and education/Phillip E. Johnson
        p.   cm.
    Includes bibliographical references.
    ISBN 0-8308-1610-0 (cloth: alk. paper)
    ISBN 0-8308-1929-0 (pbk.)
    1. Naturalism—Controversial literature.   2. Apologetics.
3. United States—Religion—1960-   4. United States—Church
history—20th century.   I. Title.
BT1200.J64   1995
239'.7—dc20   95-12620
                                                                                       CIP

19 18 17 16 15 14 13 12 11 10 9 8 7 6 5 4 3 2 1

14 13 12 11 10 09 08 07 06 05 04 03 02 01 00 99 98

Introduction *7*

1 **Is God Unconstitutional?** *19*

2 **The Established Religious Philosophy of America** *35*

3 **The Grand Metaphysical Story of Science** *51*

4 **Is There a Blind Watchmaker?** *71*

5 **Theistic Naturalism & Theistic Realism** *89*

6 **Realism & Rationality** *111*

7 **Natural Law** *133*

8 **Education** *155*

9 **The Subtext of Contempt** *173*

10 **The Beginning of Reason** *193*

Appendix: Naturalism, Methodological & Otherwise *205*

Research Notes *219*

Index *241*

Introduction

Is God the true creator of everything that exists, or is God a product of the human imagination, real only in the minds of those who believe? This book is about how people answer that question, and the consequences of answering it one way or another.

According to public opinion polls, the vast majority of Americans are *theists,* which means they believe (or at least say they believe) that we were created by God, a supernatural being who cares about what we do and has a purpose for our lives which is to be fulfilled in eternity. If God really does exist, then to lead a rational life a person has to take account of God and his purposes. A person or a society that ignores the Creator is ignoring the most important part of reality, and to ignore reality is to be irrational. That is why the Bible says the fear of the Lord is the beginning of wisdom.

The most influential intellectuals in America and around the world are mostly *naturalists,* who assume that God exists only as an idea in the minds of religious believers. In our greatest universities, naturalism—the doctrine that nature is "all there is"—is the virtually unquestioned assumption that underlies not only natural science but intellectual work of all kinds. If naturalism is true, then humankind created God—not the other way around. In that case, rationality requires that we recognize the Creator as the imaginary being he always has been, and that we rely only on things that are real, such as ourselves and the material world of nature. Reliance on the guidance of an imaginary supernatural being is called superstition.

Naturalism in the Academy

The domination of naturalism over intellectual life is not affected by the fact that some religious believers and active churchgoers hold prestigious academic appointments. With very few exceptions, these believers maintain their respectability by tacitly accepting the naturalistic rules that define rationality in the universities. They explicitly or implicitly concede that their theism is a matter of "faith" and agree to leave the realm of "reason" to the agnostics. This is true in every field of study, but especially so in natural science, the discipline that has the authority to describe physical reality for all the others. A biologist may believe in God on Sundays, but he or she had better not bring that belief to the laboratory on Monday with the idea that it has any bearing on the nature or origin of living organisms. For professional purposes, atheistic and theistic biologists alike must assume that nature is all there is.

Natural science is thus based on naturalism. What a science based on naturalism tells us, not surprisingly, is that naturalism is true. Because of the authority of science, the assumption that naturalism is true dominates all the disciplines of the university. As the famous Harvard paleontologist George Gaylord Simpson straightforwardly put it, the "meaning of evolution"—that is to say, the guiding premise of the branch of natural science that studies the history of life—is that "man is the result of a purpose-

less and natural process that did not have him in mind." Douglas
Futuyma, author of a widely used evolutionary biology textbook
for college students, is just as plainspoken: "Some shrink from the
conclusion that the human species was not designed, has no purpose, and is the product of mere mechanical mechanisms—but this
seems to be the message of evolution."

These are not idiosyncratic statements of personal opinion, but
reflections of the orthodox understanding of evolution that is un-
challenged within mainstream science. Given this understanding of
human origins, it is no wonder that the remaining theists in academic life are always on the defensive, concerned more to justify
their own existence than to influence the mainstream academic
world. If the evolutionary scientists are right, then believers in God
are deluded. People who think God is real either do not understand the meaning of evolution or for personal reasons are unwilling to follow the path of scientific understanding to its logical
conclusion in naturalism.

But what if naturalism is not true? In that case, it may be the
scientific naturalists who are deluded, and it may be that our
intellectual culture is based on a false assumption.

Naturalism in Popular Culture
The domination of the intellectual world by naturalism has important consequences for the popular culture, where theism remains
prevalent. The United States is formally a democracy, but on matters involving "religion" the Constitution is supreme, and the
judges have the authority to say what the Constitution means.
Moreover, the voters get their information about what is going on
from the newspapers and television. The judges who make the
legal decisions and the journalists who report the news get their
education at the universities, and they normally interpret events in
the light of what they have been taught. To the extent that they
have learned to take a naturalistic understanding of reality for

granted, they will tend to assume that persons who base their thinking on the premise that God is real are irrational and hence dangerous when they influence public policy.

Suppose that parents in a particular public school district want their children to be exposed to the arguments against the theory of evolution or want their teenagers to be told to save sex for marriage, perhaps because they take their morality from the Bible. Those parents are unlikely ever to get their way. The media will characterize them as religious extremists seeking to impose their (irrational) beliefs and oppressive morality on other people. The educational bureaucracies, backed by the courts, will make sure that "rationality" prevails.

In a sense the people govern, but there are powerful cultural restraints designed to prevent the people from governing "irrationally." Rational beliefs are those that are consonant with reality, and in the intellectual world of today, reality means naturalism.

Because I am myself a theist, and because knowing the true basis of rationality is important to individuals and to the social order, I want to have an open discussion about whether naturalism deserves its dominating status. It is not easy to do this, because the dominant worldview is protected by a defense that usually prevents the discussion from getting started.

The basic defense is to deflect the discussion from the categories of "true" and "false" and into categories that effectively protect naturalism from critical scrutiny. It is said that naturalism is science, whereas theism belongs to religion; naturalism is based on reason, whereas theism is based on faith; and naturalism provides knowledge, whereas theism provides only belief. Science, reason and knowledge easily trump religion, faith and belief.

The Darwinian Question
A second line of defense comes from the specialization of knowledge that is basic to the modern university. In the academic hier-

archy, authority to describe "the way things really are" belongs to natural science, and the history of life belongs to evolutionary biology. This assignment of authority implies that the question of how living organisms came into existence is a matter of specialized knowledge, knowledge that is not available to persons outside the inner circle of science. Ordinary people thus have no alternative but to accept what the experts tell them about such matters, unless they want to be thought ignorant. If the consensus of opinion among evolutionary biologists is that biological evolution produced very complex living organisms by purposeless processes like mutation and selection, then that is an end to the matter. No one has authority to say otherwise.

I challenged this consensus of expert opinion in my previous book, *Darwin on Trial*. There I examined the scientific evidence for the neo-Darwinian theory of evolution, a theory that is routinely promoted as fact in educational institutions, museums, books and television programs. The most important claim of the theory—the one that generates those sweeping statements about humans being the product of purposeless material forces—is that a combination of random genetic changes and natural selection can generate extremely complex organisms from simple beginnings. I argued that this claim is not only unproven but actually contrary to the overwhelming weight of the evidence. Despite all the inflated and oft-repeated claims, science has not shown that biological creation either can or did occur by the Darwinian mechanism, or by any other unintelligent and unguided process.

My book was reviewed widely and sparked a public debate that is still going on. The story of that debate is told in the epilogue chapter of the softcover edition of *Darwin on Trial*. Among the leading defenders of Darwinism who stepped forward as critics were distinguished scientists and philosophers of science like Stephen Weinberg, Stephen Jay Gould, David Hull and Michael Ruse. Professors identified as Christians and "theistic evolutionists" also joined the debate, mostly in defense of the orthodox view of evolution. As the debate progressed, it became clear that very little of the disagreement turned on disputes of fact, and practically everything turned on the proper rules for scientific investigation—"how science works."

Two things about my approach to the subject seemed to baffle, and sometimes infuriate, my critics. First, I insisted on distinguishing naturalism from science, whereas my critics insisted that the two are virtually the same thing. Second, I felt no obligation to offer my own theory about how life was created in the first place, or how complicated things like plants and animals might have evolved from simpler organisms—if indeed they did. My purpose was to show that what is presented to the public as scientific knowledge about evolutionary mechanisms is mostly philosophical speculation and is not even consistent with the evidence once the naturalistic spectacles are removed. If that leaves us without a known mechanism of biological creation, so be it: it is better to admit ignorance than to have confidence in an explanation that is not true. My critics regarded my purpose as perverse, or as reflecting an ignorance of "how science works."

I debated the critics in print and before audiences all over the United States, enjoying the experience immensely. The debate gave me a thorough education in the relationship between naturalism and evolutionary science and in the true cultural importance of the theory of evolution.

Conflicting Creation Stories
Darwinian evolution is not primarily important as a scientific theory but as a culturally dominant creation story. Every culture must have a creation story as a basis for things like philosophy, education and law. If we want to know how we ought to lead our lives and relate to our fellow creatures, the place to begin is with knowledge about how and why we came into existence. When there is

radical disagreement in a commonwealth about the creation story, the stage is set for intense conflict, the kind of conflict that is known as a "culture war."

For many centuries Western civilization in Europe and America was based on a creation story that said we are created by an omnipotent and omniscient being called God, who brought about our existence for a purpose and who is actively concerned with what we do. When a creation story of this kind is generally accepted, it follows that the most important knowledge to have is knowledge of the Creator's purposes, what the Creator has done and plans to do. Knowledge of the workings of material processes like gravity and blood circulation may be valuable, but still more valuable is knowledge about the ultimate values and purposes behind the mechanisms of physics and biology, and these are the values and purposes of the Creator.

In the nineteenth and twentieth centuries, a very different creation story replaced the traditional one, first among the most highly educated elites and gradually in the society as a whole. The new creation story said it is not true that God created us; on the contrary, our ancestors created God out of their prescientific imagination. According to the new story, all living creatures evolved by an unguided, purposeless material process of random genetic change and natural selection.

This naturalistic creation story implies that knowledge of the Creator's mind and purpose is inherently illusory; the true creator—evolution—has no mind or purpose. What is important to us is not why we exist—in any case no knowledge is available about a subject like that—but rather how we can learn to control our physical and social environment in order to increase our safety and happiness. Eventually we may even learn to control evolution itself, through genetic engineering, and thus become the masters of the process that made us in the first place. If and when that happens, evolution will have become for the first time an intelligently directed rather than a mindless process.

Meanwhile, we can learn to improve our lives and our societies by putting aside the illusion that we were created for a purpose and by concentrating on learning how living and nonliving bodies, including those bodies we call humans, actually behave. What we used to call knowledge of God (theology) is only human knowledge, since humans invented God to explain things before they had scientific knowledge. A consequence of the "death of God," which is simply the realization that evolution is our real creator, is the realization that we can obtain knowledge only from science—including not only physics and biology but also the human sciences, such as psychology, anthropology and sociology. Insofar as "theology" has any content, it will turn out to have been borrowed from one of these sciences.

The naturalistic creation story began to take hold in the late eighteenth century, although its main elements date back to ancient times. Naturalism was able to attain cultural dominance, however, only after 1859, when Charles Darwin provided a plausible mechanism of naturalistic creation in his theory of natural selection. Darwin's theory, to quote the words of the contemporary Darwinist Richard Dawkins, "made it possible to be an intellectually fulfilled atheist."

The culturally important element in the Darwinian theory is not the claim that there was some process of ancestral descent in biology, nor is it the claim that biological creation was a gradual and lengthy process rather than the single week described literally in Genesis. Such claims have to do only with the method of creation, not the nature of the creator. The important claim is the one that substitutes a purposeless material process for the Creator. I call that claim the "blind watchmaker" thesis, after the title of a famous book by Dawkins.

The blind watchmaker thesis says that there was no need for a Creator, because the unconscious forces of random mutation and natural selection—with an assist from prebiological chemical evolution to get life started—were capable of creating, and actually did create, all the living creatures that have ever existed. Because this thesis is the most important element in the creation story of modernist culture—a story that is promulgated aggressively in the educational world and the media with the resources of government—it is important to know whether the blind watchmaker thesis is true.

The Blind Watchmaker on Trial

In *Darwin on Trial* I examined the evidence for the blind watchmaker thesis and found it wholly unsatisfactory to persuade an unbiased mind that biological creation occurred in the way Darwinists say it did. That is not to say that all the claims that come under the label "evolution" are false. There is no question that evolution of the Darwinian kind occurs, in the sense that types of living organisms have a certain capacity for variation. This is a process commonly called microevolution, and it accounts for such things as the variant characteristics of plants and animals that have been transported to an isolated island environment. The problem is that there is no evidence for, and very much evidence against, the Darwinian assumption that some similar process of step-by-step gradual change produced the basic body plans of plants and animals in the first place or brought about the existence of complex organs like wings and eyes. Conceivably there was some mysterious process by which later groups grew out of earlier ones, but if so, we know very little about it.

Chapter four of the present book deals briefly with the current situation in evolutionary biology, but readers who want a more complete account of that subject should consult the earlier book. I had to write a book about scientific evidence first, because I had to counter the impression that evolutionary biologists have specialized knowledge that shows the important Darwinian claims to be true. In the last analysis, however, Darwinism is not really based on empirical evidence. Its true basis is in philosophy, and specifically in the metaphysics of naturalism.

Metaphysical Naturalism

Naturalism is the metaphysical position that underlies not only contemporary science but the humanities and the so-called social sciences as well. In chapters one and two of this book, I explain what metaphysical naturalism is and how powerful its implications are for culture in general—even for my own professional subject, the law.

A theory of biological origins that is in a general way like Darwinism follows fairly straightforwardly from the proposition that God is an illusion and nature is therefore all that exists. If nature is all there is, how did complex things like ourselves come into existence? Without a satisfying answer to that question, naturalism is a nonstarter. The most appealing answer is that there was a process of evolution from simple to complex and that there exists a process for generating adaptive complexity that does not require direction from a preexisting intelligence. Darwinian selection is simply the most plausible candidate for that process that has ever been suggested.

Naturalism does not have an answer for the ultimate question of why there is something instead of nothing, but then, theism does not try to answer the agnostic's question: who created God? Creation has to begin with something that is eternal, the uncaused cause of everything that follows. Theists start with God, and scientific naturalists start with matter (perhaps virtual particles emerging from a quantum fluctuation in a vacuum) and impersonal natural laws. From the ultimate beginning to the emergence of human consciousness, according to naturalistic science, purposeless natural forces of the kind already known to our science were capable of doing, and actually did do, all the work of creating formerly credited to God. This account is what I call the "grand metaphysical story of science," in which Darwinian evolution is the most important element, and it is the subject of chapters three and four.

The grand metaphysical story is the product of an epistemology—a way of knowing—called methodological naturalism. The consequences of methodological naturalism are poorly understood. Chapter five explains what this methodology is and why it is inconsistent with a meaningful theism in religion. Chapter six illustrates through the example of two prominent philosophers, John Searle and Richard Rorty, how naturalistic metaphysics leads inexorably to relativism in ethics and politics, even though many naturalists dislike relativism and try hard to avoid it.

Chapter seven returns to my own professional territory and explains how the concept of natural law takes on a new meaning in the light of naturalistic metaphysics. Chapter eight explores the consequences of naturalism for education, and chapter nine describes the changing meaning of "tolerance" in a naturalistic culture. The concluding chapter sets out the crucial choice that Christian theists have to make in consequence of the domination of the culture by naturalism.

I begin with a true story about the law of religious and intellectual freedom.

1

Is God
Unconstitutional?

N EW YORK STATE LAW ALLOWS PUBLIC SCHOOL DISTRICTS
to make their buildings generally available after school
hours for rental to community groups for "social, civic and
recreational" uses. A state court held that this broad authoriza-
tion was not broad enough to include "religious" purposes, and
so student Bible clubs and churches were not allowed to rent
rooms. A major constitutional controversy over the exclusion of
religious groups erupted when the evangelical minister of "Lamb's
Chapel" in a town called Center Moriches applied to use a school
auditorium to show a six-part film series. The series featured lectures by Dr. James Dobson, a Christian writer and speaker whose
Focus on the Family radio broadcasts attract an enormous audience.

The Dobson lectures dealt with parent-child relationships from
a conservative Christian viewpoint. Dobson urged parents to "turn
their hearts toward home" and give priority to their families dur-

ing child-rearing years. Warning that the family is "under fire" in a "civil war of values," he opposed abortion and pornography and concluded with a defense of "traditional values which, if properly employed and defended, can assure happy, healthy, strengthened homes and family relationships in the years to come." One of the lectures was by his wife, Shirley Dobson; she spoke of a difficult childhood with an alcoholic father and recalled "the influences which brought her to a loving God who saw her personal circumstances and heard her cries for help."

The school district, backed by the state attorney general, refused to permit its facilities to be used for showing the films. The minister then brought a lawsuit challenging the refusal as unconstitutional. Whether the minister had a case depended on how one categorized the film series. The district had no obligation to make its facilities available to outsiders, and if it did choose to do so it could place reasonable limitations on the kinds of uses that would be permitted. For example, the district had refused the same minister's request to hold church services on Sunday in a school building, and the legality of this refusal was not challenged.

On the other hand, Supreme Court decisions interpreting the First Amendment have imposed a ban on what lawyers call "viewpoint discrimination." This means that if the district allowed speakers to address a particular subject on school property at all, it could not discriminate in favor of some opinions and against others. If political meetings were permitted, the Socialists as well as the Republicans must be allowed to meet, and if religious services were allowed, the Buddhists as well as the Catholics would have to be welcome.

But in New York the state's policy was to ban religious activities from school property altogether. Therefore, the state argued, the Dobson film series was excluded not because its viewpoint was disfavored but because it did not fit within the categories for which use of school facilities was authorized. The federal trial court that heard the minister's lawsuit accepted this reasoning and upheld the state's position, and the court of appeals affirmed its decision.

When the case got to the United States Supreme Court, however, things went very differently. The state's legal rationale collapsed if the appropriate category for the film series was not religion, but rather family values and relationships. Not only was this latter subject legitimate for groups renting rooms after school hours; it is part of the regular school curriculum as well. Looked at that way, by excluding the films the state was discriminating against a religious viewpoint on a secular subject and thus allowing only one side of a controversial question to be presented.

And that is just the way the Supreme Court did look at it. In the words of the opinion by Justice Byron White for a unanimous court, there was no suggestion "that a lecture or film about child-rearing and family values would not be a use for social or civic purposes" as permitted by the state's rules. Denying permission to show the Dobson films on that subject for no reason "other than the fact that the presentation would have been from a religious perspective" therefore violated the constitutional principle that the government may not deny a speaker access to a public forum "solely to suppress the point of view he espouses."

The Marginalization of Religion

The *Lamb's Chapel* case illustrates how classifying a viewpoint or theory as "religious" may have the effect of *marginalizing* it. A viewpoint or theory is marginalized when, without being refuted, it is categorized in such a way that it can be excluded from serious consideration. The technique of marginalizing a viewpoint by labeling it "religion" is particularly effective in late-twentieth-century America, because there is a general impression, reinforced by Supreme Court decisions, that religion does not belong in public institutions.

Supposedly this exclusion of religion reflects a national policy of religious neutrality, but it is anything but neutral when it is employed to protect important ideas and public policies from effective criticism. The subject of family values and sexual behavior provides a powerful illustration of this point.

James Dobson's views about family values have deep roots in our religious tradition and great current public support, but they are also extremely controversial. The values he upholds center on a man and a woman who marry for life and who play distinct paternal and maternal roles. In this value system, abortion is equivalent to homicide, and sexual activity outside of marriage is a manifestation of sin. Dobson would not teach adolescents to use condoms while having sexual intercourse, because he places higher priority on teaching them to wait for adulthood and marriage before having sex at all.

Public education in states like New York tends to take a more relativistic approach to sexual morality. In what I will call the "progressive" (as opposed to the traditional) viewpoint about family life and sexual behavior, the family itself may be redefined to include any persons who live together in a sexual relationship, whether or not they are legally married. From the progressive standpoint, to advocate heterosexual marriage as morally superior to homosexual relationships, or premarital chastity as morally superior to sexual experimentation, is itself a form of viewpoint discrimination. Moreover, progressives think it irrational to spend much effort trying to get adolescents to refrain from sexual intercourse altogether, because the sexual urge is deemed to be irresistible. Progressive sex education may make favorable reference to abstinence in passing, but its main emphasis is on teaching young people to practice "safe sex," by means of explicit instruction and even hands-on practice in rolling condoms onto cucumbers.

To traditionalists, this instruction seems to be a positive encouragement to promiscuous sex, and about as rational as pouring gasoline on a raging fire. Bitter political battles have erupted, in

New York and elsewhere, between the progressives and the traditionalists.

To progressives, the Dobson approach to family values is likely to seem outdated, intolerant and aimed at undoing everything that progressive sex education aims to accomplish. Progressive educators do not deny that religiously motivated dissenters, however irrational, have a right to freedom of speech. It does not follow, however, that the state should appear to give approval to such opinions by giving them a place in the public schools. For progressives the main point, of course, is to keep extremist influences out of the school curriculum itself, but even renting a school auditorium after hours might seem like a symbolic endorsement of a viewpoint that the schools are trying to delegitimate.

The school district tried to hint at this consideration to the Supreme Court, at the cost of undermining its own denial that it was engaging in viewpoint discrimination. If religious use of school property were permitted at all, said the district's brief, the school might have to grant access to a "radical" church that meant to "proselytize," and this could lead in turn to "a volatile and destructive situation." A friend-of-the-court brief by educational organizations supporting the district's position spelled the point out more clearly: if the principle of viewpoint neutrality were applied to this situation, "the use of school facilities would have to be made available even to groups which, for example, preach racial intolerance in contravention of the educational mission of our public school system to teach pluralism and mutual respect for all people."

Was the district then denying that it was engaging in viewpoint discrimination, or was it justifying the practice of discriminating against religious viewpoints by classifying them as extremist or irrational, like the viewpoint of the Ku Klux Klan on racial issues? The state attorney general of New York, supporting the school board, embraced the latter option. The purpose of making school facilities available to the public, he argued to the Supreme Court, was to serve the interests of the public in general rather than private or sectarian interests. Ordinarily freedom of expression is thought to serve the public interest by allowing the citizenry to hear a variety of viewpoints and thus become better informed. That is not the case when a religious position is advocated, said the attorney general, because "religious advocacy . . . serves the community only in the eyes of its adherents and yields a benefit only to those who already believe."

This sweeping dismissal of the value of religious speech was all the more remarkable in that it was made in reference to a movie series directed at ordinary parents, urging them to devote their primary attention to their family relationships during the critical years when their children are growing up. Why would such a message yield no benefit to non-Christians?

For that matter, suppose the film series made a straightforward effort to convert unbelievers to the Christian faith, or to some other faith. Why would that message yield a benefit only to those who already believe, if it was specifically addressed to unbelievers who chose to attend? The implicit message of the New York attorney general's argument seemed to be that religious advocacy is valueless because it is irrational, and therefore persons outside the community of faith will not, or at least should not, take it seriously.

Creation and Evolution
The attempt to marginalize religious advocacy, or traditional family morality, failed spectacularly in this instance in the Supreme Court, although it had been successful in the courts below the highest level. The New York attorney general might well have expected a more favorable reception for his argument, however, because essentially the same line of reasoning had succeeded brilliantly in the Supreme Court a few years previously.

In its 1987 decision in *Edwards* v. *Aguillard,* the Supreme Court addressed the constitutionality of a Louisiana statute that required that when "evolution-science" was taught in the public schools, balanced treatment had to be given to the rival theory of "creation-science." With two justices dissenting, the majority opinion by Justice William Brennan held that the state law was an unconstitutional "establishment of religion," because the legislature's purpose "was clearly to advance the religious viewpoint that a supernatural being created mankind."

The issue decided in *Edwards* is clouded by the fact that the term *creationism* in newspaper and textbook usage refers to Genesis literalism and hence to the belief that the earth is no more than a few thousand years old. The Supreme Court opinion, however, addressed a much broader question than the age of the earth or the validity of the Genesis account. What Justice Brennan described as a "religious viewpoint" is the very broad proposition that a purposeful supernatural being—God—is responsible for our existence. The leading alternative to that belief is that purposeless material processes created us and that purpose and consciousness did not exist in the cosmos until they evolved naturalistically. This second viewpoint is incorporated in the scientific definition of evolution, because in contemporary usage "science" is thought to be based on a completely naturalistic understanding of reality.

To clarify the essential point, suppose the basic claim of "creationism" is that God created us, whether he did so suddenly a few thousand years ago or gradually over a much longer period of time. Suppose further that creationists claim that certain features of living organisms, such as the extreme complexity of even the simplest living organisms, give support to their claim that a preexisting intelligence was necessary for biological creation. If the Supreme Court in the *Edwards* case in 1987 had employed the same reasoning as in the 1993 *Lamb's Chapel* decision, its opinion might have said that the subject in question was not religion but human or biological origins, and that it would be unconstitutional viewpoint discrimination to exclude creationist opinion from discussion of a secular subject already included in the public educational forum.

Instead the majority opinion in *Edwards* said that the state was not only permitted to exclude the creationist viewpoint but was *required* to do so—and not because belief in a supernatural Creator is necessarily false or irrational, but precisely because it is religious. The logic implies that creationist arguments must be excluded regardless of their merits and that students may hear only the naturalistic viewpoint on the subject of origins. The creationist viewpoint was thoroughly marginalized by being confined within the category of religion.

The strategy of marginalizing "religion" succeeded in *Edwards* but failed in *Lamb's Chapel,* probably because neither the Supreme Court nor the legal community in general understood that the two cases were profoundly similar, although apparently quite different. One difference was that *Lamb's Chapel* involved the use of a school building by a community group after hours, whereas *Edwards* concerned the teaching of a theistic viewpoint in the school curriculum itself. The distinction is superficial, because the same issue of classification is critical to both situations. Put most simply, the underlying philosophical question in both *Lamb's Chapel* and *Edwards* was whether the authorities were dealing with separate subjects or with conflicting opinions about the same subject. If a high-school curriculum incorporates the subject of biological origins, and if supernatural creation is a rational alternative to naturalistic evolution within that subject, then it is bad educational policy as well as viewpoint discrimination to try to keep students ignorant of an alternative that may be true.

Of course, this reasoning does not apply if the excluded alternative is irrational or demonstrably false. We do not give the views of the Flat Earth Society a respectful hearing in geography classes, and we do not give favorable recognition in arithmetic class to the dissenting opinion that two plus two equals five. The real argument in the Louisiana creationism case, which was pressed upon the Supreme Court with great urgency by the National Academy of Sciences, was that the creationist position is irrational, the equivalent in biology of the flat-earth position in geography.

This argument was endorsed not only by all the major scientific and educational organizations and by the leading civil liberties organizations, but also by many mainstream religious groups. The extreme isolation of the creationist groups supporting the balanced-treatment legislation both reflected and furthered the public's impression that what was at stake was not the general concept of creation by God but an effort by fundamentalist extremists to import all the details of the literal Genesis account into the science curriculum.

The legal problem for the opponents of creationism was how to translate the National Academy of Science's argument into an acceptable proposition of constitutional law. The Supreme Court has no obvious authority to decide that belief in the existence of a supernatural Creator is irrational, or even that belief in the literal Genesis account is irrational. What it does have is authority to interpret the religion clauses of the First Amendment—and thus to decide that this belief is religious. In context, *religious* was implicitly a synonym for *irrational*—which is to say that the Brennan opinion in *Edwards* essentially adopted the reasoning that was later unsuccessfully advanced by the New York attorney general in *Lamb's Chapel.* Discussions about how the evidence of biology might support a creationist viewpoint were characterized as equivalent to the minutes of the Flat Earth Society or perhaps of the Ku Klux Klan. Such nonsense might appeal to those who already believe, but it has no conceivable educational value.

I am not saying that the courts cannot draw a distinction between what may be said in the classroom during school hours and what may be said in public meetings after school hours. The courts might apply the "two subjects" approach to religious speech in the regular school curriculum and the "two opinions about the same subject" approach when schoolrooms are rented to community groups in the evening or on weekends. In fact, I expect the courts probably will do something of that kind, at least for a while, in the wake of the *Lamb's Chapel* decision. For one thing, the Supreme Court's opinion in *Lamb's Chapel* itself may have implied the legitimacy of such a distinction by observing that the showing of the Dobson films by an outside group after school hours would not imply endorsement of its message by the school district. Perhaps such endorsement would be implied if a teacher showed the film in a family life class, even in combination with other materials supporting the progressive viewpoint, and in that case the long-standing prohibition against using the classroom to "further religion" would come into play.

No doubt the courts can draw a line around the classroom and order religious speakers to stay outside the line. The problem with doing this, however, is that such a line becomes difficult to defend once its rationale has been undermined. Religious groups have largely accepted the exclusion of religious speech from public schools on the basis of the official explanation that the constitutional policy reflects a genuine neutrality on religious matters rather than a hostility toward theistic religion. But that explanation is wearing thin. Excluding religious opinion from the schools was one thing when the schools taught mainly the "three R's" and when the moral principles taught or practiced in the classroom were at least in a general way consistent with those taught at home and in the churches and synagogues. A superficially similar policy has quite a different effect when the schools are actively promoting the progressive viewpoint on sexual behavior to students from traditionalist homes and actively promoting a naturalistic understanding of creation in science classes.

Under current conditions, excluding theistic opinions means giving a monopoly to naturalistic opinions on subjects like whether humans were created by God and whether sexual intercourse should be reserved for marriage. As the *Lamb's Chapel* litigation itself indicates, religious traditionalists are learning to see the exclusion of religion not as religious neutrality, but as a partisan maneuver by educators who want to promote an ideological agenda without opposition. If they pursue their protest vigorously, the courts will not long be comfortable with a formula that claims to be neutral but patently serves the interests of one side to a major cultural controversy.

The Dean Kenyon Case

That it may be difficult to justify continuing to exclude theistic opinions from the regular classroom was illustrated by a case that did not go to court but was settled in the academic government of San Francisco State University. Dean Kenyon is a distinguished senior biology professor at that institution and coauthor of a standard work on the origin of life on earth, *Biochemical Predestination*. Although his book reflected the orthodox naturalism of the contemporary scientific community, Kenyon eventually became disenchanted with efforts to explain life as a product of purposeless and unguided chemical evolution. He became a proponent of "intelligent design" as an explanation for life's inherent complexity, which is to say he argued, without necessarily endorsing a literal reading of the Genesis account, that a preexisting supernatural intelligence probably had to have been involved in some way.

When Kenyon taught the prevailing naturalistic theories of biological and chemical evolution in his large introductory biology course for nonmajors, he also explained his own skepticism about whether these theories are consistent with the evidence and argued that intelligent design is a legitimate alternative to naturalistic evolution. A handful of students complained, and the department chairman immediately endorsed their complaints. He announced that he would not allow Kenyon to teach this course in the future, on the ground that the professor was improperly introducing his "religious opinions" into the science curriculum.

Kenyon complained to the faculty senate's Academic Freedom Committee, arguing that he was merely exercising the right of a professor to question orthodox opinion in the subject of his expertise, which is exactly what academic freedom exists to protect. The committee agreed with Kenyon, despite vigorous arguments from the department chairman and the dean of the School of Science that intelligent design is inherently in the category of religion and not science. When the faculty senate voted overwhelmingly to support the committee, the administrators backed down and reluctantly reinstated Kenyon in his course, at least for the time being.

The outcome turned on how one categorized what Professor Kenyon was doing. Academic freedom does not permit a professor to neglect a subject he is assigned to teach and present a different subject instead. It does, however, permit him to express a dissenting opinion about the assigned subject, even if it is an opinion that his colleagues and the academic administrators regard as irrational. Like the Dobson film series, Kenyon's advocacy of intelligent design was an opinion about a subject already being discussed in the secular public forum, not the introduction of a new and different subject.

Science and Morality

There is a second superficial difference between the *Lamb's Chapel* and *Edwards* cases, pertaining to the subject matter. At one level, the Dobson film series was about family morality and the Louisiana creationism statute was about science education. The slogan of science educators these days is "Evolution is a fact," and on that basis creationists are often defined as persons who deny scientifically established facts. In our culture, however, morality is typically considered to be a matter not of fact but of value. In disputes about facts, one side must be in principle right and the other wrong, but in disputes over value, both sides may be equally right. That Mount Everest is taller than Pike's Peak is an objective fact; whether it is more beautiful is a subjective question of value.

Some contemporary thinkers would place both religion and morality in the category of subjective value, as distinguished from objective scientific knowledge. This was the position taken by the famous evolutionary biologist Stephen Jay Gould, for example, when he reviewed my book *Darwin on Trial*. Science and religion are separate realms of equal dignity and importance, wrote Gould, "because science treats factual reality, while religion struggles with human morality." If we were to accept that division of things, then religious leaders (but which ones?) should have roughly the same authority in the moral realm that Gould and his scientific colleagues have over the realm of factual reality. In that case, the argument for allowing religion to participate in the morals curriculum, or even to dominate it, would be very strong—and so would the argument for excluding religion from the science curriculum.

This distinction is superficial, however, because the validity of religious morality is inextricably linked to the validity of the factual propositions that support it. If God really did create us "male and female," and intended male and female to play different roles in the family, and intended sexual intercourse to be confined to the marital relationship, then the system of traditional family morality makes sense. In that case the new sexual morality taught in the progressive curriculum is inconsistent with reality and likely to end in frustration and misery.

But if God is merely a projection of human desires—or worse, a concept invented by patriarchal authorities to rationalize their oppressive rule—then the death of God is like being released from a prison. All the rules promulgated in the name of the illusion that deprived us of our freedom lose their authority when the illusion is exposed. Some elements of the prison moral code might be retained in the new situation: a ban on polygamy, for example, might be kept as a protection for gender equality. But the outlook on family morality as a whole rightly becomes entirely different once the death of God becomes fully assimilated as knowledge.

The rationality of any moral code, in other words, is linked to a picture of reality that contains both fact and value elements. That picture of reality can probably best be expressed in the form of a story. The Christian story is one of human beings who are created by God, but who are separated from God by their own sin and must be saved from that sin to become what they were meant to be. The Enlightenment rationalist story is one of human beings who escape from superstition by mastering scientific knowledge and eventually realize that their ancestors created God rather than the other way around. Currently some women have been telling a naturalistic story of gender oppression by patriarchal males throughout history, rationalized through religious and scientific mythology, and of consciousness raising that permits women to see through the myths and assert their natural equality.

I mentioned earlier that Shirley Dobson spoke in one of the Dobson films of her difficult childhood with an alcoholic father and recalled "the influences which brought her to a loving God who saw her personal circumstances and heard her cries for help." Her personal story makes perfect sense if the Christian story about reality in general is true. But if the Enlightenment story is true, a loving God is no more than a product of her imagination; and if the radical feminist story is true, it was probably a product of patriarchal tradition that was forced upon her.

In a sense the New York attorney general was right: Christian family morality looks like oppressive nonsense if you take for granted that Christian metaphysics has been shown to be false. Since the Supreme Court had implicitly agreed in the *Edwards* opinion that supernatural creation is an inherently irrational concept, why should it require a public school system, dedicated to the promotion of rationality and democratic freedom, to make room in its buildings for the promotion of irrationality and oppression?

It is apparent from legal cases that the dominant judicial philosophy of late-twentieth-century America views theism, particularly traditional Christian theism, with considerable ambivalence. On the one hand, naturalistic thinking rules the intellectual world, including the National Academy of Sciences, the public schools, the universities and the elite of the legal profession. On the other hand, it would be unthinkable for the Supreme Court or any other official body to declare explicitly that "a supernatural being did *not* create humankind." An official posture of religious neutrality is essential not only because atheists and agnostics are outnumbered by theists but also because our constitutional order is genuinely committed to freedom of religion and of religious expression. Yet what cannot be done explicitly can often be done implicitly, by the imposition of categories and definitions that are anything but neutral in their impact.

The courts may express tolerance and even respect for "religion," but this does not necessarily mean that they take the existence of God as anything but a comforting fantasy. If the courts contrast "religious belief" in God with "scientific knowledge" of naturalistic evolution, they imply that the former is a subjective feeling and the latter is an objective fact. Even people who believe in God tend to accept these categories, because the surrounding culture teaches them to do so, and when they accept the categories of naturalistic metaphysics they admit naturalistic thinking into their own minds.

The decisive question for First Amendment religious law, then, is one of metaphysics rather than legal doctrine. Is the Constitution genuinely neutral between scientific naturalism and theism? In that case both positions should be admitted to public discussion, in the schools and elsewhere, and protected from "viewpoint discrimination." Or is naturalism the established constitutional philosophy? In that case naturalism will have a monopoly in the public arena, while theistic dissent will be restricted to private life. If the latter alternative is taken, then the Supreme Court will in effect have established a national religion in the name of First Amendment freedoms.

2

The Established
Religious
Philosophy
of America

T HE UNITED STATES OF AMERICA DOES NOT HAVE AN ESTAB-
lished church, but it does have (and always has had) an
established religion, or at least a dominant religious philosophy, an established way of thinking about religion. For our purposes here, *religion* may be defined as a way of thinking about
ultimate questions. A person's religion answers questions such
as how and why we (and everything else) came into existence,
whether the purpose of life has been established by a Creator or
is up to us to decide, and how we can have reliable knowledge
about the world and about ourselves. The officially recognized
answers to these questions make up a society's established religious philosophy, its culturally dominant way of thinking about
religious topics.

There is nothing sinister or inherently unconstitutional about
the existence of a de facto established public philosophy on religious questions. The philosophy is *established* not in the sense that

it is formally enacted or that dissenters are subject to legal punishment, but in the sense that it provides a philosophical basis for
lawmaking and public education. The content of the established
philosophy may often be controversial and may change over time,
but something of the kind must necessarily exist or government
will become incoherent and even chaotic. For example, one culture may endeavor to encourage its schoolgirls to look forward to
lives as mothers and homemakers, while another may encourage
them to reject traditional gender stereotypes and pursue formerly
masculine careers. To encourage either choice reflects a dominant
public philosophy about human nature and gender roles. Similarly, any community that operates a public school system must have
a policy of some kind concerning sexual morality, even if the
policy is merely to encourage adolescents to choose for themselves.
Relativism itself is a policy choice, and it rests on assumptions
about reality.

A Shift in Religious Philosophy
During the second half of the twentieth century, the United States'
established religious philosophy changed drastically from what it
had been previously. In the nineteenth century, Americans overwhelmingly assumed that the Protestant version of the Christian
religion was true, at least in a general way. Soldiers marched to
the "Battle Hymn of the Republic"—a song that would probably
be banned from most public schools today—and judges unabashedly referred to Christianity and the Bible as the foundation
of the legal order. When Utah joined the Union, the Mormons did
not have to change their theology, but they did have to give up
polygamy, because a Christian nation would not tolerate the practice. A great deal of whatever schooling ordinary citizens had was
provided by churches, or by public schools that were on very
friendly terms with Protestant Christianity.

The degree to which this Protestant-dominated culture was

tolerant of groups like Catholics and Jews varied greatly depending on place and time, but on basic moral questions there was little dispute, because Protestants, Catholics and Jews agreed upon a common tradition stemming from the Bible. There were differing doctrines on divorce, for example, but there was an overwhelming consensus that divorce was a great evil that should be legally and socially discouraged. There was plenty of room for argument over specific questions, but there was nearly universal agreement that the Bible and the Judeo-Christian tradition furnished the materials on the basis of which the argument would be conducted.

Today things are very different. Many people would say that we have progressed from a de facto religious establishment to a position of neutrality toward religion, but, as I have said, that would be a superficial and misleading way of describing the contemporary situation. What has really happened is that a new established religious philosophy has replaced the old one. Like the old philosophy, the new one is tolerant only up to a point, specifically the point where its own right to rule the public square is threatened.

When I want a long and fully descriptive name for it, I call the established religious philosophy of late-twentieth-century America "scientific naturalism and liberal rationalism." When I just want a convenient label, I shorten this cumbersome term and call the ruling philosophy simply "naturalism" or "modernism." Modernism as an intellectual condition begins when people realize that God is really dead and that humankind is therefore on its own.

Naturalism is a *metaphysical* doctrine, which means simply that it states a particular view of what is ultimately real and unreal. According to naturalism, what is ultimately real is nature, which consists of the fundamental particles that make up what we call matter and energy, together with the natural laws that govern how those particles behave.* Nature itself is ultimately all there is, at least as far as we are concerned. To put it another way, nature is a permanently closed system of material causes and effects that can never be influenced by anything outside of itself—by God, for example. To speak of something as "supernatural" is therefore to imply that it is imaginary, and belief in powerful imaginary entities is known as superstition.

Naturalism gives priority to natural science as a way of describing reality, because everything we know about nature, other than by direct observation, is the product of scientific investigation. Science may not be able to answer all questions, at least for the time being, but some of the most visionary scientists already speak of a "theory of everything," or "final theory," which will in principle explain all of nature and hence all of reality. Because (in this view) science is by far our most reliable source of knowledge, whatever conflicts with scientific knowledge is effectively false, and whatever is in principle closed to scientific investigation is effectively unreal. We might say that any supernatural reality or nonscientific knowledge is "immaterial," meaning both that it is not based on matter and that it is of no concern to us.

Scientific naturalism, as I have just described it, provides modernist culture with its picture of reality. Liberal rationalism, the other half of the equation, provides its ethical and social viewpoint. Everyone agrees that government policy in such matters as lawmaking and education should be based on reason. Reason im-

---

*"Naturalism" is similar to "materialism," the doctrine that all reality has a material base. I prefer the former term because it avoids any confusion caused by the ordinary language distinction between matter and energy (both are ultimately made up of the somewhat ghostly subatomic entities studied by particle physicists). Moreover, particle physicists sometimes write and speak as if what is ultimately real is not the particles themselves but the grand unified theory that explains the movements and interactions of the particles. The essential point is that nature is understood by both naturalists and materialists to be "all there is" and to be fundamentally mindless and purposeless. This distinguishes naturalism from both pantheism (God is all there is, and God is identified with nature) and theism (God created the natural world for a purpose).

plies more than logic, however, because logic is merely a way of getting from premises to conclusions. Logic works from metaphysical assumptions, or pictures of reality, and it leads in very different directions depending on the starting point.

For much of Western history, lawmakers assumed that authoritative moral guidance was available to them in the Bible and in the religious traditions based on the Bible. From a naturalistic standpoint, however, the Creator God of the Bible is every bit as unreal as the gods of Olympus, and the commands of an unreal deity are in reality only the commands of an ancient priesthood. Such human commands derived from the conditions and problems of primitive societies can hardly furnish authoritative guidance to lawmakers and educators of modern societies, who, having the benefit of modern scientific knowledge, are presumably much better informed than their remote ancestors.

This does not mean that supposedly God-given rules like the Ten Commandments are necessarily irrational—some of them may have a sound basis in human experience. But it does mean that premodern standards need to be evaluated by the standards of naturalistic reason. Thus modernist culture retains the prohibition of theft and murder, retains the sabbath merely as a secular day of recreation, discards the admonition to have "no other gods before me" as meaningless, and regards ambivalently the prohibition of adultery and the command to honor parents. Adultery, for example, may be damaging to human relationships and a breach of contract. In that case an individual should avoid it for secular reasons, but to condemn adultery merely because God forbids it would be, in modernist terms, irrational.

Naturalistic rationalism provides modernist societies with either a socialistic or a liberal morality. The former starts with the needs of the society or the government; the latter starts with the needs of the individual. Because socialist ideologies are currently undergoing hard times, and because my main concern is with the individualistic culture of late-twentieth-century America, the liberal alternative is more important for present purposes.

The term *liberal* itself is unavoidably confusing, however, because in America it is often used in a partisan sense. Thus to defend large government spending on social programs is said to be "liberal," whereas to urge greater reliance on the free market is said to be "conservative"—even when the so-called conservatives are the ones advocating radical change and the liberals are defending the existing structures of government.

Liberal Rationalism
In the philosophical sense in which I employ the term, *liberalism* refers not to a position about the level of government spending or to the desirability of change, but to the secular legacy of philosophers such as Thomas Hobbes, John Locke, David Hume, Adam Smith and John Stuart Mill. Its essence lies in a respect for the autonomy of the individual. Because liberalism starts with the individual, the most characteristic liberal political doctrines are the social contract as the foundation of legitimate government and individual rights as the basis of liberty. Contemporary liberals will speak enthusiastically of natural rights, but they tend to reject the concept of natural laws, in the sense of obligations that are superior to those created by governments. Obligations in contemporary liberalism come not from nature, and certainly not from God, but from society, and they are clearly legitimate only to the extent that individuals have in some sense consented to be bound by them. Rights, on the other hand, are founded directly on our assumed status as autonomous beings.

Although the initial founders of liberalism were theists, the dominant contemporary form of liberal rationalism incorporates the naturalistic doctrine that God is unreal, a product of the human imagination. The famous "death of God" is simply the modernist certainty that naturalism is true and that human beings must therefore create their own standards rather than take them from some divine revelation. We cannot look to anything higher than ourselves, because there *is* nothing higher, at least until we encounter superior beings from other planets. That means we have to start with human society (socialism) or with the individual (liberalism) as the unit that is fundamentally real. Of course the two units will tend to be mixed in practice, because any enduring governmental system must take into account both the needs of society and the needs of the individual. For example, John F. Kennedy's famous exhortation "Ask not what your country can do for you, but what you can do for your country" appears to be a thoroughly socialistic utterance. It was directed by a liberal president to an overwhelmingly individualistic nation, however, as a corrective to the selfishness that rampant individualism tends to spawn.

Because liberalism starts with individual rights and autonomy, its morality tends to become progressively more relativistic and even permissive. The exercise of individual freedom is limited primarily by the rights of others, and to a lesser extent by abstract social policies, which are usually debatable. We may all agree that a man's freedom to swing his fist ends at his neighbor's nose, but it is much less obvious that he has violated any liberal norm if he opens a pornographic movie theater or divorces his children's mother to marry someone more attractive.

The current battle over the morality of abortion exemplifies the liberal approach to moral issues. Nearly everyone agrees that the deliberate killing of a newborn infant is murder, but there is intense disagreement about the morality of early, middle and late abortions. In the face of such disagreement the liberal rationalist position is "prochoice," as it presumably will be if one day a substantial body of opinion—especially articulate and well-educated opinion—develops in favor of infanticide. How could it be otherwise, if morality rests ultimately on human decisions rather than external authority?

So far I have given a brief description of the nature of scientific naturalism and liberal rationalism, which I will henceforth designate by the less cumbersome term *modernism*. When I say that this religious philosophy is "established," of course I do not mean that people are literally compelled to believe it, any more than people were compelled to believe in Protestant Christianity when Alexis de Tocqueville described that creed as the de facto established religion of America in the early nineteenth century. A religious establishment is consistent with a large degree of tolerance, but there is a very important difference between being tolerated and being allowed to govern. The established religious philosophy is the creed of the people who do the governing, or most of them. They are the ones who decide how much tolerance will be extended to others.

The Supreme Court cases discussed in the preceding chapter provide an illustration of the limits of tolerance. A naturalistic establishment may think it the wiser course to allow a Christian film to be shown in a rented public schoolroom in the evening, because to engage openly in viewpoint discrimination would be inconsistent with liberal rationalist principles, which ostensibly reject the idea of an officially established orthodoxy and protect freedom of expression for all viewpoints. The prospect of allowing creationists to challenge the naturalistic account of biological creation in science classes, on the other hand, was sufficiently alarming to inspire determined efforts from the major organizations of the scientific, educational and legal elites to repel the challenge. Providing an ideological faction a platform in public education gives a disfavored creed a kind of official certification of legitimacy and also supplies it with public resources for recruitment (this explains why multiculturalists, feminists and gay liberationists have placed so much importance on gaining such a platform at all levels of education). Allowing a James Dobson film to be shown by a "fringe group" in the evening once in a while is thus relatively harmless; adopting the same film officially in the high-school curriculum of New York State would signal a cultural revolution—even if the curriculum also included other films expressing a different viewpoint.

The establishment of a particular religious philosophy does not imply that competing philosophies are outlawed, but rather that they are relegated to a marginal position in private life. The marginalization is most effective when formal government actions are supplemented by a variety of intimidating acts by nongovernmental institutions such as the news media. The media uproar surrounding the "creationist" policies of the locally elected Vista District school board in San Diego County, California, provides a good example.

Before 1989, the California State Board of Education's official policy simply forbade the "dogmatic" teaching of any scientific theory, a stance that in context discouraged textbook publishers from giving as much emphasis to evolution as many science educators thought appropriate. In 1989 the science educators persuaded the state board to adopt a new policy statement on the teaching of science. Without explicitly mentioning evolution, this policy encouraged textbook publishers and teachers to give much greater emphasis to accepted scientific doctrines and to relegate any consideration of nonscientific subjects such as divine creation, ultimate purposes and the ultimate cause of the physical universe to literature and social studies classes.

When a majority of conservative Christians won election to the Vista District school board, they took language directly from the 1989 state policy statement and employed it in their own local policy, which provided that "discussions of divine creation, ultimate purposes, or ultimate causes [the 'why'] shall be included at appropriate times in the history-social sciences and/or English-language arts curricula" (but not in science classes). The new local policy mandated "exploration and dialogue" of "scientific evidence that challenges any theory in science" and stated that "no student shall be compelled to believe or accept any theory presented in the curriculum."

The Vista policy seemed on its face to comply with the state guidelines, and a representative of the state board acknowledged that there would be a conflict only if the local policy in practice was used to promote Christianity instead of giving equal treatment to all religious viewpoints. In fact, the board faced so much hostility from the teachers' unions that the policy had little effect. Nonetheless, press, radio and television accounts of the controversy continually portrayed the Vista policy as defying the state guidelines and as a covert attempt to evade constitutional standards by introducing biblical creationism (which was not mentioned in the local policy) "through the back door."

The basis for this portrayal was that the local board members were known to be sympathetic to the creationist viewpoint and hence must have been motivated by a desire to get that viewpoint taken seriously. The prospect that they might succeed was so alarming to the defenders of modernism that national and even international media took an intense interest in this local controversy. The influential *Los Angeles Times* mounted a campaign in its editorial and news columns, and vigorous editorial denunciations of the Vista board came from as far away as London. As the historian Ronald Numbers put it in his book *The Creationists,* the attitude of the educational elites toward creationism can be summed up as "We've got to stop these bastards!" In this case the campaign succeeded, and the offending school board members were defeated at the next election.

The elite attitude examined by Numbers is a clear sign that modernist culture finds creationism—as distinguished from, say, the New Age mysticism of a Shirley MacLaine—genuinely threatening. The problem is not with the detailed Genesis literalism of the fundamentalists, which is relatively easy to marginalize, but with the broader doctrine that, one way or another, God brought about our existence for a purpose and cares about what we do. The vast majority of Americans at least say that they believe in such a God, and if that belief were to emerge as a serious contender at the intellectual level, there could be important consequences. If God is more than a myth or a figure of speech, then modernist culture is ignoring something really important, and its ruling philosophy may be in serious trouble.

On the other hand, defenders of modernism cannot openly ban the advocacy of theism without contradicting their own commitment to freedom of expression and unfettered intellectual inquiry. Modernist discourse accordingly incorporates semantic devices— such as the labeling of theism as "religion" and naturalism as "science"—that work to prevent a dangerous debate over fundamental assumptions from breaking out in the open. As the preceding chapter showed, however, these devices become transparent under the close inspection that an open debate tends to encourage. The best defense for modernist naturalism is to make sure the debate does not occur.

It would be inadequate and misleading, however, to account for modernist rule as if it were a kind of plot by agnostics to rule the United States by employing deceptive techniques. Modernism is not a conspiracy, but a way of thinking that is taken for granted not only by agnostics but also by millions of people who consider themselves theists but have to some extent adopted modernist ways of thinking about theism. In fact, the authority of modernism rests largely on theists' tacit acceptance of modernist premises. It is possible to make so strong a case for modernism that it may seem futile and self-destructive for theists to challenge modernism as a public philosophy.

The Advantages of Modernism

I believe that the case for modernism can be answered convincingly, but the case that has to be answered is a powerful one, and it will not do to underestimate the difficulty of the task. There are at least five reasons that advocates of modernist naturalism can (and do) give to justify their right to rule, and I will state them as persuasively as I can.

1. Modernism's metaphysical foundation rests firmly on scientific naturalism, which is "the way things really are." Through science we now know that nature, of which we are a recently evolved part, really *is* a closed system of material causes and effects, whether we like it or not. Any other system—particularly one based on the supposed commandments of a supernatural being—would therefore be founded on illusion rather than reality. God is a product of the human imagination, not the Creator of us all. Once science has established the facts, we have eaten the fruit of the tree of knowledge and there is no going back to prescientific beliefs, however great a sense of loss some of us may feel.

2. Modernist naturalism is equivalent to rationality because it excludes consideration of miracles, defined as arbitrary breaks in the chain of material causes and effects. This argument is particularly important to scientists, who see the success of science as inextricably linked to the presumption that no supernatural mind or spirit ever interferes with the orderly (but purposeless) course of natural events. Most modernists' identification of naturalism with rationality is so complete that they do not think of naturalism as a distinct and controversial metaphysical doctrine, but simply assume it as part of the definition of *reason.*

3. Modernist naturalism is liberating, especially in the area of gender roles and sexual behavior, because it frees people from the illusion that outdated cultural norms have permanent validity as commands of God. Persons who attack scientific naturalism or the theory of evolution probably do so as part of a disguised agenda to reestablish a stifling patriarchal code of sexual behavior. I have found that any discussion with modernists about the weakness of

the theory of evolution quickly turns into a discussion of politics, particularly sexual politics. Modernists typically fear that any discrediting of naturalistic evolution will end in women being sent to the kitchen, gays to the closet and abortionists to jail. That kind of consideration explains why any perceived attempt to undermine the teaching of evolution as fact in the schools is met with such fierce opposition; much more than a scientific theory is deemed to be at stake.

4. Modernist naturalism supplies the philosophical basis for democratic liberty, because it relies only on knowledge that is in principle available to every citizen. Modernists characterize persons who wish to make public policy on the basis of some divine revelation as inherently undemocratic, because they assert authority on the basis of a knowledge that has been revealed only to them and hence is not available to others. In contrast, the observations and methods of reasoning employed by science are universally accessible in principle, although in reality the special study (and funding) required to practice science limits citizens' ability to judge scientific questions for themselves. If public debate is carried out only on the basis of knowledge derived from sensory experience and scientific investigation, then in principle everyone can participate on equal terms. Modernists think debates between competing supernaturalistic ideologies can be settled only by force, whereas debate on naturalistic principles is open to reason and hence to peaceful solution.

5. Finally, modernist government is acceptable even to many religious people, including Christian theists of relatively high intellectual standing. Modernism is not inherently antireligious or even antitheist, provided that "belief in God" is relegated to its proper place in private life. Under liberal rationalist principles of tolerance, believers may have their own churches and may even send their children to private religious schools if they can afford to do so—provided that they do not attempt to force their beliefs

on other people by seeking, for example, to advocate them in the public schools. Modernists think that this is as much authority as believers with a proper respect for the autonomy of nonbelievers should want. The restriction of religion to private life therefore does not threaten the vital interests of the majority religion, and it positively protects minority religions from the tyranny of the majority.

The tacit understanding that religion has to do with subjective feelings rather than objective facts allows scientific naturalists to exempt religion from all-out scientific scrutiny; thus modernism compassionately protects the cherished illusions of religious believers. Modernists warn Christian theists who want to dispute naturalism in the public arena that they are making a big mistake and are inviting a conflict with science that they cannot win. As the example of creationism illustrates, modernist tolerance stops at the point where the religious people start demanding that public institutions treat their subjective beliefs as if they might possibly be objectively true.

Theistic Realism

That is a formidable list of advantages and justifications, but in the end everything depends on the first argument: the God of Christian theism and of the Bible is unreal, the product of a prescientific human imagination. Grant that premise, and everything else follows. But reject that premise, and everything on the list becomes doubtful.

Of course a social order should be founded on reality and not unreality, but if God exists, a naturalistic order is founded on unreality and naturalistic rationalism is an illusion.

Of course science likes to assume that the cosmos is rationally understandable and not arbitrary, but how better to guarantee a rational cosmos than to recognize that it was created by a rational mind? If such a Creator really does exist, then science itself is ignoring the most important aspect of reality.

Of course people should be freed from arbitrary restrictions, but if the supposedly arbitrary restrictions are in reality necessary to restrain our irrational passions, we can expect to get something other than freedom when we abolish them. We should also expect something other than rational government when the governors break their connection to the source of reason.

Finally, if God is real, then those theists who meekly accept their assigned place in the naturalistic order of things may be like sailors who choose not to disturb the captain by informing him that the ship is about to sink. It may be rational to argue about whether God is real or unreal, but it is clearly irrational to assume that a God who is real can safely be ignored.

I am not a modernist; a modernist would call me a "religious believer," but I call myself a *theistic realist*. The term signifies that I am convinced that God is objectively real, not merely a concept or fantasy in my own mind. This is a shocking proposition to many people, including many churchgoers and professional clergy. I have been told by many modernists that to assert the reality of God as Creator is dogmatic and arrogant, since it is to imply that I have knowledge that is unavailable to scientific naturalists. Modernists do not think it arrogant to declare that "evolution is a fact," although the statement seems to imply that creationists are wrong. That is because in their metaphysics, naturalistic evolution falls in the category of scientific knowledge, whereas creation is a matter of religious faith. It is not arrogant or dogmatic to insist that things be placed in their proper categories.

Arrogant or not, I think that the Creator is real and naturalism is untrue. The strongest argument against my position is that science is based on naturalism, and the success of science has proved that naturalism is, if not absolutely true, at least the most reliable way of thinking available to us. Scientific naturalists do not claim to have proved that God does not exist, but they do claim to have demonstrated that God as Creator is superfluous, because purely natural forces were capable of doing and actually did do all the work of creation. This is not a case of a purposeful Creator's making use of secondary causes, as an artist uses brushes and paints, but of the material causes acting on their own without intelligent guidance. If the brushes and paints can draw the picture without assistance, then it does not seem that any hypothetical artist would ever have had anything important to do.

Whether a purely naturalistic account of creation is consistent with "religious belief" or not, the general assumption that science has actually provided such an account clearly has a great deal to do with the fact that naturalism has become so widely identified with reason. But let us take a good look at exactly how successful science has been in its attempt to give a complete naturalistic account of creation.

3

The Grand
Metaphysical
Story
of Science

S TEPHEN HAWKING'S BOOK *A BRIEF HISTORY OF TIME* WAS
one of the greatest surprise successes of publishing history,
having sold an estimated five million copies worldwide by
1992, after an initial printing of only five thousand in 1988. This
level of success had to be due to something other than the scientific
content of the book. Very few of the millions of purchasers could
have understood Hawking's descriptions of relativity theory and
quantum mechanics, which are difficult for nonphysicists to follow
even in popularized form. In any case, essentially the same information was available in many other popular books about physics
and cosmology.

What Hawking's book offered that the others did not was
Hawking himself, a man who had triumphed over a horribly crip-
pling disease to reach the pinnacle of scientific fame. It also offered

one of the most ambitious programs for the scientific enterprise that has ever been stated.

Theories of Everything

In Hawking's expansive vision, theoretical physics promises to provide humanity with something more than mathematical theories understandable only to specialists, and something much more important to ordinary people than possible technological benefits like new sources of energy. What Hawking envisions is a kind of universal human wisdom attainable under the tutelage of physicists. The goal is nothing less than "a complete understanding of the events around us, and of our own existence."

The first big step toward this goal is a unified theory of the four fundamental forces of nature, the final theory that particle physicists dream of. Once the unified theory is discovered, Hawking thinks, it will be possible to teach philosophers and even ordinary people something of what the theory means. Eventually this knowledge will enable everyone to take part in a great conversation about such grand questions as why it is that we and the universe exist. Finding the answer to the riddle of existence, Hawking concludes, "would be the ultimate triumph of human reason—for then we would know the mind of God."

To have a complete understanding of everything that happens, and even why the universe exists at all, can certainly be described as knowing the mind of God—or more precisely, attaining the omniscience previously attributed to God. Perhaps it is not surprising that a book captures the public imagination when it holds out even a distant prospect of omniscience to the world at large and seems to back the promise with the authority of science. But how much can scientific investigation really contribute to an understanding of the meaning of our existence, particularly a science that is as incomprehensible to nonspecialists as theoretical physics?

The scientific side of the Hawking story begins with the work of another great mathematical physicist, Roger Penrose, famed as the discoverer of "black holes." Penrose demonstrated that the existence of these exotic astronomical entities follows as a matter of logic from the gravitational principles of Einstein's general theory of relativity. According to Hawking's account, Penrose

> showed that a star collapsing under its own gravity is trapped in a region whose surface eventually sinks to zero size. And, since the surface of the region sinks to zero, so must its size. All the matter in the star will be compressed into a region of zero volume, so the density of matter and the curvature of space-time become infinite. In other words, one has a singularity contained within a region of space-time known as a black hole.

Hawking's own scientific fame began with a 1970 paper, coauthored with Penrose, which applied the black hole theory to the universe as a whole. Just as a black hole is a dying giant star collapsing into a point of zero volume, the universe is now thought to be expanding from a similar infinitesimal point. As the black hole ends in a singularity, the universe must have begun with one. The existence of a singularity at the beginning of time had previously been thought to be a possible implication of general relativity; Hawking and Penrose demonstrated that it was an inevitable implication.

This conclusion of theoretical physics has great philosophical and religious significance. The big bang theory itself had to overcome considerable resistance from scientists: they objected to the implication that the universe had a definite beginning in time, because such a moment of creation was previously associated more with religion than with science. Indeed, the proposition that the universe began in an unimaginably vast explosion of energy sounds to many like a rendering in modern scientific language of what the book of Genesis said long ago: "God said, Let there be light!"

Despite these metaphysical objections, the big bang theory triumphed because it fit the evidence better than any rival. An expanding universe seems to follow from the logic of general relativity, the expansion seems to be confirmed by observations of the Hubble "red shift," and the primeval explosion seems to have left an "echo" in the form of a universal background radiation that was first detected in 1965.

Still, Hawking and Penrose's demonstration that the universe must have begun with a singularity significantly increased the metaphysical uneasiness. A singularity is defined in relativity jargon as a point at which the space-time curvature becomes infinite, which sounds innocent enough, but the disturbing implication is that at such a point all relativity-based laws of nature break down. The existence of a singularity at the absolute beginning thus could be taken to imply that there was a time when the most fundamental laws of science did not exist. How, then, did the laws come into existence? Whatever the scientists might prefer to think, it was inevitable that the popular culture would infer that God—a supernatural entity unknown to science—must have created the laws.

That kind of answer is intensely disliked by many scientists, including Hawking, because to leave any room for the supernatural seems to leave science incomplete. The search was on for some way to discard the singularity. The search involves the attempt to provide a grand unified theory (GUT) of physics, a project that has been celebrated in so many books and educational television programs that most readers have undoubtedly heard of it.

Physicists recognize four fundamental forces. Three of these—electromagnetism, the weak nuclear force and the strong nuclear force—operate at subatomic levels and are understood through the mathematics of quantum theory. The fourth, gravity, is important for large-scale bodies and is understood in terms of Einstein's general theory of relativity. In our world the forces are distinct, but many physicists think that they were unified at the earliest moment of the big bang, when the universe was unimaginably hot and dense.

A satisfactory "electroweak" theory unifying electromagnetism and the weak nuclear force already exists, and it has achieved some experimental confirmation. Although the strong nuclear force has its own theory, called quantum chromodynamics, physicists think they have made some progress toward a unification of quantum chromodynamics with the electroweak theory. The great difficulty lies in extending the program of unification to the fourth force, gravity, because the principles of relativity and quantum mechanics are contradictory.

Whether a unified theory can ever be achieved is in dispute. One possibly insuperable obstacle is the extreme difficulty of carrying out the experiments needed to test the work of theoreticians. According to David Lindley's *The End of Physics: The Myth of a Unified Theory,* particle physics is becoming more like myth than science, because its mathematical constructions are so distant from any conceivable experimental confirmation. If the Texas Supercollider had been built, it might have found the famous Higgs particle, which would have provided further support for the electroweak theory—and thus for the proposition that the physicists are in general on the right track. The Supercollider has been canceled, however, and in any case the experiments needed to pursue the unification project to the next stages would require energy levels that cannot be produced on earth, especially at any cost that the public is likely to be willing to fund.

In consequence a proposed final theory could not be confirmed by experiment, but only by agreement among the theoreticians, which makes the theory sound more like philosophy than science. But the inspiration provided by past success overcomes such practical obstacles in the minds of theorists, and so popular books by Hawking and other leading physicists imply confidence that the grand unification project can be carried out—possibly even while the authors are still alive to enjoy the triumph.

The extraordinary metaphysical significance of a unified theory of the four forces is illustrated by the names physicists give to it: "the holy grail of physics," "the final theory" and especially "the theory of everything." These romantic titles are not justified by any tangible accomplishments expected to flow directly from the theory itself, since even a successful unified theory is not expected to tell us anything in particular about such mysteries as how galaxies and galactic clusters form, how life arose or why people behave as they do. The immense imaginative appeal of a unified theory stems entirely from the position it occupies in the naturalistic philosophy that scientists generally assume in their work.

If nature is really a permanently closed system of physical causes and effects, then everything that has happened in the entire history of the cosmos must be determined (or at least permitted) by the conditions that existed at the beginning. If in the beginning nothing existed except the laws and the particles, and nothing fundamentally new has entered the universe subsequently, then a complete understanding of conditions at the beginning is in principle the key to a complete understanding of everything that followed. The unified theory is therefore what might be called the opening chapter in the grand metaphysical story of science, and the set of laws described by the unified theory is the scientific equivalent of a creator. That is why religious language permeates the books about the theory, and why Hawking thinks that to achieve a complete understanding of the theory would be to know the mind of God—in the sense of knowing all that there is to know.

To be truly like God, though, the theory has to be eternal, and the existence of a singularity at the beginning implies a time when the laws described by the theory did not exist. Hawking's greatest contribution to what might be called the religious unification of physics was to propose a theory that gets rid of the awkward singularity whose existence he and Penrose had established in the first place. What he suggested was that the big bang singularity might merely imply that at the earliest moment the gravitational field was so strong that general relativity was not applicable, and scientists may be able to employ a "quantum theory of gravity" (if one is ever discovered) to understand the beginning. A quantum theory of gravity would probably involve "imaginary time," a mathematical concept employed to resolve certain problems in quantum mechanics. In imaginary time, explains Hawking, "the distinction between time and space disappears completely." Accordingly, a theorist can do away with the embarrassing singularity at the beginning by doing away with the need for a beginning. Here is how Hawking puts it:

> The quantum theory of gravity has opened up a new possibility, in which there would be no boundary to space-time and so there would be no need to specify the behavior at the boundary. There would be no singularities at which the laws of science broke down and no edge of space-time at which one would have to appeal to God or some new law to set the boundary conditions for space-time. One could say: "The boundary condition of the universe is that it has no boundary." The universe would be completely self-contained and not affected by anything outside itself. It would neither be created nor destroyed. It would just BE.

Hawking freely concedes that the no-boundary concept of space-time is "just a *proposal:* it cannot be deduced from some other principle." He goes on to say that such a proposal may be put forward for aesthetic or metaphysical reasons, but the test of its status as a scientific theory is whether it makes predictions that can be verified by observation.

Obviously, the no-boundary proposal cannot make such predictions at the present time. That is not only because the necessary unification of relativity and quantum theory has not been achieved, but also because any model that described the whole universe would be too complicated mathematically to permit exact predictions. Theorists therefore would have to make simplifying assumptions and approximations, and Hawking concedes that "even then, the problem of extracting predictions remains a formidable one." One could never know whether any hypothetical predictive success was due to the particular simplifying assumptions that the theorist chose to make. David Lindley seems to be right; without experimental confirmation, theoretical physics takes on the qualities of myth.

The no-boundary proposal is therefore properly labeled as an element in a grand metaphysical story rather than as a scientific theory. When metaphysical stories are told by world-famous physicists, however, they take on an air of authority and may have profound consequences on the thinking of persons who do not distinguish between "stories scientists tell" and "scientific theories."

Paul Davies, another prominent mathematical physicist, explains the importance of Hawking's no-boundary proposal in his book *The Mind of God,* in a chapter titled "Can the Universe Create Itself?" Davies candidly states at the outset, "This particular explanation may be quite wrong," but immediately adds that the correctness of any particular explanation does not matter. According to Davies, "What is at issue is whether or not some sort of supernatural act is necessary to start the universe off. If a plausible scientific theory can be constructed that will explain the origin of the entire physical universe, then at least we know a scientific explanation is possible, whether or not the current theory is right."

But an untestable metaphysical story that makes no predictions is not a scientific theory, and such speculation cannot prove that a true naturalistic explanation for the ultimate beginning exists. Davies's statement amounted to saying that even a myth is sufficient to reassure scientific naturalists that they do not have to worry about the supernatural.

Scientists and philosophers of science frequently say that God is a subject outside of science, but such statements are seriously misleading. It would be more accurate to say that the scientists who think about the big picture are obsessed with the God issue, and it is natural that they should be. The aim of historical scientists—those who attempt to trace cosmic history from the big bang or before to the present—is to provide a complete naturalistic picture of reality. This enterprise is defined by its determination to push God out of reality, because naturalism is defined by its exclusion of the supernatural. Particle physicists and cosmologists tend to be very religious people in their own way, but their religion is often science itself, and so the only creation story they will accept is one in which all the elements of reality are in principle accessible to scientific investigation. An imaginative story that makes the universe itself eternal is hence preferable to a scientific theory that requires a disturbing singularity at the beginning, and for this reason the former may attain the status of scientific knowledge on its imaginative appeal alone.

That removing God from the history of the cosmos is the central point of *A Brief History of Time* is pointed out to readers by the astronomer Carl Sagan, in the closing lines of his Introduction to the book, although Sagan presents the conclusion as if it were an unanticipated experimental result rather than the conscious purpose of the author:

> The word God fills these pages. Hawking embarks on a quest to answer Einstein's famous question about whether God had any choice in creating the universe. Hawking is attempting, as he explicitly states, to understand the mind of God. And this makes all the more unexpected the conclusion of the effort, at least so far: a universe with no edge in time, no beginning or end in time, and nothing for a Creator to do.

Mind and Matter

One element in the imaginative dimension of *A Brief History of*

Time consists of its telling a story about the ultimate beginning of the universe in a way intended to relieve scientific naturalists of their fear of the supernatural, while holding out to the public the prospect of eventual omniscience. A second element concerns Hawking's personal story, particularly visible in the publicity surrounding the book—and especially in the outstanding BBC television movie that was made from and about Hawking's phenomenal bestseller.

When as a young man Stephen Hawking was diagnosed with what Americans call Lou Gehrig's disease, he had every reason to give up on life. Instead, not only did he live much longer than the doctors had predicted, but he married, had children and achieved preeminence in science. Today he occupies the Lucasian Professorship of Mathematics at Cambridge, a chair that once belonged to Sir Isaac Newton. That Hawking's publisher considers Hawking himself to rank with the greatest of scientists is suggested none too subtly to readers of *A Brief History of Time* by the inclusion of brief biographies of Einstein, Galileo and Newton at the end of the slender volume.

When we see Hawking in person in the television adaptation of his book, his disease has left him almost totally helpless, unable to move from his wheelchair or even to speak normally. He speaks through a voice synthesizer by entering words into a computer program, producing an effect rather like a modern incarnation of the oracle of Delphi, or perhaps the supercomputer called Hal in the movie *2001: A Space Odyssey.* The thought that such a ruined body might hold a mind capable of penetrating the ultimate secrets of the universe is genuinely inspiring. In this sense Hawking's life is an archetype of the entire saga of science, for science is the story of the power of the mind to penetrate the fog of superstition and ignorance to discern the invisible reality beyond. The story of the man Stephen Hawking, in the mythological dimension that has so much to do with his immense popular success, is the story of mind over matter.

The irony is that what this heroic mind ends up producing is a reductionist science that reduces the mind itself to a trivial side-show in a materialist universe. Hawking does not address this problem directly, but it surfaces in his book, for he recognizes that a physical theory of everything is inherently self-referential and hence potentially incoherent. The enterprise of science assumes that human beings—or scientists, at any rate—are rational beings who can observe nature accurately and employ logical reasoning to understand the reality behind the appearances. If a theory of everything exists, however, the laws it describes determine even the thoughts and actions of the scientists who aim to discover the theory. How then, wonders Hawking, can the scientists trust their own powers of reasoning? How can they know that the laws of physics predict or permit the discovery of a true theory?

Naturalistic philosophy offers one line of escape from this co-nundrum, and Hawking takes it. The only validation of the mind's reasoning power that science can provide is Darwin's principle of natural selection, which explains all adaptive features of organisms in terms of reproductive success. The theory posits that evolution rewarded those organisms that were best at drawing correct conclusions about the world and acting accordingly to escape predators, find mates and so on. Right-thinking organisms would presumably excel at surviving and reproducing, and hence would leave more offspring than competitors who were more inclined to err. Eventually the ability to come to correct conclusions would become widespread in every population. In Hawking's words, "Provided the universe has evolved in a regular way, we might expect that the reasoning abilities that natural selection has given us would be valid also in our search for a complete unified theory, and so would not lead us to the wrong conclusions."

But one cannot avoid the problem of self-reference by invoking another theory in this way. Darwin's theory is just another product of the human mind, whose reasoning is still governed by the hypothetical theory of everything, so the problem of reliability is merely displaced rather than solved. In any case, Darwinian selection rewards only success in leaving offspring, and the presumption that abstract mental powers cause their possessor to leave more viable offspring than creatures who are more modestly endowed is neither borne out by experience nor even remotely plausible. By Darwinian criteria, the brains of rats and cockroaches are every bit as conducive to reproductive success as human brains, particularly when one reflects that the "fitness" of the human brain would have to be judged in the primitive conditions in which it supposedly evolved. One has only to consider Hawking's own hereditary disease to appreciate how little advanced mathematical gifts have to do with the ability to leave viable offspring.

There are ways of meeting this kind of objection, of course. An ingenious Darwinist can always suppose that the capacity to solve equations involving imaginary time evolved as a serendipitous byproduct of more modest mental traits that did increase reproductive success. The problem with this sort of explanation is not that it can be proved wrong, but rather that it is vacuous because it can "explain" any trait whatsoever. One might as well speculate—without any evidentiary support whatever—that the ability to solve equations is a secondary effect of a gene that also codes for a high sperm count or a pleasantly shaped nose.

Although invoking Darwinian selection does not solve the problem of self-reference, it is to Hawking's credit that he brought the problem to the attention of his readers, because what it really demonstrates is that a theory that is the product of a mind can never adequately explain the mind that produced the theory. The story of the great scientific mind that discovers absolute truth is satisfying only so long as we accept the mind itself as a given. Once we try to explain the mind as a product of its own discoveries, we are in a hall of mirrors with no exit. It is as if a disciple of Sigmund

Freud were to explain his master's theory of the Oedipus complex as a product of Freud's own unconscious wish to murder his father and marry his mother. The theory could still conceivably be true of men in general, because Freud might just happen to be like others in this peculiar respect, but we would certainly not rely on Freud's authority to establish the point.

Attributing an idea to irrational unconscious desires or physical forces has about the same effect as showing that a judge received a huge cash payment from a litigant. The fact does not absolutely prove that the verdict was against the law or the evidence, because the litigant might conceivably have bribed the judge to do the right thing, but it mightily suggests the likelihood.

Materialist Theories of the Mind
It is in the nature of explanation that one thing is explained in terms of something else that is assumed valid, and to explain the latter as nothing more than a product of the former is to create a logical circle. Yet naturalistic metaphysics is so seductive that eminent scientists and philosophers frequently do employ their own minds to attempt to prove that the mind is "nothing but" a product of physical forces and chemical reactions.

One of these is Francis Crick, the biochemist who as codiscoverer of the structure of DNA is almost as famous as Hawking himself. In his later years Crick has been drawn to the problem of consciousness, and he expressed his thoughts in the 1994 book *The Astonishing Hypothesis.* Here is how Crick states his own starting point:

> The Astonishing Hypothesis is that "You," your joys and your sorrows, your memories and your ambitions, your sense of personal identity and free will, are in fact no more than the behavior of a vast assembly of nerve cells and their associated molecules. . . . The hypothesis is so alien to the ideas of most people alive today that it can truly be called astonishing.

Of course the hypothesis is not astonishing at all to anyone acquainted with the recent history of science, because neuroscientists in particular have long taken for granted that the mind is no more than a product of brain chemistry. As Crick says, what makes the hypothesis astonishing is that it conflicts with the commonsense picture of reality most people assume as they go about the business of making decisions, falling in love or even writing books advocating materialist reductionism.

The conflict with common sense would become apparent if Crick had presented his hypothesis in the first-person singular. Imagine the reaction of his publisher if Crick had proposed to begin his book by announcing that "I, Francis Crick, my opinions and my science, and even the thoughts expressed in this book, consist of nothing more than the behavior of a vast assembly of nerve cells and their associated molecules." Few browsers would be likely to read further. The plausibility of materialistic determinism requires that an implicit exception be made for the theorist.

Whatever common sense may have to say about the matter, the deconstruction of the mind advocated by Crick is implicit in the metaphysical materialism and naturalism that dominate the scientific community. Most biologists who express opinions on the subject in public take for granted that living organisms contain no "vital force" or other nonmaterial component, that complex organisms evolved from simpler predecessors by Darwinian selection, and that the human mind is therefore a product of material forces that valued nothing but success in reproduction. Given that understanding of things, what could the mind and its thoughts conceivably be but a product of the biochemistry of the brain, whatever the unlearned might think?

Crick does not claim that the materialistic understanding of the mind has been proved (the scientific part of his book limits itself to stating some tentative proposals for research into the mechanisms of vision). What he does claim is that the materialistic theory of the mind is the only possibility worth taking seriously. The only alternative he can envisage is some hangover from religion, which he characterizes contemptuously as "the superstitions of our ancestors."* Although Crick insists that scientists hold their hypotheses only as provisional beliefs and not by "blind faith," it is not clear what, if anything, could convince him that there is more to the mind than matter. Materialism to Crick is equivalent to science, and science to rationality.

Crick's reductionism is no idiosyncrasy; the same prejudice dominates contemporary science, regardless of reservations that individual scientists (who also have to live in the commonsense world) might express in private. It is not that workaday scientists are necessarily as enthusiastic about materialism as Crick is. The problem is that they do not know how to challenge materialism in principle without seeming foolish or sentimental. The materialists are intimidating because they seem to have the logic of science on their side. The same materialists are frustrated, however, because so many people are perversely unwilling to accept conclusions that a reductionist science necessarily implies. As the famous Stanford biochemist Arthur Kornberg complained to a 1987 meeting of the American Academy for the Advancement of Science, it is astonishing "that otherwise intelligent and informed people, including physicians, are reluctant to believe that mind, as part of life, *is* matter and *only* matter." On Kornberg's own premises, however, his astonishment was unjustified. Presumably, one kind of chemical reaction in the brain causes Kornberg to accept materialist reductionism, while another kind of reaction causes those physicians to doubt it.

---

*Crick's village-atheist level of understanding of religion is illustrated by the following comment: "Not only do the beliefs of most popular religions contradict each other but, by scientific standards, they are based on evidence so flimsy that only an act of blind faith can make them acceptable. If the members of a church really believe in a life after death, why do they not conduct sound experiments to establish it?" Religious people may take some comfort from the fact that Crick is nearly as contemptuous of philosophers: "Philosophers have had such a poor record over the last two thousand years that they would do better to show a certain modesty rather than the lofty superiority they usually display."

There is a great deal at stake in the argument about whether the mind can really be explained as a strictly material phenomenon. The authority of the scientific priesthood rests on public acquiescence in the grand metaphysical story of science, but the public is manifestly inclined to doubt. In this delicate situation the rulers of science cannot afford to leave any openings for rival stories. They do not have to be able to supply a reductionist explanation of the mind today, or even tomorrow, but they do have to claim that their methods, and no others, are based on a correct understanding of what the mind really is. If they were to concede even tacitly that mental activity has its ultimate roots in something beyond physics and chemistry, the resulting opening for the supernatural would be far larger and more dangerous than that involved in a singularity at the beginning of time.

If science cannot explain consciousness, the way is open for some rival discipline—religion, in particular—to fill the vacuum with a different metaphysical story of great emotional or imaginative appeal. This explanation would be a better candidate for the title of "theory of everything" than anything particle physics or evolutionary biology can provide, because science itself is a product of the mind. Whoever explains the mind explains science, and gains authority to say how great or small a role science should play in the life of the mind. That is not an authority that scientists will voluntarily surrender to philosophers or theologians.

Evaluating the Story of Science

How are we to evaluate the grand metaphysical story of science? It would be a mistake to take the easy way out and dismiss the story because some of its key elements are not proved. Of course the elements are not proved; Hawking and Crick themselves are emphatic on that point with respect to the no-boundary proposal, the unified physical theory and the materialist theory of the mind. The grand metaphysical story is not itself even conceivably subject to proof. Rather, it encapsulates the scientific way of thinking about the work that science has yet to accomplish.

The point of the materialist theory of the mind, for example, is not that such a theory exists (except in the most primitive and speculative form). It is that biochemists who are materialist reductionists fiercely want to believe that real progress toward understanding the mind comes only from learning the principles of biochemistry and not from listening to priests or philosophers. Similarly, the point of assuming that supernatural action played no role in the history of the cosmos is to inspire scientists with faith that nothing is beyond the scope of science.

A second mistake would be to underestimate the importance of the grand metaphysical story because subjects like ultimate origins are remote from the day-to-day concerns of practicing scientists. It is perfectly true that most scientists do not spend much time thinking about the ultimate metaphysical implications of the scientific enterprise, and I am sure that many are embarrassed by the hubris of the "theory of everything" school of physicists and the dogmatic materialism of the "DNA is everything" school of molecular biologists. But this is beside the point. Most people, whether they are scientists or not, go about day-to-day life without thinking about metaphysics, but their thinking is nonetheless influenced by metaphysical assumptions. In fact, metaphysical assumptions are most powerful when they are unconscious and do not come to the surface because everyone in the relevant community takes them for granted.

Relatively few scientists explicitly advocate the grand metaphysical story, but any scientist who explicitly challenged it would quickly earn a reputation as an eccentric. Francis Crick's hypothesis may be astonishing to the general public, but when I spoke on a panel at a huge neuroscience convention, I found that his basic premise was unreflectively taken for granted by almost everyone I met. Some neuroscientists are modest about what they expect to achieve in the foreseeable future, although an expansive optimism was more in evidence, but I saw no willingness to challenge in principle the premise that mind, as part of life, *is* matter and *only* matter. After all, what else could it be?

The grand metaphysical story is therefore important, and it deserves to be taken seriously as a metaphysical story. The question is whether we have good reason to believe that the story is true, or at least more probably true than the rival metaphysical story that we were created by a supernatural being called God who cares about what we do and gives ultimate meaning to our lives.

When this question comes to the surface, which it rarely does except when scientists are debating creationists, the answer that scientific naturalists usually give is that science's past successes justify a continuing confidence in the metaphysical vision that inspired those successes. This is potentially a good argument (I will call it the argument from success), but not all kinds of success are equally relevant.

The crudest version of the argument from success relies on the technological achievements of science, like airplanes, nuclear bombs, antibiotics and computers. From this it is only a short step to the contemptuous argument that persons who dispute the grand metaphysical story of science ought to try to travel by flying carpet or to cure their children's illnesses by faith healing. One of anthropologist Donald Johanson's popular books made the point in a memorable non sequitur: "You can't accept one part of science because it brings you good things like electricity and penicillin and throw away another part because it brings you some things you don't like about the origin of life." That reasoning overlooks the important consideration that all statements made in the name of science are not equally reliable. We believe in the efficacy of electricity and penicillin on the basis of experimental verification; many of us disbelieve claims that scientists know how life originated because we know how inadequate the experimental evidence is to justify those claims. To insist that claims be tested and not just promoted as fact because they are made by persons labeled "scientists" is simply to insist that the scientific method be followed and not just counterfeited.

In any case, the technological achievements of science have very little relevance to the vast theoretical scenarios of cosmology and evolutionary biology. Very likely the public is impressed by what theoretical physicists say about the origin of the universe mainly because an earlier generation of physicists invented the bomb that destroyed Hiroshima. But that is a fact about the public, not a fact about the origin of the universe.

The success that really matters for confirming the grand metaphysical story is the degree of success that has been achieved by historical science itself. If the scientists have actually confirmed many of the most important elements of the story, so that only a few gaps remain to be filled, then there are solid grounds (short of absolute proof) for believing that the story itself is fundamentally correct. For example, many scientists freely concede that the origin of life is still an unsolved mystery and that the materialistic theory of mind is only a hypothesis. On the other hand, even these scientists are usually confident that the neo-Darwinian theory of evolution is fundamentally correct and that science therefore knows in principle how today's complex plants and animals, including humans, evolved from the simplest life forms by natural selection. Granted this Darwinian premise, and granted the validity of the astronomers' model of stellar evolution and the formation of the solar system and the earth, scientists have good reason to be confident that naturalistic solutions to the origin of life and consciousness problems exist to be found.

It is conceivable that God intervened twice in cosmic history, once to create the first life and subsequently to insert human consciousness into a hominid, leaving everything in between to naturalistic evolution, but scientists who think they have succeeded so brilliantly in solving most of the puzzle understandably are not impressed by a "God of the gaps" who seems likely to be replaced before long by another successful naturalistic theory.

Suppose, however, that we were to learn that the accepted theory of biological evolution is fundamentally untrue. Suppose that the Darwinian mechanism of mutation and selection cannot really create complex organs and organisms from simple beginnings, and that the problem of biological complexity has not been solved after all. If an error of that magnitude had to be confessed, the entire part of the grand metaphysical story that deals with the history and nature of life would be called into question. The confidence scientists feel that they can eventually provide a materialistic explanation for the origin of life and for consciousness would have no basis once its essential Darwinian foundation was removed. Why devote prodigious effort to speculating about how a primitive form of RNA might be produced in a chemical soup if you have no idea how such a molecule could evolve into a cell? Why assume that mind is only matter if you have no idea of how the brain could have evolved? Instead of a generally satisfactory picture of the history of life with a few gaps, science would confront a vast mystery that would become increasingly stark with the gathering of more biological data. When we imagine the consequences that would follow from a discrediting of the Darwinian theory, it is easy to understand why scientists defend the theory so fiercely.

Modernism rests on the grand metaphysical story of science, and the degree to which the story has been successfully told rests largely on the Darwinian theory of evolution. For scientific naturalists the story and the theory are virtually sacrosanct, but a theistic realist can afford to take a critical look at both. And so we will.

4

Is There
a Blind
Watchmaker?

T HE MAY 8, 1994, ISSUE OF *THE NEW YORK TIMES SUNDAY*
Magazine carried a short article by Jonathan Weiner, titled
"The Handy-Dandy Evolution Prover." Weiner began by
telling stories about fundamentalist Christians he had met who did
not believe in evolution and insisted that the earth was less than
ten thousand years old. He thought it extremely odd that such
people still existed, since he himself had seen evolution actually
in progress. Weiner had written a book about his time in the
Galápagos Archipelago with Peter and Rosemary Grant, two
Princeton scientists who study finches. The distinctive characteristics of "Darwin's finches" on these islands have long been
an important example of what Julian Huxley called "evolution

in action," although Charles Darwin himself did not seem to perceive their significance when he visited the islands on his famous voyage. The Grants observe, measure and record the characteristics of the finch populations, especially their beaks, and note variations that appear from time to time due to environmental changes.

The most spectacular example of evolution that the Grants witnessed involved a finch species that was greatly reduced in numbers during the terrible drought year of 1977 on Daphne Island. The beaks of the next generation following the drought were on average 4 to 5 percent larger, and better shaped for opening the last tough seeds that remained on the island. Then in 1983 spectacular floods came, many finches died, and the island turned rapidly from desert to jungle. The first postflood generation of finches again had smaller beaks, which fitted them to enjoy the multitude of tiny seeds that became available. Beak size thus went through a cycle, caused by environmental changes, from smaller to larger and then back to smaller.

A laudatory review of Weiner's book *(The Beak of the Finch: A Story of Evolution in Our Time)* appeared in the *Times* book-review section a week later. Like Weiner's essay, it began by commenting on the astonishing persistence of biblical creationism among persons who appear to be otherwise perfectly reasonable. The reviewer attributed this to a lack of knowledge of the overwhelming proof of evolution which scientists have discovered. "Although there is abundant hard proof of natural selection and the origin of species in the form of fossils embedded in the rock of ages," said the reviewer, "the evidence is far more subtle among living creatures." The review praised Weiner for demonstrating that evolution is not just a theory about changes that happened in the remote past but a process that we can watch, because it goes on all around us all the time. As Weiner himself wrote, after one has seen evolution actually happening, "debating the reality of the process seems as absurd as debating the existence of gravity."*

A Caricatured Debate

The Weiner article and book review illustrate what I would call the "official caricature" of the creation-evolution debate, a distortion that is either explicit or implicit in nearly all media and textbook treatments of the subject. According to the caricature, "evolution" is a simple, unitary process that one can see in operation today and that is also supported unequivocally by all the fossil evidence. Everyone accepts the truth of evolution except a disturbingly large group of biblical fundamentalists, who insist that the earth is no more than ten thousand years old and the fossil beds were laid down in Noah's flood. These baffling persons either are uninformed about the evidence or perhaps choose to disregard it as a temptation placed before us by God to test our faith in Genesis. There is no conceivable intellectual basis for their dissent, because the evidence for evolution is absolutely conclusive.

According to the official caricature, the finch-beak variation that the Grants observed on Daphne Island is fundamentally the same process that brought birds into existence in the first place. Essentially the same process, extended over immense stretches of geological time, produced complex plants and animals from single-celled microbes. Biological evolution at all levels is thus fundamentally a single process, which one either accepts or (irrationally) rejects.

This scientific understanding of evolution, according to the car-

---

*Readers who are at all familiar with the literature of evolution will have noticed that the case of the finch beak is a variation of the most famous textbook example of "evolution in action": a phenomenon called "industrial melanism" in the peppered moth. In a population containing both light and dark moths, the light moths were predominant while the background trees were light in color, but the dark moths tended to predominate when the trees became darkened due to industrial smoke. The example does not illustrate moths in the process of changing to something else, or even changing in color. It illustrates an essentially stable population that can vary cyclically to adjust to conditions.

icature, does not threaten theistic religion. As the *New York Times* book reviewer put it, "The secret of life is that it can change with [environmental changes] and continue to thrive, and if I were searching for signs of an infinitely wise creator, I might find them here."

Of course the official caricature utterly misrepresents the scope of the controversy. Creationists are not necessarily Genesis literalists or believers in a young earth, nor do they necessarily reject "evolution" in all senses of that highly manipulable term. A creationist is simply a person who believes that God *creates*—meaning that the living world is the product of an intelligent and purposeful Creator rather than merely a combination of chance events and impersonal natural laws. Critics of evolutionary theory are well aware of the standard examples of microevolution, including dog breeding and the cyclical variations that have been seen in things like finch beaks and moth populations.* The difference is that we interpret these observations as examples of the capacity of dogs and finches to vary within limits, not of a process capable of creating dogs and finches, much less the main groups of plants and animals, in the first place.

This skepticism about the extrapolationist view of evolution is hardly unreasonable, because many distinguished evolutionary biologists have also written that large-scale evolutionary change cannot be explained as a product of merely the accumulation of generation-to-generation variations. As any creationist (and many evolutionists) would see the matter, making the case for "evolution" as a general theory of life's history requires a lot more than merely citing examples of small-scale variation. It requires showing how extremely complex biological structures can be built up from simple beginnings by natural processes, without the need for input or guidance from a supernatural Creator. Perhaps evolu-

---

*The Daphne Island finch-beak example is discussed on page 25 of my book *Darwin on Trial* as a typical example of cyclical variation.

tionary biologists can show how that could happen, but the finch-beak example does not even begin to do it.

The caricature also misleads by implying that Darwinian evolution, when properly understood, points to the existence of "an infinitely wise creator." All the major authorities of modern Darwinism have said otherwise, from the founders of the neo-Darwinian synthesis (Theodosius Dobzhansky, George Gaylord Simpson, Julian Huxley, Ernst Mayr) to contemporary authorities such as Richard Dawkins, Stephen Jay Gould and Douglas Futuyma. Gould, for example, has remarked, "Before Darwin, we thought that a benevolent God had created us." After the acceptance of Darwinism, however, that belief became intellectually untenable. According to Gould,

No intervening spirit watches lovingly over the affairs of nature (though Newton's clock-winding god might have set up the machinery at the beginning of time and then let it run). No vital forces propel evolutionary change. And whatever we think of God, his existence is not manifest in the products of nature.

Similar sentiments have been expressed by just about all the other leading Darwinists who write for the general public (the professional audience doesn't need to be told). In terms of the creation-evolution controversy, the main point of "evolution" is not the study of natural variations or domestic animal breeding, although evolutionary biologists certainly do study these things. The main point is that the entire history of life can be understood as part of the grand metaphysical story of science. To that end evolutionary biology must establish that a combination of random events and impersonal natural laws—"chance and necessity," in the famous words of Jacques Monod—actually performed the work of biological creation.

Dawkins's Blind Watchmaker

I call this main point the "blind watchmaker thesis," after the title of the famous book by Richard Dawkins, which in its American edition is subtitled *Why the Evidence of Evolution Reveals a Universe Without Design.* Among modern Darwinists, Dawkins has achieved enormous acclaim for presenting orthodox neo-Darwinism persuasively. Francis Crick has advised the public, "If you doubt the power of natural selection I urge you, to save your soul, to read Dawkins' book." In 1990 Dawkins received the Michael Faraday Award from the British Royal Society as "the scientist who has done the most to further the public understanding of science." In 1992 he gave the Royal Institution's Christmas lectures for young people, televised by the BBC, arguing the same naturalistic worldview that he presents in *The Blind Watchmaker.* I mention these accolades to dispel any illusion that Dawkins's explicitly naturalistic presentation of Darwinism amounts to a mere personal philosophy. He certainly is promoting metaphysical naturalism, but, like his American counterpart Carl Sagan (who received the Public Welfare Medal in 1994 from the National Academy of Sciences for his contributions to public education), he does so with the wholehearted support of the scientific establishment of his nation.

Dawkins begins *The Blind Watchmaker* by acknowledging, "Biology is the study of complicated things that give the appearance of having been designed for a purpose." The complexity is indeed enormous; according to Dawkins, even a single cell contains more information than all the volumes of the *Encyclopaedia Britannica* put together, and an encyclopedia is definitely the kind of thing that in our experience is produced only by a preexisting purposeful intelligence. Dawkins insists, however, that the genetic information required for complex plants and animals not only can be but actually has been built up by natural selection in the course of evolution. He writes,

Natural selection is the blind watchmaker, blind because it does not see ahead, does not plan consequences, has no purpose in view. Yet the living results of natural selection overwhelmingly impress us with the appearance of design as if by a master watchmaker, impress us with the illusion of design and planning.

Whether natural selection actually can produce that illusion of design and planning remains to be seen, but at least there is no doubt that Dawkins is posing the right question. If natural selection can perform the wonders Dawkins promises, there is no need to posit a supernatural Creator and it is possible, in Dawkins's words, to be "an intellectually fulfilled atheist."* The truth or falsity of Dawkins's blind watchmaker thesis is thus a matter of immense cultural importance.

The Replicator and Its Offspring

But exactly how did natural selection create the enormously complex forms of life that exist today? In Dawkins's telling, the story begins when a "Replicator," probably a primitive form of RNA molecule, somehow emerged by a combination of chance and chemical laws from a process of prebiological evolution. The essential characteristic of the Replicator was that it reproduced and therefore left offspring more or less like itself. The process of replication required the copying of the Replicator's genetic information, and in the process of copying, errors occurred in the genetic sequences.

The errors led to variation, and thus to some Replicators that were more successful at leaving offspring than others. Natural selection favored the advantaged group, and as more copying errors (mutations) and resultant variations occurred, there eventu-

---

*The blind watchmaker thesis makes it *possible* to be an intellectually fulfilled atheist by supplying the necessary creation story. It does not make it *obligatory* to be an atheist, because one can imagine a Creator who works through natural selection. Since the consensus of contemporary evolutionary biologists is that evolution is purposeless and unguided, however, it is doubtful that a Creator would have anything to do. A Creator who merely sets a process in motion and thereafter keeps hands off is easily ignored.

ally emerged Replicators whose genes (segments of the genetic material) produced not only proteins but complete bodies (phenotypes).

In the Dawkins scenario, phenotypes are merely devices produced by genes to ensure their own reproductive success. A gene that produces a body is more likely to produce offspring than a naked gene at the mercy of the chemical elements, and a gene that contributes to the production of a more adaptively successful body will leave behind more successor genes than a gene that is trapped in a body less fitted to survive and reproduce. By this essentially simple "blind watchmaker" mechanism, given enough time and the right environmental conditions, the original Replicator can give birth through disparate lines of succession to creatures as complex and different as orchids, trees, giraffes, ants and human beings.

In *The Blind Watchmaker* Dawkins's chosen example for how this process must have worked at relatively advanced levels is the bat. Many complicated changes must occur to make a flying bat from a hypothetical four-footed ancestor, but let's just look at one small part of the picture for illustration. How did the bat get its wings? Here is the Dawkins story:

How did wings get their start? Many animals leap from bough to bough, and sometimes fall to the ground. Especially in a small animal, the whole body surface catches the air and assists the leap, or breaks the fall, by acting as a crude aerofoil. Any tendency to increase the ratio of surface area to weight would help, for example flaps of skin growing out in the angles of joints. . . . [It] doesn't matter *how* small and unwinglike the first wingflaps were. There must be some height, call it h, such that an animal would just break its neck if it fell from that height, but would just survive if it fell from a slightly lower height. In this critical zone, any improvement in the body surface's ability to catch the air and break the fall, however slight the improvement, can make the difference between life and death. Natural selection will then favor slight, prototype wingflaps. When these small flaps have become the norm, the critical height h will become slightly greater. Now a slight further increase in the wingflaps will make the difference between life and death. And so on, until we have proper wings.

Gene Selection with No Selector?

According to the doctrines of orthodox Darwinism and Mendelian genetics, the "improvements"* in this and all other Darwinian scenarios come from gene mutations that are random in the sense that they are not directed either by God or by the needs of the organism (such as its wish or need to become a flying creature). This point is important because if an unevolved intelligent or purposeful force directed evolution, the blind watchmaker would not be blind and a supernatural element would be introduced into the system. "Evolution" in which the necessary mutations were directed by a preexisting intelligence (which did not itself evolve naturalistically) would be a soft form of creationism and not really evolution at all, in the sense in which Dawkins and other leading Darwinists use the term.

Another essential element in the blind watchmaker model of evolution involves what biologists call the unit of selection. According to Dawkins, what natural selection selects is not just the whole organism (the bat itself) but, more importantly, the gene or gene combination that produced the wing improvements. Selection of the whole organism is not sufficient to propel creative evolution, because the organism dies. However successful at sur-

---

*I am using the term *improvement* because it is convenient and Dawkins employs it. I should warn readers, however, that some Darwinists object to such words because they suggest that evolution is inherently progressive. In Darwinian terms, complex creatures like bats and human beings are not really an improvement over (say) bacteria; after all, bacteria have survived and reproduced successfully for billions of years. Among complex animals the greatest evolutionary success might be the cockroach, which has been around for a very long time and is probably much better equipped than *Homo sapiens* to survive a planetwide catastrophe.

viving and reproducing the individual-organism-on-the-way-to-becoming-a-bat might have been, when it died its components decayed and nothing was left. What the primitive bat passed on to its descendants were its genes (reshuffled in the process of sexual reproduction), specifically including the evolving genetically encoded information that supposedly produced the incipient wings in each stage of development. The blind watchmaker model of evolution is therefore a "gene selection" model, and this, as we shall see, is controversial.

Can blind watchmaker evolution as described by Dawkins actually produce complex adaptive improvements like the bat's wings? The answer depends on the validity of the factual assumptions that underlie the model. Several conditions must be met before evolution of the blind watchmaker sort can occur, and each one is highly problematical.

First, gene mutations of the necessary complexity-building type must occur sufficiently frequently to build the improvement. Unfortunately, mutations having a favorable effect on the organism are extremely rare. Dawkins himself says that the mutations in question would probably have to be too small in effect to be observable, because "virtually all the mutations studied in genetics laboratories—which are pretty macro because otherwise geneticists wouldn't notice them—are deleterious to the animals possessing them."

The mutations that the blind watchmaker model requires must be not only favorable, but favorable in the very strong sense that they provide exactly what is needed for the next stage of the wing-building project. That each individual mutation is supposed to produce only a slight effect in the desired direction implies that there will have to be an enormous number of exactly the right kind of mutations to finish the job—and wings are only one of myriad alterations needed to modify a tree climber into a bat. The only reason to believe that mutations of the kind and quantity needed for blind watchmaker evolution actually occur is that the theory requires them.

Second, the genes that mutate must reliably produce the hypothesized adaptive changes (in this case, skin flaps growing into wings) *without also producing maladaptive side effects.* This condition seems very difficult to meet, because in most cases there is no specific gene that directs the production of a corresponding body part—such as a gene for a specific wing component. Rather, important properties of the animal are typically the result of interactions among various genes, and each individual gene may contribute an effect to various different properties. This pattern of multiple effects helps to explain why mutations are not likely to be favorable, since a destructive effect on one essential bodily function would be likely to produce a fatality in the organism, even if some other effect happened to protect the creature from the consequences of a fall.

Whether the problems of multiple effects are fatal to the gene-selection model depends on your attitude toward the model. If blind watchmaker evolution simply has to be the explanation for adaptive complexity, because no alternative is available, then there has to be a way to overcome the problems. That is essentially Dawkins's position, and he does have speculative answers to the objections. He suggests that what natural selection preserves is a relatively short piece of DNA that is small enough to be passed on intact for many generations despite the reshuffling that occurs in sexual reproduction. He supposes that these discrete genetic units have some tendency, in cooperation with other genetic units, to produce some predictable trait in the organism, "other things being equal." Whether any of this is more than wishful thinking has yet to be demonstrated.

Third, blind watchmaker evolution can occur only if the effects of differential survival (natural selection) are sufficiently strong and consistent over time to encourage long-term change in the hypothesized direction. Natural selection must in effect operate as consistently as artificial selection, where human breeders select for the woolliest sheep or the largest dog, preserving the desired characteristic even if the breeding results in a variety that is in other respects overspecialized and hence vulnerable to disease, injury and predators.

In nature, however, the selective advantage of something like a tiny, incipient wing flap would probably be very weak, especially if most climbing creatures die from causes other than falls or if the presence of the flap causes an awkwardness in climbing. The actual efficacy of natural selection in preserving hypothetical incipient structures cannot be determined, and so Dawkins illustrates how it might work primarily with illustrations involving *artificial* selection—that is, intelligent design. For example, he points out that some industrial designers use random-search techniques to design the most efficient wings or pipeline systems. The most famous example of this sort is Dawkins's own popular Blind Watchmaker computer program, in which viewers select the characteristics of "evolving" computer figures. When the selection is done by a purposeful human agent and the mutations are supplied by the computer program, the biological problems with blind watchmaker evolution are assumed away.

The Fossil Record
There is an additional evidentiary problem that advocates of blind watchmaker evolution need to address, although it is of a different character from the ones just discussed. If the proposition being tested is not only that blind watchmaker evolution *could* produce complex adaptations but that it also *actually did so,* scientific investigation must include an evaluation of the fossil record. If the blind watchmaker thesis is true, fossil evidence should on the whole support the claim that today's complex organisms evolved step-by-gradual-step from specific common ancestors.

It is generally conceded today, however, that fossil species are remarkably stable over long periods of time and that the appearance of new forms is typically abrupt. Moreover, many authorities now attribute extinctions primarily to freakish catastrophes, rather than to the hypothetical Darwinian process by which ancestors are supposedly being supplanted continually by better-adapted descendants. Advocates of blind watchmaker evolution accordingly take a defensive stance toward the fossil record, typically arguing that it is good enough to show that "evolution has occurred" but insufficiently complete to demonstrate the exact steps by which simple organisms developed new complex adaptations like wings.

Accounting for Complexity
Despite the enormous evidentiary problems faced by the blind watchmaker model of evolution, the model's great virtue is that it actually does address the main point at issue, which is how a vast increase in biological complexity might have occurred over time. I emphasize this virtue because, as we have seen, many popular "proofs" of evolution that uncritical Darwinists find completely satisfactory do not address the complexity question at all. For uncritical Darwinists who accept the official stereotype, the issue is not complexity or increase in genetic information, but simply variation. In their simplistic view, variations in finch beaks constitute "evolution" and hence illustrate a process capable of evolving a human being from a bacterial ancestor, when compared to the standard straw-man alternative that all species were created fixed and immutable a few thousand years ago.

Dawkins's blind watchmaker model is infinitely preferable to such oversimplifications, even if it has to make unsupported assumptions about crucial factors like the frequency of helpful mutations. Moreover, Dawkins has argued, without serious contradiction as far as I am aware, that his kind of model is the only naturalistic theory that can account for biological complexity even in principle. If rival models of evolution cannot even in principle explain complexity, Dawkins's blind watchmaker model deserves to be called *the* theory of evolution. That is exactly what his protégé Helena Cronin did call it in her book *The Ant and the Peacock,* where she referred to the Dawkins model simply as "modern Darwinism."

Arguing for Catastrophism

By using that term Cronin implicitly relegated all other understandings of Darwinism to the trash can of history, and for that she drew a furious reaction from the most famous American advocate of evolution, Harvard professor Stephen Jay Gould. In his angry review of Cronin's book, Gould denied that most evolutionary biologists accept the gene-selection model and declared, for reasons similar to those I have already discussed, that genes cannot possibly be the exclusive unit of selection. Gould asserted forcefully that most important bodily characteristics are "emergent properties" of organisms which are not produced in any direct way by individual genes or even combinations of genes. Instead, these properties are products of such complex interactions among genes that they cannot *even in principle* be adequately known or predicted at the genetic level.

If Gould is correct on that point, then to select for individual genes or even gene combinations is not to select for predictable properties in the adult organism. But in that case, how can the complex adaptations that Dawkins and Cronin seek to explain be built up by a process of mutation and selection?

Gould did not ask himself that question, nor did he draw his readers' attention to the problem. Instead he went on to reject what he called the "uniformitarian vision of extrapolation," which is the fundamental Darwinian principle illustrated by the finch-beak example with which this chapter began. To classical Darwinists, the entire story of evolution and extinction is basically an extrapolation from the examples of random variation and natural selection that can be observed in the living world. In this story random variations appear more or less continually, but only those that confer increased fitness survive to spread through a population by natural selection. There is thus a continual gradual process by which favored organisms crowd out those less capable of leaving fit offspring. As the fitter organisms survive, the less fit die off, and this equally gradual process is what we call extinction. The whole system is propelled by chance variations, but over time natural selection inexorably governs all the important characteristics of living organisms.

According to Gould, however, "the main excitement in evolutionary theory during the last twenty years has not been . . . the shoring up of Darwinism in its limited realm (by gene selectionism or any other patching device), but rather the documentation of the reasons why Darwin's crucial requirement for extrapolation has failed." Gould explained that for one thing, molecular studies have indicated that most variations at the molecular level are neutral as far as fitness goes, and so selection plays little part in molecular evolution. The most important evidence against extrapolation, however, concerns the frequency and importance of mass extinctions—which are increasingly attributed to sudden catastrophic accidents such as asteroid impacts. Such extraordinary events, which may account for a high percentage of extinctions, destroy the continuity of natural conditions assumed by Darwin and the extrapolationists of today.

Environmental conditions in normal times may consistently encourage change of the Darwinian kind for a while, but even the fittest organisms are not necessarily protected from extinction in a catastrophe that changes all the conditions. Once a catastrophe occurs, the lucky survivors, which may have been only marginally fit under precatastrophic conditions, will inherit the earth in spite of their modest capabilities.

After this review of his own version of "modern Darwinism," Gould concluded, "The Darwinian struggle does not extrapolate to the tree of life."

Competing Models

My purpose here is not to take sides between Dawkins and Gould. Indeed, I would say that these two eminent Darwinists were dealing with different subjects, although both called the subject "evolution." Gould was writing about the changes that scientists actually observe, either in the living world of today or in the fossil record of the past. Their observations do include instances of Darwinian evolution by natural selection, but they observe it only at the relatively modest level of the finch-beak example. In biochemistry laboratories they observe molecules accumulating variations by chance, with natural selection so rarely a factor of importance that a "neutral theory of molecular evolution" has taken center stage. In the fossil record, paleontologists observe mass extinctions and the subsequent sudden appearance of new kinds of organisms. They do not observe new organs like bat wings in the process of gradual formation, and they do not observe one kind of organism changing into something fundamentally different through a step-by-step process.

If the fossil record is a reliable guide, "evolution" seems to be a process in which new forms of life appeared abruptly, remained fundamentally unchanged throughout their tenure on the earth and then often became extinct—not because they were gradually supplanted by improved descendants, but because they were in the wrong ecological niche at the time of a mass extinction. That is evolution Gould-style. Because it is derived primarily from observation, rather than the more abstract theoretical need to account for complex adaptations, I call it "empirical evolution" to distinguish it from "blind watchmaker evolution."

The advantage of empirical evolution is that it squares pretty well with observations. The disadvantage is that it does not explain the main point that a theory of evolution needs to explain, which is the origin of adaptive complexity. Living organisms are packed with complex parts that have to work together, and the genetic information required to keep those parts working properly to serve the needs of the organism must be enormous. Where did it come from? To stick with Dawkins's chosen example, how did the bat get its wings, or its echolocation (bat sonar) system, or its breathing apparatus, or any of the myriad other complex things that bats need to have? Extinctions might clear the way for surviving organisms to occupy new environmental niches, but extinction events only kill, they do not create.

Neutral evolution *by definition* does not explain the growth of adaptive complexity. If adaptive complexity is to be explained at all, it must be by a model like that provided by Dawkins. Gould can discard that model only at the cost of leaving adaptive complexity unexplained. Probably that is why Gould is evasive about whether he is rejecting the Dawkins model or merely supplementing it with other kinds of evolution.

Perhaps the best example of the incompatibility of empirical and blind watchmaker evolution is the Cambrian explosion, which is memorably pictured in Gould's book *Wonderful Life*. Nearly all the animal "phyla" (basic body plans) appear suddenly and without apparent ancestors in the rocks of the Cambrian era, dated around 540 million years ago. These animals are all complex multicellular organisms, with highly complex adaptations like the famous trilobite eyes. Where did these complex features come from? Before the Cambrian era, with a few exceptions, we have evidence of nothing but simple, unicellular life.

If one assumes that a process of gradual, blind watchmaker evolution produced the Cambrian phyla, then one has to assume also that a universe of transitional species that once lived on the earth has vanished mysteriously from the fossil record. Gould, a paleontologist who refuses to treat the fossil record so cavalierly, can only declare that the transitionals (or at least most of them) never existed and that something called a "fast-transition" filled the gap.

Gould is faithful to the observable evidence, where a blind watchmaker theorist is not, but the price he has to pay is that he has only an empty term to account for the complexity. When pressed on this point (as I have had occasion to observe), he has no alternative but to retreat to blind watchmaker evolution for as long as it takes to protect his home base.

The differing evolutionary theories of Gould and Dawkins cannot be resolved, because the observations that scientists have been making are at odds with the presuppositions of the blind watchmaker thesis. This situations places evolutionary scientists and popularizers of evolution in a dilemma: should they support the official caricature of the evolution-creation debate even though they must know it is simplistic nonsense—or should they make the scientific objections known and thereby give an opening to "irrational" (that is, nonnaturalistic) people and organizations who want to attribute our existence to a supernatural being called God?

What is at stake is not a mere scientific theory but a concept of rationality, or perhaps the survival of the established naturalistic religious philosophy.

5

Theistic Naturalism & Theistic Realism

I F ONE LOOKS AT THE GRAND METAPHYSICAL STORY OF SCI-
ence with a critical eye, it is easy to find reasons to be skeptical
of the whole project. Astrophysics seems to point to a creation
event; the much-hyped physical theory of everything may never be
more than a myth (and in any case would explain disappointingly
little); natural selection is absurdly inadequate to explain the existence of conscious, reflecting, equation-solving and poetry-writ-
ing minds; and most important, the whole theory of blind watchmaker evolution relies on very dubious assumptions and virtually
ignores the weight of the fossil evidence. This is not to deny that
scientists pursuing the grand project have come up with some very
useful and interesting knowledge, but they seem also to have produced some myth and fantasy, precisely because they have refused
to consider that there may be limits to what can be learned about
reality through their methodology.

Blind Theorymakers

Perhaps their dogmatic metaphysical naturalism has even led scientists to disregard some aspect of reality that is virtually staring them in the face. Could it be, for example, that living organisms (in Richard Dawkins's wording) "give the appearance of having been designed for a purpose" because in fact they *are* designed?

Scientific naturalists meet this shocking suggestion with one of two inconsistent responses. One is to make a few superficial debater's points against design and then declare the subject closed. The most famous example of this approach is an article by Stephen Jay Gould called "The Panda's Thumb," which relies on a few selected examples and a spectacularly shallow theology to establish the "fact of evolution." The panda's "thumb" is not a true opposable thumb like our own but an extension of the wristbone. Gould thinks that a supernatural designer could have found a more elegant solution to the panda's need for an efficient bamboo-stripping tool; therefore the thumb is not designed; therefore it is the product of evolution.

Gould's approach implicitly concedes that intelligent design is a legitimate hypothesis, subject to proof and disproof. If a genuine public debate on that subject were to occur, the shaky premises of blind watchmaker evolution would get a lot of unwanted attention.

That debate is not likely to occur, though, because the main line of argument against intelligent design in biology is not that the possibility has been impartially considered and refuted, but that intelligent design is inherently ineligible for scientific consideration because it implies the existence of a supernatural entity. To postulate an unevolved intelligence to explain the characteristics of living organisms is allegedly to abandon science for religion. And one of the curiosities of contemporary academic life is that most Christian theists with respectable academic appointments will enthusiastically unite with agnostics to defend the exclusion of intelligent design from science.

The very atheistic physicist Steven Weinberg described the central point at issue, in commenting on my critique of Darwinism in his own book, *Dreams of a Final Theory.* Weinberg did not dispute any of my specific scientific arguments against the validity of blind watchmaker evolution. He was willing to concede that evolutionary theory may be encountering some difficulties with the evidence, but he thought that to make very much of this is to misunderstand the nature of science. In his own words:

> Johnson argues that naturalistic evolution, "evolution that involves no intervention or guidance by a creator outside the world of nature," in fact does not provide a very good explanation for the origin of species. I think he goes wrong here because he has no feeling for the problems that any scientific theory has in accounting for what we observe. Even apart from outright errors, our calculations and observations are always based on assumptions that go beyond the validity of the theory we are trying to test. . . . In the writings of today's paleontologists and evolutionary biologists we can recognize the same state of affairs that is so familiar to us in physics; in using the naturalistic theory of evolution biologists are working with an overwhelmingly successful theory, but one that is not yet finished with its work of explication. It seems to me to be a profoundly important discovery that we can get very far in explaining the world without invoking divine intervention, and in biology as well as in the physical sciences.

The Excluded Middle

To my argument that blind watchmaker evolution owes its support more to naturalistic philosophy than to empirical science, Weinberg responded in effect that science and naturalism are basically the same thing, because "the only way that any sort of science can proceed is to assume that there is no divine intervention and to see how far one can get with that assumption."

If Weinberg means that any divine intervention brings science to an end, his statement exhibits what in logic is known as the fallacy of the excluded middle. The possibility that divine intervention may occur sets limits to the scope of scientific understanding, but it emphatically does *not* imply that all events are the product of an unpredictable divine whimsy. On the contrary, the very notion of "natural law" grew out of the concept of a lawmaker. If that lawmaker also created our minds in the image of his own, then it is not surprising that we have the reasoning powers that make science possible.

As we have seen, the existence of conscious, reasoning minds has no logical connection to a natural order ruled by a blind watchmaker that cares for nothing but survival and reproduction and therefore ought to have been satisfied with cockroaches and weeds. The universal lawmaker has the power to make exceptions, just as a worldly sovereign has the power to pardon lawbreakers, but such exceptional acts do not make the laws unimportant. Medical science, for example, remains a very useful discipline whether or not there are instances of miraculous cures that are in principle beyond scientific explanation.

Similarly, the discipline of biology will not only survive but prosper if it turns out that genetic information really is the product of preexisting intelligence. Biologists will have to give up their dogmatic materialism and discard unproductive hypotheses like the prebiotic soup, but to abandon bad ideas is a gain, not a loss. Freed of the metaphysical chains that tie it to nineteenth-century materialism, biology can turn to the fascinating task of discovering how the intelligence embodied in the genetic information works through matter to make the organism function. In that case chemical evolution will go the way of alchemy—abandoned because a better understanding of the problem revealed its futility—and science will have reached a new plateau.

Pressing the Limits

What Weinberg probably meant to say is that the only way to find out whether there are any limits to scientific knowledge (or exactly what the limits are) is to assume that there are no limits and forge ahead as far as one can go. Up to a point, I agree. Employing the heuristic assumption* that no limits exist is useful to people who want to push the limits, for the same reason that it may be useful for a military commander facing overwhelming odds to refuse to consider the possibility of defeat. If there really is a materialist explanation for the origin of life, or the human mind, it surely will be found by a scientist who resolutely ignores the objections of people like me and persists in looking for it.

The danger of heuristic assumptions, though, is that they so easily turn into facts in the eyes of those who rely on them. Previously successful military commanders may convince themselves that defeat really is impossible and continue a suicidal campaign, arbitrarily refusing to credit intelligence reports documenting the overwhelming strength of the enemy. Behavioral psychologists may train themselves to think that all human behavior really can be explained as responses to rewards and punishments. Economists may become convinced that people really are economically rational, and particle physicists may flatter themselves that they really are capable of discovering the ultimate secrets of the universe. The professionals always tend to exaggerate their successes, especially when they are competing for funding or public respect, and they have a corresponding ability to forget about facts that do not fit their theories. At some point, outsiders need to come in and audit the books.

But an audit that is done at the wrong time may be misleading.

---

*A heuristic assumption is one that is useful in providing aid or direction in the solution of a problem but that is not independently justifiable or provable.

The books may look pretty shaky today, but the managers of the enterprise may be confident that a smashing success is just around the corner. The big problem is deciding when to stop believing their promises of eventual success, particularly when the managers have been successful in the past. As Weinberg observes, outsiders like me may lack feeling for the problems that any scientific theory has in accounting for all the observations. Outsiders may think that discordant observations have invalidated the theory, while the insiders are facing the situation with confidence, convinced that their approach to the problems is fundamentally sound and will lead to eventual success.

How can we tell who is correct? It's a good question, but the solution is *not* to grant the insiders the exclusive privilege of auditing themselves.

The Need for Outside Criticism

Weinberg's point takes on added significance in view of certain difficulties with big bang cosmology that became apparent shortly after his book appeared. The best known of these is that new measurements seem to indicate that the universe as a whole is substantially younger than the oldest stars within it, a logical contradiction. Dispute about the measurements is still going on, but the paradox has set some cosmologists to speculate about reintroducing a "cosmological constant" into the equations to reconcile the figures, even though Einstein once did something of the sort and later called it the greatest mistake he had ever made.

As if that were not enough, recent observations with the Hubble space telescope indicate that faint red dwarf stars are very rare. The observation is important because current gravitational theories require that at least 90 percent of the mass of the universe be invisible to our telescopes, and red dwarfs had been the leading candidates to supply the missing mass. If the missing mass does not exist, then a scientific revolution may be in prospect.

On the other hand, the missing mass may yet be found, the paradox about the age of the universe may be resolved by still better measurements, and the current standard model may go on to new triumphs. What is a crisis to one group of investigators may be a golden opportunity to another. Indeed, the *New York Times* article that reported the red dwarf problem quoted a prominent astrophysicist as saying, "This is a day for particle physicists to celebrate"—because their theories about the existence of exotic particles take on greater importance now that the search for more conventional solutions to the missing-mass problem is at an apparent dead end.

I can imagine Steven Weinberg asking me, "Should scientists pursue these problems according to their best judgment, or should they give up on science and just say that God did it?" The answer is easy: I do not urge scientists to give up on any theory or research agenda until they themselves are convinced that further efforts would be fruitless. In view of the cultural importance of the naturalistic worldview, however, and its status as virtually the official philosophy of government and education, there is a need for informed outsiders to point out that claims are often made in the name of science that go far beyond the available evidence. The public needs to learn to discount those claims, and the scientists themselves need to learn how profoundly their interpretations of the evidence are influenced by their metaphysical preconceptions. If the resulting embarrassment spurs scientists on to greater achievements, leading to a smashing vindication of their basic viewpoint, then so be it.

Outsiders to the research community need to provide criticism on the fundamental issues, because debate within that community operates within definite limits. Scientists are highly vulnerable to peer pressure because their careers depend on favorable peer reviews. To become a scientist at all requires satisfying dissertation and appointment committees. Thereafter, professional standing depends on one's ability to satisfy the anonymous referees who decide what is to be published in journals and the study groups that decide what projects are to be funded. The system of peer review has important virtues, but it means that even a very esteemed scientist who goes too far in criticizing fundamental assumptions can be effectively excluded from the research community. (I have personally seen this happen.) Disagreement within professional boundaries is accepted, of course, but disagreement that seems irrational to powerful colleagues can ruin even the most brilliant career.

That is why it is important for each independent professional community to check its rivals and neighbors. Sometimes this happens within the boundaries of science. For example, claims by molecular biologists about the discovery of a "molecular Eve" ancestor of all humans, whose descendants allegedly emerged from Africa relatively recently, were effectively criticized by fossil experts who thought that their cherished older specimens from Europe and Asia should not be excluded from the line of human descent. Personal motives and ideologies abounded on all sides, as they tend to do in human disputes, but the existence of an opposition party sparked an enthusiastic (and successful) search for deficiencies in the way the molecular biologists interpreted their evidence.

What is missing from the contemporary intellectual world is a qualified opposition party that is willing and able to challenge the established religious philosophy itself, the metaphysical naturalism that is so successfully promoted in the name of science by such as Weinberg, Hawking, Sagan, Gould, Dawkins and Crick. The logical opposition party would consist of scientifically informed theologians, or perhaps theologically informed scientists, who respect the experimental method within its limits but who do not assume a priori that all of reality can be understood in naturalistic or materialistic terms.

The need for such an opposition party is implied by Weinberg's own logic: the only way to find out what the limits of naturalistic science may be is for some persons to act as if there were no limits and see how far they can go—and then for other persons who are free of naturalistic preconceptions to evaluate their results and consider whether limits have been revealed.

Theistic Naturalism

The power of scientific naturalism in the academic world is so intimidating, however, that hardly anyone is willing to challenge it. Theologians (or theistic scientists) survive in academia not by challenging naturalism with a rival interpretation of reality but by trying to find a place for theology within the picture of reality defined by scientific naturalists. They write books with titles like *Religion in an Age of Science* (Ian Barbour), *Theology for a Scientific Age* (Arthur Peacocke) and *Theology in the Age of Scientific Reasoning* (Nancey Murphy). I call this genre "theistic naturalism," because to accommodate successfully the theists must accept not just the particular conclusions that scientists have reached but also the naturalistic methodology that generated those conclusions.

A representative example is Nancey Murphy, who received her Ph.D. degree at the Graduate Theological Union adjacent to the Berkeley campus. Her dissertation-based first book received an award from the American Academy of Religion, and she thereafter became professor of Christian philosophy at an evangelical Christian institution, Fuller Theological Seminary in southern California. Murphy is therefore particularly well placed to assess the arguments of *Darwin on Trial* from the viewpoint of those Christian scholars who have found a respectable place on the periphery of the academic mainstream by developing an approach to theology that supports rather than challenges the identification of science with naturalism.

Murphy's review of *Darwin on Trial* criticized the book for failing to observe the crucial distinction between religion and science on which scientific naturalists are so insistent. She particularly objected to my suggestion that scientists should consider the possibility that "life is what it so evidently seems to be, the product of creative intelligence." That option is impermissible, Murphy answered, because "for better or worse, we have inherited a view of science as *methodologically* atheistic." It follows that

> anyone who attributes the characteristics of living things to creative intelligence has by definition stepped into the arena of metaphysics or theology. Some might reply that the definition of science, then, needs to be changed. And perhaps it would be better if science had not taken this particular turn in its history. Could the nature of science change again in the near future to admit theistic explanations of natural events? There are a number of reasons for thinking this unlikely. A practical reason is the fact that much of the funding for scientific research comes from the federal government. The mixing of science and religion would raise issues of the separation of church and state.
>
> A second reason for thinking such a change unlikely is that many Christians in science, philosophy, and theology are still haunted by the idea of a "God of the gaps."... Many Christians are wary of invoking divine action in any way in science, especially in biology, fearing that science will advance, providing the naturalistic explanations that will make God appear once again to have been an unnecessary hypothesis.

The great virtue of Murphy's review is that she is so candid in acknowledging that the issue is one of cultural power and intimidation, not truth. Because she is familiar with contemporary trends in philosophy, she knows better than to suggest that science inherently *must* have any particular characteristic, as if there were some "essence" of science located in a Platonic heaven. A cultural phenomenon like science is defined by human beings, and the definition can and does change from one era to another. What humans have defined, other humans can redefine—if they have sufficient cultural power to force the change.

Murphy does not argue, as Weinberg undoubtedly would, that methodological atheism* ought to rule science because atheism is *true.* On the contrary, we are entitled to presume that a professor of Christian philosophy at Fuller Theological Seminary would insist emphatically that atheism is *false.* In that case, the reason that valid scientific theories can be achieved only by making the counterfactual assumption that atheism is true is not immediately obvious—to put it mildly. In a free intellectual environment, we might expect that Christian theists would vigorously assert that some conclusions of the methodological atheists who rule science may be as faulty as the unsound premise from which they were derived. The reason theists do not (should not?) do this, it seems, is they are afraid—for both legal and intellectual reasons—to enter the debate.

Murphy's suggestion that the constitutional separation of church and state prevents publicly funded scientists from considering intelligent design should not be taken seriously. As pointed out in the opening chapters, some people do have the impression that it is virtually illegal to offer scientific arguments for intelligent causes in biology, at least when public funding or property is involved. This impression exists, however, only because the very religion-science dichotomy that Murphy is defending temporarily obscures the decisive consideration that the Constitution exists to protect freedom of inquiry and expression, not to impose a philosophical straitjacket upon scientists or anyone else.

Its dedication to the separation of church and state notwithstanding, the American Civil Liberties Union (which sided with

---

*For present purposes, there is no need to distinguish between atheism and naturalism. Atheism makes the strong statement that God does not exist; naturalism says merely that no supernatural entity has influenced the world of nature. *Methodological* atheism and naturalism are identical.

the evangelical minister in the Lamb's Chapel case discussed in chapter one) is not going to send lawyers into court to argue that while God may be free to create life elsewhere in the world, within the boundaries of the United States he must respect the Constitution's establishment of naturalism in science.

The likelihood of coercion and retaliation against theists is real enough, but it will come from within the scientific community, in the form of tenure denials and unfavorable peer reviews, not from civil liberties lawyers. To be sure, it takes courage for theists to challenge the domination of naturalism, especially if they are scientists with families to support. But if it becomes sufficiently apparent that the rulers of science are trying to punish rational dissent, the Constitution will be on the side of the dissenters. I am also confident that if the issues are sufficiently clarified, the scientific community will choose overwhelmingly to join the party of intellectual freedom.

Murphy's second point is of the same order. Why should theistic scholars be haunted by the fear that invoking divine action in biology is inherently futile, assuming they believe that such divine activity could have occurred? (If they do not believe divine action could have occurred, then they are naturalists, not theists.) The answer goes back to the very requirement of methodological atheism that Murphy defends. If the atheists make the rules, the atheists are surely going to win the game, regardless of what is true. The rules limit science to naturalistic theories and provide that the best available naturalistic theory can be considered successful even when it rests on unverifiable assumptions and conflicts with some of the evidence. If those are the rules of the game, then it is indeed futile for theists to try to play—but why should theists accept such rules, except that they lack the courage to challenge them?

The presence of so much irrational fear is understandable, although the formal controls on dissent would collapse the moment they were challenged by a determined minority with rational arguments to make. The real power of naturalism consists of its presence in the minds of its natural adversaries. Scientific naturalism is the spirit of the age, at least in the universities, and even many Christian intellectuals are at least half convinced that naturalism is true. Some abandon their theism for just this reason, while others think about the contradiction as little as possible or struggle in various ways to reconcile theism in religion with naturalism in science.

Seeking Space for Theology

The simplest way to resolve the contradiction is to withdraw one's personal theism from the world of objective reality. Perhaps the consequences of divine action are inherently invisible to science, although they may be apparent enough to the eye of faith. If evidence of divine action in the history of the universe is conspicuous by its apparent absence, then we may still choose to believe that the universe would disappear if God did not constantly uphold it with his mighty (but scientifically undetectable) word of power. Wise metaphysical naturalists will smile at these transparent devices, but they will not openly ridicule them. Why should they—when theists implicitly comply with the naturalistic doctrine that "religion" is a matter of faith, not reason?

More interesting is the possibility that theology might make a desperate last stand at the ultimate beginning of time. This is an option Nancey Murphy considers, following Arthur Peacocke. There is a commonly recognized hierarchy of the sciences, ranging from those that study the supposedly most fundamental constituents of nature (such as particle physics) to those that study more complex interactions (such as biology). According to Murphy,

Peacocke proposes that at the top of the hierarchy of the sciences we reach theology, the science that studies the most complex system of all—the interaction of God and the whole of creation.

Peacocke's suggestion provides the groundwork for an exciting account of the relations between science and theology. We can examine the kinds of relations that hold between two hierarchically ordered sciences, and then look for analogous relations between theology and one or more sciences. One relation we may expect to find is that when a science reaches an inherent limit, there may be a role for theology to play at that point. For example, it *may* be inherently impossible for science to describe what happened "before" the Big Bang.

I fear that Murphy's hopes are doomed to disappointment. The metaphysicians of science have no intention of cooperating with any plan to leave a metaphysical space for theology—a reality that is illustrated by a marvelously revealing story told by Steven Hawking in *A Brief History of Time.* To set the context, Hawking explained that the concept of a big bang commencement of the universe was unwelcome at first to many scientific naturalists, on strictly *theological* grounds:

> Many people do not like the idea that time has a beginning, probably because it smacks of divine intervention. (The Catholic Church, on the other hand, seized on the big bang model and in 1951 officially pronounced it to be in accordance with the Bible.) There were therefore a number of attempts to avoid the conclusion that there had been a big bang.

The discovery of the universal background radiation, however, turned the scales decisively in favor of the big bang, leaving naturalists with the problem of finding a way to eliminate the obnoxious hint of divine intervention. Hawking could not have been clearer about how unwilling the physicists were to throw a bone to theology:

> Throughout the 1970s I had been mainly studying black holes, but in 1981 my interest in the questions about the origin and fate of the universe was reawakened when I attended a conference on cosmology organized by the Jesuits in the Vatican. . . .

At the end of the conference the participants were granted an audience with the Pope. He told us that it was all right to study the evolution of the universe after the big bang, but we should not inquire into the big bang itself because that was the moment of creation and therefore the work of God. I was glad then that he did not know the subject of the talk I had just given at the conference—the possibility that space-time was infinite but had no boundary, which means that it had no beginning, no moment of Creation. I had no desire to share the fate of Galileo, with whom I feel a strong sense of identity, partly because of the coincidence of having been born exactly 300 years after his death! In this story it was not the pope who resisted scientific knowledge on religious grounds, but naturalists who disliked the big bang because it "smacks of divine intervention." What the pope was trying to restrain was not scientific investigation but scientific pretenses to omniscience, pretensions based on metaphysical preference rather than on observation or experimental testing.

The fundamental issue between the pope and the physicist was whether God is real or imaginary. If God is real, then a naturalistic science that insists on explaining everything is out of touch with reality; if God is imaginary, then theologians have no subject matter. If theologians are willing to allow the reality of God to be decided by scientific naturalists according to the rules of methodological atheism, they do not deserve even the modest position in academic life which they presently occupy.

The Governing Discipline

If God is real, however, and if theologians are prepared to assert that reality as a fact rather than a mere subjective reflection, then theology has a very important place in the world of knowledge. Whatever we may call it, there is a need for a discipline at the top of the hierarchy of sciences which studies knowledge itself in the most general sense and for that reason governs the more specialized disciplines. The governing discipline takes respectful account of specialized knowledge, of course, but it evaluates that knowledge in the light of more general principles, which may be scientific or moral or aesthetic. It decides such questions as whether scientifically valuable experiments on prisoners (or humans generally, or fetal tissue, or animals) are ethically permissible; whether research into heritable differences in intelligence should be discouraged because the results might be misunderstood or abused; whether in the light of other needs it is worth ten billion dollars or more to build a Supercollider to find the Higgs particle; and whether scientific investigation should be based on naturalism or whether intelligent creation is also entitled to consideration.

The governing discipline is not the exclusive property of any academic specialty, or even of professors and scholars as a class. It is essentially a governmental activity, the government of the mind. Competition to exercise this governmental power is understandably fierce. Physicists, judges, politicians, biologists, literary critics, journalists, economists and many others enthusiastically join in the contest. Which discipline has the best claim to priority over the others depends on which subject matter is the more fundamental.

If the human need for bread is fundamental, then economics is the base and all else is superstructure, as the Marxists said. If human communication through language is what knowledge is really all about, then literary theory, the discipline that interprets texts, is more fundamental than the others. If ultimate reality consists of elementary particles, and if everything that has happened is in some sense determined by some great law that governed events at the beginning of the big bang, then the search for the final theory is not just a game that particle physicists play but a quest of immense importance to humanity. In that case we might say that "physics" and "metaphysics" are at bottom the same thing. But if God is real and constitutes the true basis of all knowledge, then we call the governing discipline *theology.*

Those who explicate fundamental reality are the rulers of knowledge, for those that acknowledge their claim. That implies that if God really exists and has revealed something of his nature and will to humankind, then the interaction of God and the whole of creation is not just the most complex of subjects but by far the most important, and theology is by right the "queen of the sciences."

Defining to Exclude

In the contemporary university, however, theology barely has the status of a pawn—perhaps a captured pawn. That is because the other disciplines, rivals though they may be in many other respects, have united to define reality as "nature." Physics is the traditional senior partner in the naturalistic enterprise, although the better-funded discipline of molecular biology is a credible competitor and literary criticism is beginning to make a bid for power. Regardless of which of these disciplines has precedence, there is no need or place for a department of theological science, because the topic of "religion" is adequately covered by the departments of psychology and anthropology, or perhaps by Francis Crick's materialist "brain science." If humankind really did create God, as the contemporary university assumes, this way of treating the subject is eminently reasonable.

The key element in the cultural authority of the scientific naturalists is their power to set the standards by which theories are evaluated. That power explains why theists are so paralyzed by fear of the "God of the gaps" fallacy. Darwinism became unchallengeable scientific orthodoxy not because the creative power of the mutation/selection mechanism was experimentally demonstrated, but because the scientific community adopted standards of evaluation that made something very much like Darwinism inevitable. Naturalistic rules require that theories employ only two kinds of forces—chance and necessity, random variation and impersonal law. The only debate is over details like the relative importance of chance (mutation) and necessity (natural selection), or the mechanism of heredity. The rules also provide that a theory retains its authority even in the teeth of a great deal of nonconforming evidence unless critics can provide a better theory.

Because of this way of thinking, even the notorious discrepancies between the facts of the fossil record and Darwinian expectations do not matter so long as there is *some* evidence *(Archaeopteryx,* Lucy, the "mammal-like reptiles") that can be interpreted to fit the paradigm—and the critics are unable to propose a credible mechanism for evolution by big jumps. If the contest is between Darwinism and supernatural creation, or between Darwinism and "we don't know," Darwinism wins.

Given those rules, it is no wonder that theists think it futile to assert the possibility of divine action or influence in the history of life. It is not just that science will "plug the gaps" in the future: the gaps are *already* plugged, by philosophy. Finch-beak variation will do quite nicely as proof of biological evolution until something better comes along. Prebiological evolutionists may not have a theory comparable to neo-Darwinism, but they do not need to have one to defeat the theists. In the words of a 1984 booklet of the National Academy of Sciences attacking creationism,

> For those who are studying aspects of the origin of life, the question no longer seems to be whether life could have originated by chemical processes involving nonbiological components but, rather, what pathway might have been followed. The data accumulated thus far imply selective processes. Prebiological chemical evolution is seen as a trial-and-error process leading to the success of one or more systems built from the many possible chemical components. The system that evolved with the capability of self-replication and mutation led to what we now define as a living system.

Translated into plain English, this means that scientific fashion as of 1984 recognized that chance alone cannot account for the origin of life, and so something comparable to Darwinian selection had to be assumed—even though Darwinian selection by its very nature can appear only when life processes (use of nutrients and reproduction) are already in existence. That life evolved by a combination of chance and necessity is axiomatic for naturalistic science and requires no proof. Science does not need a good theory (that is, a theory genuinely backed by empirical testing) to defeat creationism (theistic realism). The battle has been won in the definitions, before the empirical testing even gets started.

Steps Toward Theistic Realism

If naturalism is true, the scientific naturalists deserve their cultural power, and theologians whose professional mission is to propound knowledge about an imaginary God deserve their lowly status. If theologians hope to win a place in reality, however, they have to stop seeking the approval of naturalists and advance their own theory of knowledge. My intention here is to start the process rather than to finish it, but readers are entitled to expect me to provide a concrete proposal as a basis for further discussion. Here, then, is what I think to be the essential, bedrock position of Christian theism about creation.

The most important statement in Scripture about creation is not contained in Genesis but in the opening verses of the Gospel of John:

In the beginning was the Word, and the Word was with God, and the Word was God. He was in the beginning with God. All things came into being through him, and without him not one thing came into being. (John 1:1-3)

This statement plainly says that creation was by a force that was (and is) intelligent and personal.

The essential, bedrock position of scientific naturalism is the direct opposite of John 1:1-3. Naturalistic evolutionary theory, as part of the grand metaphysical story of science, says that creation was by impersonal and unintelligent forces. The opposition between the biblical and naturalistic stories is fundamental, and neither side can compromise over it. To compromise is to surrender.

Because in our universal experience unintelligent material processes do not create life, Christian theists know that Romans 1:20 is also true: "Ever since the creation of the world [God's] eternal power and divine nature, invisible though they are, have been understood and seen through the things he has made." In other words, there is absolutely no mystery about why living organisms appear to be the products of intelligent creation, and why scientific naturalists have to work so hard to keep themselves from perceiving the obvious. The reason living things give that appearance is that they actually are what they appear to be, and this fact is evident to all who do not cloud their minds with naturalistic philosophy or some comparable drug.

The rest of that passage (Romans 1:20-23) is also true:

So they are without excuse; for though they knew God, they did not honor him as God or give thanks to him, but they became futile in their thinking, and their senseless minds were darkened. Claiming to be wise, they became fools; and they exchanged the glory of the immortal God for images resembling a mortal human being or birds or four-footed animals or reptiles.

What these words plainly mean is that those who turn away from God and toward naturalistic philosophy give up their minds in the process and end up endorsing sophisticated nonsense and nature worship.

Naturalistic science tells us something completely different from what Romans 1 tells us, something that contradicts not just the Genesis account but the fundamental principle of creation that is the common ground of all creationists—Christian, Jewish and Islamic. It tells us not that we collapse into intellectual futility and confusion when we discard the Creator as a remnant of prescientific superstition, but that it is precisely by the "death of God" that humankind comes of age and becomes ready to receive the truth that Darwinism is all too ready to provide.

Which is the beginning of wisdom? Biblical theism says that wisdom begins with the "fear [proper understanding] of God." Naturalism and its evolutionary satellite declare that the "death [intellectual discrediting] of God" is the essential metaphysical prelude to a true understanding of "how things really are." The difference between the two ways of thinking is fundamental, and theists who try to bridge it by a superficial compromise end up by tacitly accepting naturalism.

It is misleading to say that there is a conflict between "creation" and "evolution": such wording makes it appear that the conflict is over facts rather than over ways of thinking. Where scientists sympathetic to Christian theism have been unable honestly to interpret the empirical evidence in a manner consistent with the Genesis chronology or a worldwide flood, that is a genuine empirical problem that intellectually honest Christians cannot ignore in deciding how to interpret the Bible or understand biblical authority. The situation is entirely different when scientists insist that their empirical claims be evaluated by standards derived from naturalistic philosophy. Where scientists have made an a priori commitment to metaphysical naturalism and endorsed the power of mindless material processes to create living organisms because that power is implied by their philosophy, it is the right and duty of theologians to point out that there is another way of looking at the evidence. If theology is to have the grand role envisaged by Nancey Murphy and Arthur Peacocke, or even any role at all in a competitive intellectual community, theologians must have the courage to defend their proper intellectual territory.

To enter the field of intellectual argument is to accept the risk that we may lose by being proved wrong. But accepting the risk of being wrong is the inescapable price for making any meaningful statements about the world. The best scientists have never feared to accept that risk—which is why they have learned so much and also why they have placed themselves at risk by overextending their territory. Those who will not take a risk end up saying nothing at all, like a violinist who stops playing for fear of hitting a wrong note.

If Christian theists can summon the courage to argue that preexisting intelligence really was an essential element in biological creation and to insist that the evidence be evaluated by standards that do not assume the point in dispute, then they will make a great contribution to the search for truth, *whatever the outcome*. Possibly the scientific naturalists will come back with genuinely convincing evidence that unintelligent processes were sufficient—although if they were capable of doing that, I do not think they would fight so hard to keep the concept of creation off the table. No matter how the debate unfolds, we will come to know a great deal more than we know now, and the outcome will be no worse for Christian theism than the theistic naturalists already assume it to be.

6

Realism
& Rationality

THE ACCEPTANCE OF NATURALISTIC ASSUMPTIONS IN SCIENCE by Christian and secular intellectuals alike has moved God steadily into some remote never-never land ("before the big bang") or even out of reality altogether. In consequence theology has practically no standing in the modern university, and all the prestigious disciplines interpret reality solely in naturalistic terms. Nowadays a biology professor who publicly doubted that chemicals in a prebiotic soup can combine to form life without divine assistance would stand a good chance of being driven out of science teaching. A professor in a history class who asserted that the resurrection might actually have happened would gain a reputation as an eccentric, and probably also as a bigot.

At the same time, ideas that *are* widely accepted in university life sometimes seem so strange to people unfamiliar with academic ways that they find it difficult to believe that well-educated people really take them seriously. When I describe postmodernism or deconstruction or radical feminism to nonuniversity groups, many listeners are tempted to make the mistake of disregarding the whole business as harmless academic claptrap.

Ways of thinking that seem very strange at first, however, may have their roots in more fundamental ideas that are widely accepted in the general culture. People often do not understand the full implications of what they have been taught to believe. Claptrap or not, ideas have consequences. What is fashionable in the secular academic culture soon becomes fashionable in the media, and even in Christian colleges and seminaries, which tend to follow trends in the mainstream academic world. For example, in 1991 a Presbyterian denominational commission, advised by seminary professors, recommended that the Bible should be interpreted according to a "hermeneutic of justice-love" and that when so interpreted it actually approves certain sexual relations outside of marriage. The stage had been set for this reversal by academic theories about textual interpretation and the nature of truth. Hence it is worth paying attention to how truth is viewed in academia.

The Campus Culture War

John Searle, professor of the philosophy of language and the mind at the Berkeley campus of the University of California, is a frequent and insightful commentator on the current campus culture war. The war is fundamentally over what kinds of knowledge universities should encourage their students to acquire; important secondary skirmishes involve the standards for admitting students and hiring or promoting faculty. While no brief description of the conflict could be adequate, the war at the simplest level is between two groups that Searle calls the "traditionalists" and the "challengers." The former value the classic works presented in courses with titles like "Western Civilization," while the latter want to reform the curriculum in the name of concepts like multicultural-

ism, postmodernism, feminism and gay and lesbian studies.* The
resulting conflict over "the canon" (the list of great books deemed
particularly worthy of study) and "political correctness" has been
brought to the attention of the world at large by two books in
particular: Allan Bloom's *The Closing of the American Mind* and
Dinesh D'Souza's *Illiberal Education.* Both of these weigh in on
the traditionalist side.

John Searle, too, is a traditionalist. Being a distinguished philosopher, however, he aims to go beyond current political polem-
ics to find the underlying philosophical roots of the battle. In his
published lecture "Is There a Crisis in American Higher Education?" Searle set out the interrelated assumptions behind the traditionalist position, to make clear what it is that the challengers
are challenging.

First, traditionalists say that some masterpieces (like those of
Aristotle and Milton) are included in the canon—in preference to
(say) the works of contemporary feminists or African-Americans—not because of cultural or political bias but because of their
inherent excellence and importance.

Second, traditionalists say that there are objective standards of
"rationality, intelligence, truth, validity, and general intellectual
merit."

Third, they believe that a major purpose of higher education is
to liberate students from their parochial backgrounds and introduce them to the general intellectual culture.

Fourth, the tradition that the traditionalists are defending com-
bines an extreme devotion to individual rights and expression on
the one hand with an equally extreme devotion to a universal
human culture on the other hand.

Fifth, the tradition encourages a relentlessly critical stance

---

*I am borrowing Searle's terminology, but I should note that the so-called challengers often
hold positions of administrative power. Which side is in the driver's seat is itself a matter
of dispute.

toward prejudice, including the individual's personal prejudices and the prejudices of the community to which he or she belongs.

All these points are worthy of discussion, but it is the sixth presupposition of academic traditionalism that is all-important for present purposes, and so I will state it in Searle's exact words:

> A sixth and final feature that I will mention is this: objectivity and truth are possible because there is an independently existing reality to which our true utterances correspond. This view, called realism, has often been challenged by various forms of idealism and relativism within Western philosophy, but it has remained the dominant metaphysical view in our culture. Our natural science, for example, is based on it. A persistent topic of debate is, How far does it extend? For example, is there an independently existing set of moral values that we can discover, or are we just expressing our subjective feelings and attitudes when we make moral judgments?

Various challengers—Afrocentrists, gender feminists, gay liberationists and so on—dispute these assumptions. They say that the "canon" of writers deemed worthy of study systematically favors dead white males, that supposed "objective" standards mask race, gender and class bias, and that the most important thing about an individual is his or her membership in a subgroup (gays, women, African-Americans) rather than his or her identity either as an individual or as a member of a general scholarly culture. Some of them say that the purpose of education, at least in the humanities, is political transformation and empowerment, not learning a tradition that is allegedly responsible for their own oppression.

Most important, some of them even challenge the metaphysical realism and scientific rationalism that provides the philosophical foundation for the traditionalist position. According to Searle,

> [The challenge to the sixth presupposition] involves a marriage of left-wing politics with certain anti-rationalist strands derived from recent philosophy. The idea is that we should stop think-

ing there is an objective reality that exists independently of our representations of it, we should stop thinking that propositions are true when they correspond to that reality, and we should stop thinking of language as a set of devices for conveying meanings from speakers to hearers. In short, the [contradiction of the] sixth presupposition is a rejection of realism and truth in favor of some version of relativism, such as pragmatism. This is a remarkable guise for left-wing views to take, because until recently extreme left-wing views claimed to have a scientific basis. The current challengers are suspicious of science, and equally suspicious of the whole apparatus of rationality, objective truth, and metaphysical realism that goes along with the scientific attitude.

The reason the conflict over metaphysical realism is all-important is that it turns what would otherwise be a squabble over who gets what into a debate about the fundamental nature of knowledge and rationality. Traditionalists like Searle are willing in principle to concede that the challengers may be right that the current curriculum reflects certain prejudices—Eurocentrism or whatever—and that some writers or thinkers of merit may have been unfairly neglected due to their race or gender. If the challengers can argue persuasively that this has happened, then the canon should be revised accordingly. If there is disagreement about whether their arguments are persuasive, then a compromise can be arranged. That kind of discussion is squarely within the academic tradition, because it assumes an objective, transcultural standard of merit that works by Asians, African-Americans or feminists might or might not meet.

Some of the challengers would be satisfied to negotiate on that basis, but others would not be. Their more radical challenge is to the notion of transcultural objectivity itself. The challenge is supported by some very influential white male academics, notably deconstructionist literary critic Jacques Derrida and philosophers

Thomas Kuhn and Richard Rorty. Searle describes the simplified
version of these thinkers' ideas that has influenced the campus
culture war:

> The idea, roughly speaking, is that Kuhn is supposed to have
> shown that science does not give us an account of an indepen-
> dently existing reality; rather, scientists are an irrational bunch
> who run from one paradigm to another for reasons that have
> no real connection with finding objective truths. What Kuhn
> did for science, Rorty supposedly also did for philosophy. Phi-
> losophers don't provide accounts that mirror how the world is,
> because the whole idea of language mirroring or corresponding
> to reality is flawed from the beginning. . . . Whether or not this
> is the correct interpretation of the works of Kuhn, Rorty, and
> the deconstructionists, the effect has been to introduce visions
> of relativism, antiobjectivism, and skepticism about science and
> the correspondence theory of truth into various humanities de-
> partments.

To Searle the existence of an objective reality—and a definition
of truth as correspondence to that reality—is fundamental to rationality itself and thus to the university's reason for existing.
Searle puts it this way: Metaphysical realism is not a thesis, but
rather a precondition for the whole process of public debate. To
hold a general conversation we must have a general frame of reference, a sense that we all inhabit the same conceptual world.
"Thus it is self-refuting for someone to claim that metaphysical
realism is false, because a public language presupposes a public
world, and that presupposition is metaphysical realism." To put
the point another way, to insist that there is no such thing as
objective truth is to state a purportedly objective truth, and this
is self-contradictory.

Richard Rorty and Neopragmatism
As I have indicated, the philosopher most often cited by Searle

and other rationalist/realists as epitomizing the rejection of realism is Richard Rorty of the University of Virginia. Rorty has told
his own side of the story in a readable and revealing autobiograph-
ical essay titled "Wild Orchids and Trotsky." Rorty's father broke
with the American Communist Party over Stalin's crimes in 1932;
thereafter the family's loyalties, including Richard's, were with
Leon Trotsky and the anti-Stalinist left. From childhood Rorty
knew that "poor people would always be oppressed until capital-
ism was overcome" and that "the point of being human was to
spend one's life fighting social injustice."

Rorty and his father admired not only Trotsky but also John
Dewey, the leading figure of American philosophical pragmatism.
As a young man Dewey had turned away from the evangelical
Christianity of his childhood to embrace a neo-Hegelian pantheism; then, because he took Darwinism seriously, he had abandoned the quest for moral absolutes to pursue a career as a social
and educational reformer. As Rorty describes his philosophical
hero,

> Dewey thought, as I do now, that there was nothing bigger,
> more permanent and more reliable, behind our sense of moral
> obligation to those in pain than a certain contingent historical
> phenomenon—the gradual spread of the sense that the pain of
> others matters, regardless of whether they are of the same fam-
> ily, tribe, religion, nation, or intelligence as oneself. This idea,
> Dewey thought, cannot be shown to be true by science, or re-
> ligion, or philosophy—at least if "shown to be true" means
> "capable of being made evident to anyone, regardless of back-
> ground." It can be made evident only to people whom it is not
> too late to acculturate into our own particular, late-blooming,
> historically contingent form of life.

This philosophical outlook leads directly to some elements of the
challengers' position as described by Searle: there is no objective
reality accessible to everyone; the perspective of the cultural mo-

ment is all-important; and the purpose of university teaching is political transformation of the students, those persons whom it is not too late to acculturate into "our" historically contingent way of thinking. The Dewey/Rorty philosophy manages to be both egalitarian and elitist. The pain of everybody matters, but only the perspective of a philosophical elite governs what is to be done about it.

After social justice, the young Rorty's second love was for the wild orchids he found in his country home. Most people have some private passion of this sort—perhaps for the music of Bach, or for antique cars, or for climbing mountains. Rorty aspired to connect his private passion with some grand scheme about the nature of reality, mixing up notions derived from Darwin, Freud and Romantic poetry.

> I was not quite sure why those orchids were so important, but I was convinced that they were. I was sure that our noble, pure, chaste North American wild orchids were morally superior to the showy, hybridized, tropical orchids displayed in florists' shops. I was also convinced that there was a deep significance in the fact that the orchids are the latest and most complex plants to be developed in the course of evolution. Looking back, I suspect that there was a lot of sublimated sexuality involved.

But was it right for a young leftist to spend his time admiring orchids when there was so much social injustice to be overcome? Young Rorty went to college at the University of Chicago, whose precocious students he fondly recalls as "the biggest collection of juvenile neurotics since the Children's Crusade," to find some philosophical system that could define the nature of beauty and social justice, thus unifying wild orchids and Trotsky with a single set of concepts. At Chicago he imbibed at first a generous dose of Aristotelian rationalism, the philosophy behind the "great books" approach to higher education, and with his classmates was attracted to the Anglo-Catholic Christian elements in T. S. Eliot's poetry.

He found himself unsuited to Christianity, however, and so his search for absolutes took him to Platonism, which "had all the advantages of religion, without requiring the humility that Christianity demanded, and of which I am apparently incapable."

Up to the age of twenty Rorty did his best to become a Platonist, but eventually he decided that the quest for absolutes was a wild-goose chase. Philosophers could trace their conclusions back to first principles that were incompatible with the first principles of their opponents, but they could never find any neutral standpoint from which competing first principles could be evaluated. Therefore "the whole Socratic-Platonic idea of replacing passion by reason seemed not to make much sense." Rorty came to believe that the test of philosophical truth was overall *coherence* rather than correspondence to objective reality or deducibility from universally granted first principles. That meant that there can be competing truths based on different first principles, mutually contradictory but equally coherent and hence equally "true."

This relativist definition of truth led Rorty to the philosophy of G. W. F. Hegel, who had said that philosophy could be no more than "its time held in thought," that is, the most coherent expression of the spirit of the age. From Hegel's historicism Rorty went on to the philosophy of Martin Heidegger, the founding spirit of postmodernism, and finally back to his childhood hero John Dewey. Rorty's own philosophy, sometimes labeled neopragmatism, takes Dewey's thought to a point where it seems to abolish philosophy altogether.* Rorty decided that the "whole idea of holding reality and justice in a single vision had been a mistake," because only belief in God, "a surrogate parent who embodied love, power,

---

*Rorty thinks that literary critics and storytellers will increasingly take over what had been the work of philosophers, as part of a general turn against theory and toward narrative: "that is why the novel, the movie, and the TV program have, gradually but steadily, replaced the sermon and the treatise as the principal vehicles of moral change and progress." When I think of what this means in practice—the music videos of MTV come to mind—I want to ask, "Progress toward what?"

and justice in equal measure," could provide such a vision. Since Rorty couldn't imagine believing in God, he concluded that "there is no way to weave together one's personal equivalent of Trotsky and one's personal equivalent of my wild orchids." Some people care for wild orchids and others don't; some groups want to realize a Trotskyite (or Deweyesque) vision of social justice and others don't. That seems about all there is to say about it.

A Vacuum at the Heart

Of course that is not all there is to say, because one has to deal with the question of when and to what extent the coercion of others is justified. It is easy to be a relativist only with respect to those private passions that are a matter of taste. If Rorty likes wild orchids and you prefer tacky artificial flowers, no doubt he will be happy to leave you to your vulgar pleasures. But suppose you resist his vision of social justice, which allows you to satisfy your private wants only if you are "using no resources needed by those less advantaged." Perhaps the ruling neopragmatists think the savings you have accumulated by hard work should be taken by the government to be redistributed to the homeless, while you feel entitled to spend the money on a family vacation. If compulsory wealth redistribution is something more than legalized theft, it must be based on a moral obligation that binds even the dissenters, but the main point of neopragmatism is to deny that such obligations have any basis in reality.

Even a relatively modest program of wealth redistribution implies a lot of coercive measures, including at a minimum a bureaucracy with the power required to collect high taxes from unwilling payers. If one has as expansive a vision of what social justice requires as Trotsky did, one has to be prepared to go the distance with thought reform, firing squads, concentration camps and other mechanisms of terror. In that situation, relativism means not universal tolerance for differing opinions but a lack of any good reason for restraining the secret police.

I think Rorty would say that the restraining principle is the instinctive tendency of liberals like himself to hate cruelty and to sympathize with the pain of others, but this does not tell us whose pain matters most when hard choices have to be made. To a radical redistributionist it is the pain of the poor that counts, and to heed the protesting squeals of the exploiters is mere squeamishness that leads to more misery in the end. If Rorty is too tenderhearted to countenance the infliction of pain in the fight for social justice, then I do not think Trotsky would reciprocate his admiration.

In one of his best-known essays, "The Priority of Democracy to Philosophy," Rorty explains that according to pragmatists "what counts as rational or as fanatical is relative to the group to which we think it necessary to justify ourselves—to the body of shared belief that determines the reference of the word 'we.' " Persons who belong to the category "they" rather than the category "we" have no voice in the decisions about what we do to them, nor are "our" decisions limited by any principle we do not choose to accept. Rorty denies that this view is relativistic, but the terms of the denial practically admit the charge. In his words,

> [My] view is often referred to dismissively as "cultural relativism." But it is not relativistic, if that means saying that every moral view is as good as any other. *Our* moral view is, I firmly believe, much better than any competing view, even though there are many people whom you will never be able to convert to it. It is one thing to say, falsely, that there is nothing to choose between us and the Nazis. It is another thing to say, correctly, that there is no neutral, common ground to which a philosophical Nazi and I can repair to argue out our differences.

When a philosopher uses a straw-man opponent like the Nazis to illustrate a thesis of general applicability, he is usually cheating. Rorty would do better to imagine himself trying to find common ground with Trotsky for a discussion about whether it was justifiable to murder the Russian czar and all his family to further the fight against oppression.* In any case, the claim of moral realists is not that Nazi philosophers or ruthless collectivists can be persuaded by sound moral arguments, but that morally rational persons are objectively justified in declaring Nazis and Bolsheviks alike to be fundamentally wrong rather than merely currently out of fashion.

The test of moral realism, or scientific realism, is not whether everybody is willing to listen to reason. No doubt there will always be people who think the earth is flat, and even people high in government have been known to consult astrologers. We rightly judge such people irrational. But whether we can extend metaphysical realism from the factual realm of natural science to the moral realm is, as Searle noted, highly questionable for those who accept modernist metaphysics. If morality, like wild orchids, is just a matter of taste, it is hard to see what Rorty could even mean by the statement that "our" (liberal) morality is better than any competing view. To say it is better because it is ours is to say nothing, and to say it is better on some objective standard is to deny the essential premise of neopragmatism.

The vacuum at the heart of Rorty's philosophy becomes more apparent if we invoke as an example not a demon from the past but a true living alternative to agnostic liberalism like the Roman Catholic teaching of Pope John Paul II. On what basis could Rorty's "we" claim to have a better morality than that of the pope? If Rorty means that his morality is better because it is in accord with ultimate reality (metaphysical naturalism) whereas the pope's morality is founded on a delusion (the divinity of Christ), then

---

* Trotsky's comment in 1935 on the murder of the Romanov family and their servants was that "the execution of the Tsar's family was needed not only to frighten, horrify, and dishearten the enemy, but also in order to shake up our own ranks, to show them that there was no turning back, that ahead lay either complete victory or complete ruin." From *Trotsky's Diary in Exile: 1935,* quoted in Robert Payne, *The Life and Death of Lenin* (1964), p. 468.

Rorty is basing his philosophy on exactly the kind of strong metaphysical position he claims to have abandoned. If he does not realize this, it is probably because he associates only with a narrow academic elite that takes naturalism so much for granted that it seems merely "the way we think today" rather than a controversial statement about the nature of reality.

The abandonment of realism in morality is supposed to produce a kindlier, more tolerant society, but what it actually does produce is tribalism or partisanship. In keeping with his conviction that he needs to justify himself only within his self-chosen group, Rorty engages in genuine dialogue strictly within an ideological party, composed of those whose politics are liberal to radical and whose minds were formed by the philosophical tradition extending from Hume through Kant and Hegel to Dewey and Heidegger.

To outsiders Rorty speaks only propaganda. He defines liberalism platitudinously as an aversion to cruelty, with the implicit (and often explicit) dismissal of nonliberals as people who either are indifferent to cruelty or positively endorse it. Those who believe in traditional biblical sexual morality—whom Rorty caricatures as "the people who think that hounding gays out of the military promotes family values"—are "the same honest, decent, blinkered, disastrous people who voted for Hitler in 1933." It doesn't take much imagination to see that Rortian liberalism in practice implies marginalizing "them"—that is, the many millions of Americans who he thinks constitute Hitler's natural constituency—by employing the techniques of conceptual manipulation available to those who control education.

The mixture of extreme partisanship with relativism is what has created that absurd fanaticism of the victims which goes by the name of "political correctness." The campus speech codes and sensitivity-training sessions seem fanatical only to outsiders, of course, and "they" are by definition oppressors. If the elite university campuses of today are providing a preview of the postmod-

ernist society of tomorrow, we may be in for an era of self-righteous bullying.

What About Reality?
The question I want to address is not whether Rorty's philosophy
has unpleasant consequences, though, but whether it is true—that
is, in accord with objective reality. This is admittedly a very un-
Rortian question to ask, but it is inescapable, and Rorty himself
has told us why. If God as Creator exists and cares about what
human beings do, then metaphysical realism is true, and a common frame of reference for disputes about value and justice also
exists. If God does not exist, and if there also is no Platonic
metaphysical realm of divine essences, then there may be no absolute reference point from which to judge competing interpretations of reality.

What is in question is not the real existence of a world of material objects "out there," at least for everyday purposes. Neopragmatists drive their automobiles just as carefully as do materialist
rationalists, and they expect just as confidently to sustain damage
if they collide with a solid object. On the other hand, the pragmatists and rationalists both realize that according to the best available scientific interpretation, those objects are not really what they
appear to be. To a physicist they are largely composed of the
spaces between particles, and the individual particles have the dis-
concerting quality of seeming to be in one place and another at
the same moment, depending on whether we happen to be looking.

External reality exists, but what it really *is* requires sophisticated interpretation. When disputes about interpretation arise, we
naturally consult the interpretive community we judge to be best
qualified. This is true even with regard to scientific questions of
"fact," but it is easiest to see when we address questions of value,
because materialist rationalists agree with pragmatists that values,
unlike particles, are created by human beings.

Reductionists and Their Hierarchies

That Rorty's philosophy is hard to refute—granted the starting point in naturalism—is confirmed by an examination of the metaphysics of his rationalist/realist adversary, John Searle. In his recent book *The Rediscovery of the Mind* Searle had this to say about the origin of the human mind and its capacities:

> Our brains are the products of certain evolutionary processes, and as such they are simply the most developed in a whole series of evolutionary paths that include the brains of dogs, baboons, dolphins, etc. . . . It's a good idea to ask ourselves, who do we think we are? And at least part of the answer is that we are biological beasts selected for coping with hunter-gatherer environments, and as far as we know, we have had no significant change in our gene pool for several thousand years. Fortunately (or unfortunately), nature is profligate, and just as every male produces enough sperm to repopulate the earth, so we have a lot more neurons than we need for a hunter-gatherer existence. I believe that the phenomenon of surplus neurons—as distinct from, say, opposed thumbs—is the key to understanding how we got out of hunter-gathering and produced philosophy, science, technology, neuroses, advertising, etc. But we should never forget who we are; and for such as us, it is a mistake to assume that everything that exists is comprehensible to our brains. Of course, methodologically we have to act as if we could understand everything, because there is no way of knowing what we can't: to know the limits of knowledge, we would have to know both sides of the limit. So potential omniscience is acceptable as a heuristic device, but it would be self-deception to suppose it a fact.

Searle wrote that paragraph in a book whose main purpose was to criticize the excesses of the materialist reductionism that currently dominates neuroscience, roughly the philosophy of Francis Crick. One of the attractions of materialist reductionism is that by declaring mental activity to be no more than a particularly complex application of physical and chemical processes in the brain, it promises in principle that scientists can understand the mind in the same way that they understand the movements of planets in the solar system or the combinations of chemicals in a test tube. In the more logically relentless formulations of the materialist program, mental states like intention and love are regarded as mere place-holders that can be eliminated from consideration when science understands the chemical mechanisms that produce these subjective phenomena.

At the opposite pole from reductive materialism is dualism, or vitalism, the doctrine that mental activities or the life processes involve some fundamental "stuff" in addition to matter and the laws of physics and chemistry. In the halls of science, dualism and vitalism are regarded with nearly as much disgust as outright creationism, and for the same reason: they imply the existence of something supernatural, which is forever outside the knowledge and control of science.

If the reductive materialists are right, then biology can ultimately be reduced to something like "DNA science" and the philosophy of mind can be reduced to neuroscience. Such a reductive move would not imply the outright abolition of academic departments of zoology and philosophy, since reductionists concede that for certain purposes things like ideas and whole organisms will always need to be studied. But reductionism definitely places the professors of those subjects in a subordinate position in the knowledge industry's chain of command. One sees evidence of the knowledge hierarchy in the outright contempt that reductionists like Weinberg and Crick express toward philosophers, and in the patronizing way well-funded molecular biologists tend to refer to their poor relations who study whole plants and animals in departments of integrative biology.

The Emergence Argument
Philosophers and integrative biologists who are not content with

such subordination have to fight it by setting up a barrier to reductionism that is sufficiently impermeable to provide the advantages of dualism while being sufficiently flexible to avoid serious
metaphysical trouble. The code word for this "now you see it, now
you don't" barrier is *emergence,* a term that refers to the tendency
of surprising new properties to emerge when substances are combined. Thus we saw in chapter four that Stephen Jay Gould insists
that the properties of organisms are mostly emergent, meaning
that they cannot be predicted at the genetic level, without clarify-
ing how this assertion affects the blind watchmaker mechanism for
creating complex organs. Similarly, John Searle insists that "one
can accept the obvious facts of physics—for example, that the
world is made up entirely of physical particles in fields of force—
without at the same time denying . . . that our conscious states
have quite specific *irreducible* phenomenological properties."

All this means in Searle's terminology, however, is that consciousness is an emergent or irreducible property of brain chemistry only in the "utterly harmless sense" in which H_2O (water) has
emergent properties not found in oxygen or hydrogen. Emergence
in this harmless sense is no barrier to reductionism. It merely says
that we do not fully understand hydrogen or oxygen until we
understand the properties that each element has which enable it
to produce new properties in combination with other elements. No
one argues that water contains, in addition to hydrogen and oxygen, *something else* that is not reducible to chemistry. Crick
called his materialist theory of the mind an "astonishing hypothesis," however, precisely because many people do think something
like that about the mind.

The concept of emergence is harmless to reductionism as long
as it refers merely to properties of higher-level systems (like organisms or minds) which are not yet fully understood in terms of the
lower-level entities (particles, molecules) of which they consist.
Everybody agrees that the reductionist program has a long way to

go. The question is whether it can succeed in principle or whether the pathway to eventual reductionist omniscience is permanently blocked by the introduction of something really different.

On this crucial point Searle produces a waffle worthy of a presidential candidate. He first says that is unrealistic to assume we can know everything (that is, pursue the reductionist program to the end) for the thoroughly reductionist reason that a baboon with surplus neurons has no solid basis for confidence in its own mental powers. Then he endorses the same reductionist dream of omniscience on the pragmatic ground that we have to assume we can learn everything in order to find out how far we can go. That is all that any reductionist would insist on.

How Things Really Are

Reductionism is intimately connected with the metaphysical realism that Searle asserts, correctly, to be an essential foundation for speech about knowledge. Such speech—whether it be by materialists, theists, Freudians, Marxists or whatever—always asserts something about how things really are, as opposed to how they seem to those who lack knowledge. The earth seems to be stationary, but in reality it moves in orbit around the sun. People think they act from rational intentions, but they really are acting out an Oedipal complex or rationalizing their class interest. You might think that humans are created in the image of an omniscient God, magnificently endowed with minds that fall far short of their potential because they are flawed by sin, but what we really are is baboons with surplus neurons that caused us to imagine God before science gave us knowledge. All these statements, right or wrong, are about two things: the way things seem and the way things really are. For statements about the difference between appearances and reality to be meaningful, there must truly be a way things really are, and this is metaphysical realism.

Pragmatism aims to displace metaphysical statements about

how things really are with pragmatic statements about what it is useful for us to think for the time being. The flight from metaphysics is only apparent, though. Even pragmatism is founded on a vision of how things really are, and it is precisely the vision enunciated by Searle: Preferences for things like wild orchids and Trotsky's politics are at bottom only notions produced by the surplus neurons that a particular animal species happens to possess. Such concepts as beauty and goodness do not and cannot exist outside the brains of particular animals, although it may be useful for the animals to pretend that they do. "Truth" for any animal is therefore whatever its brain happens to find satisfying, and the validity of this truth can be judged only by its usefulness in meeting the challenges of the world, in the judgment of the individual and the interpretive community that individual wishes to satisfy.

Even the foundational knowledge that humans really are just animals with surplus neurons is established on pragmatic grounds. Searle apparently adheres to Darwinism, despite its fatal consequences for metaphysical realism (at least on issues of value), because the authority structure of his university culture, based as it is on the pragmatic requirements of natural science, regards Darwinism as foundational. If Searle has private doubts, he would be well advised to conceal them, because to challenge "what everybody knows" is to be labeled a crank.

Searle avoids this fate by opposing reductionism on reductionist grounds and pragmatism on pragmatic grounds. That kind of reasoning is like trying to get to outer space by ascending in a balloon. The very conditions that allow the device to work at all guarantee that it will never leave the atmosphere that sustains it, and that it will eventually return to the level where it started.

What Is Knowledge?
The crisis in the university that John Searle described comes down

to the very justification for having universities in the first place. A university is fundamentally about *knowledge*. Without a strong sense of what knowledge is and why the increase of it is good for everyone, it may seem that the university is little more than a playground for intellectuals. Technical training in subjects like engineering and business may continue to be supported on pragmatic grounds, but why should taxpayers, donors and tuition-paying parents support a department of literature?

When I went to college as a literature major almost forty years ago, the answer was clear. By studying great literature with proficient scholars, one supposedly learned something about what is really good and beautiful and why the really good works are better than the ones that seem good to persons whose tastes are uninformed. If the literature and philosophy professors now believe that "good" is just what the most influential people happen to like, or if they start from assumptions that make relativism hard to avoid, the rationale for paying their salaries may well be called into question.

Forty years ago the city of Berkeley, California, was called "the Athens of the West." Now it is known everywhere as "Berserkly," and the other university cities of America are equally notorious for irrational, self-indulgent, self-righteous behavior. The problem goes far beyond adolescent high jinks, which up to a point are a proper feature of a community of adolescents learning to become mature citizens of the culture of reason. Universities are centers of unreason in the much more profound sense that they are based on a metaphysical position that will not support a concept of rationality in the value realm, and hence ultimately will not support it anywhere.

The pragmatism of Richard Rorty is just an unusually well-thought-out version of what many university people unconsciously take for granted, or at least don't know how to oppose. Knowledge is that which is useful for whatever you want to do, or perhaps it is what the fashionable people happen to like.* Truth apart from utility cannot be known to us, because at bottom we are merely animals whom a profligate nature happened to endow with more neurons than were strictly necessary to survive in a hunter-gatherer environment. As long as the scientists continue to produce useful technology and maintain their own social unity, they can preserve in their own domain the rationalist culture that is going out of fashion in the humanities. If the scientists should hit a snag or perhaps be caught in a really important mistake, literary critics will have a marvelous time deconstructing their texts.

Most university people are not happy with the growth of irrationalism and hope that the situation is not as serious as it appears. At the same time that they are caught up in the reductionist and pragmatist way of thinking, people with good minds are dissatisfied and long for something better. The problem is that any seemingly new approach that is based on naturalistic metaphysics never provides more than an illusory means of escape. Promising notions appear from time to time, and people climb on board enthusiastically, but what they eventually find out is that they are on one of those balloons struggling upward to reach outer space. To end up somewhere really different, you have to start with something really different.

In short, the crisis in the universities is a metaphysical crisis. As we shall see, the same crisis infects the law.

---

*In science, knowledge is increasingly what the granting agencies happen to like, and they like what they can get Congress to pay for.

7

Natural
Law

WHEN PRESIDENT GEORGE BUSH NOMINATED JUDGE CLARence Thomas to a vacancy on the United States Supreme Court in 1991, liberals opposed to confirming the nomination at first directed critical scrutiny to statements Thomas had made in favor of employing "natural law" in constitutional interpretation. Democratic Senator Joseph Biden, chairman of the Judiciary Committee, which had to pass on the nomination, emphasized that he too believed in the existence of natural law. Indeed, he had successfully opposed a previous Republican nominee to the Supreme Court, Judge Robert Bork, in part because Bork denied that the Constitution protects certain natural rights that are not mentioned in the document itself. At that time Biden had insisted, "My rights are not derived from any government. . . . My rights are because I exist. They were given to me and each of our fellow citizens by our Creator and they represent the essence of human dignity."

Good and Bad Natural Law

Biden feared, however, that Thomas might believe in the wrong
kind of natural law. He explained the difference between good and
bad natural law in a newspaper article that expanded on a theme
first advanced in *The New York Times* by Harvard Law School
professor Laurence Tribe, a very influential liberal legal scholar.
According to Biden's article, good natural law is subservient to the
Constitution—that is, to positive, human-produced law—and its
use is therefore restricted "to the task of giving meaning to the
Constitution's great, but sometimes ambiguous, phrases." Second,
good natural law does not dictate a moral code to be imposed on
individuals; instead, it protects the right of individuals to make
moral decisions free from dictation by either legislators or judges.
Finally, good natural law is not a static set of "timeless truths" but
rather an evolving body of ideals that changes to permit government to adjust to new social challenges and new economic circumstances. Bad natural law, by negative implication, would be an
unchanging moral code that restricts either the freedom of individuals to do as they think best or the freedom of government to
do whatever the public interest requires.

As a legal scholar, I hoped Thomas would accept Biden's challenge and articulate a vision of natural law with real content, but
this was not to be. Bork had debated his legal theories with the
senators candidly, with disastrous results, and political strategists
had concluded from that experience that the way to get confirmed
is to say as little as possible. Thomas took their advice and stuck
to a simple set of unilluminating answers when the senators tried
to probe his judicial philosophy.

The resulting stalemate illustrated the ambivalence with which
our contemporary legal culture regards the proposition that there
exists some objective standard of right and wrong against which
human legal standards can be measured. Anyone who says that
there is such a standard seems to be denying that we are morally

autonomous beings who have every right to set our own standards and depart from the traditions of our ancestors. If one attributes the enduring moral commandments to God, one invites the accusation that one means to force one's religious morality on persons with different views. On the other hand, anyone who denies that there is a higher law seems to embrace nihilism and therefore to leave the powerless unprotected from the whims of the powerful. Either alternative is unacceptable. The safest course for a judicial nominee in Thomas's position was to be impenetrably vague or platitudinous on the subject.

Abortion and Natural Law

The specific issue behind all this philosophical fencing was, of course, abortion. Biden and other liberals feared (with good reason) that Thomas believed in a natural law-based right to life for unborn children, derived from a tradition reflecting a merger of Judeo-Christian teaching with classical Greek philosophy. According to this natural-law view, the sixth commandment's prohibition of murder, like the New Testament's "golden rule," gives divine sanction to a moral principle that is independently accessible to human reason. Pagans and agnostics as well as religious Jews and Christians know, or should know, that the killing of another human being is wrongful in the absence of justifying circumstances like self-defense.

That the fetus developing in the womb already is a fellow human creature—and not just a bundle of tissues that might become human at some point in the future—is established by a particular conception of what a human being is. A human being is created in the image of God and endowed from the earliest moment of development with that divine image. In more scientific terms, we might say that the important thing about the developing fetus is not the physical state it has reached but the genetic information, present from the start and unique to each individual, which directs not only embryonic development but eventually such processes as puberty and even aging. To nurture and respect such a wondrous thing is obligatory not only because of the unborn child's right to life but also because of the reverence due to its Creator.

From these propositions it does not necessarily follow that abortion is unjustifiable in all circumstances, but it certainly does follow that abortion is something about which a legislature may make laws, just as it makes laws about other forms of homicide.

If Judge Thomas held views anything like those just delineated, advocates of a virtually absolute right to abortion had every reason to want to keep him off the Supreme Court. At the time of his confirmation, it appeared that the new justice might soon be in a position to cast the crucial fifth vote to overturn the controversial decision in *Roe* v. *Wade,* thus abolishing the right to abortion and returning the whole issue to the usual lawmaking process.*

Abortion was also the most immediate issue behind Senator Biden's modernist formulation of natural law. Biden attributed the natural right of humans to "our Creator," but the Creator he had in mind was a modernist entity whose commands evolve along with circumstances and never stand in the way of what the most enlightened human beings think is appropriate. With respect to abortion, this means that humans are entitled to autonomy in moral choices and hence to protection from moral coercion.

What Is the Fetus?
The limits of this position are not completely clear, since no one asserts a general right to kill other human beings, even if they are very young children. Behind the right to abortion must stand some doctrine about what the fetus is, and why it is not the same sort

---

*Months after his confirmation, Thomas did vote as expected, but other conservative justices joined with liberals to reaffirm the *Roe* v. *Wade* decision, and so the right to abortion survived. See *Planned Parenthood* v. *Casey,* 112 S.Ct. 2791 (1992).

of entity as a newborn infant. This doctrine may also be described as a proposition of natural law, in the sense that it purports to be a fact about the nature of the fetus that legislators—and even Supreme Court justices—are not free to disregard.

If the fetus up until birth (or at least until viability) were not an independent human being at all but a mere bodily part of the mother, then a virtually unlimited right to abortion would follow straightforwardly. The problem with justifying abortion on this basis is that outside the abortion context the law often does treat the fetus as a human being with a right to life. In some states, this protection goes so far that killing of an unborn child by anyone but its mother or her abortionist is murder. A 1994 California Supreme Court decision, for example, held that a robber who shot a pregnant woman, causing a miscarriage, was guilty of murder even if the fetus was not viable (capable of survival outside the womb) at the time of death.

The California court, like other courts that have upheld fetal homicide statutes, did not consider this result to be contrary to *Roe* v. *Wade*'s doctrine that an abortionist acting with the consent of the mother has a constitutional right to kill the same fetus. Legal authorities agree that the constitutional right to abort is based on a balancing of the state's interest in protecting unborn life on the one hand and the expectant mother's constitutional right to privacy in procreative choice on the other hand. At least before viability, and as a practical matter before birth, the mother's right to privacy always outbalances the state's interest. When the mother's privacy right is not involved, however, the state may serve its interest in protecting unborn life by punishing a person who kills a fetus for murder.

The conceptual shift that underlies this modernist approach to abortion is the substitution of a mere "interest"—the state's interest in protecting unborn life—for what traditionalists would call a human being's right to life. The state's interest in preserving fetal

life is difficult to describe coherently. In an age of international
conferences adopting urgent population-control measures, the
state's interest seems to be in encouraging abortions as a backstop
when other birth-control measures fail, rather than in preventing
them. And whatever its moral obligations, the state has no apparent "interest" in protecting the lives of physically or mentally de-
fective unborn children who may require expensive treatment and
care if they are born.

The courts say that on the one hand, the state's interest in protecting unborn life is so weak that the mere desire of a woman to
have an abortion overrules it, regardless of her reasons. On the
other hand, they also say that the same interest is powerful enough
to justify sentencing a killer of a fetus to life in prison, or possibly
even to death. Few modernists are troubled by this logical anom-
aly, because the present situation makes perfect sense politically.
Powerful social groups support both a right to abortion and a
heavy-handed crackdown on violent crime. Attempting to satisfy
both groups has led the law to treat the fetus as if it were a mere
bodily part in one situation and as if it were a human being with
a right to life in another.

Law and the Moral Order

The traditional and modernist conceptions of law differ not just
in their positions on specific matters like abortion but in their
basic understanding of what morality is and how it influences law.
For the traditionalist, morality provides the essential background
to human lawmaking. In Sir William Blackstone's classic definition, human law is "a rule of civil conduct, prescribed by the
supreme power in a state, commanding what is right and prohib-
iting what is wrong." This definition requires much elaboration
before it can explain law adequately, but it captures a profound
point. For the traditionalist there is a moral order independent of
what human rulers may from time to time prefer, and law is just

to the extent that it comports with that moral order.

This does not mean that morality leads directly to law, because considerations of practicality, compassion and even privacy may intervene. For example, the pre-*Roe* traditionalist practice was to punish abortion as a crime much less serious than murder and to direct enforcement efforts primarily at abortionists rather than at their clients. Criminal law was thus in a general way consistent with morality, but not necessarily coextensive with it. In such a system it would be nonsense to speak of a general right to freedom from moral coercion. That would be like saying that the fundamental law is that there must be no laws.

From a modernist standpoint, morality is subjective. Some people may have the opinion that certain conduct is immoral, but others have an equal right to disagree. The term *morality* in modernist usage is usually associated with sexual morality, and therefore with traditional prohibitions of sodomy, fornication, adultery and abortion. With respect to such matters involving personal taste and one's own body, consenting adults must be free to do as they like.

Modernist lawmaking is based not on morality but on "utility" and "rights." The state has authority to regulate personal conduct to the extent necessary to serve the general welfare (utility) or to protect rights (such as a right to be free from discrimination). Otherwise, the most basic modernist right is the right to do as one likes—as long as one is not thereby damaging the general welfare or infringing on the rights of others. In the modernist context, a general right to be free from moral coercion makes perfect sense. It merely means that an individual does not forfeit her freedom merely because other people happen to disapprove of what she wants to do.

Probably the most influential American statement of the modernist understanding of law is a famous lecture titled "The Path of the Law," by the revered American jurist Oliver Wendell

Holmes Jr., delivered at the Boston University Law School in 1897. This lecture has been so influential in shaping the thinking of American lawyers that it might be described as almost part of the Constitution. Holmes urged his audience of future lawyers to put aside all notions of morality and approach law as a science, basically the science of state coercion. The reason people ask lawyers for advice, said Holmes, is not because they want to hear about morality but because they want to escape the unpleasant consequences that the law will inflict on them if they violate some rule. Therefore, "if you want to know the law and nothing else, you must look at it as a bad man, who cares only for the material consequences which such knowledge [of the law] enables him to predict, not as a good one, who finds his reasons for conduct, whether inside or outside of it, in the vaguer sanctions of conscience."

Mao Zedong's famous dictum that all power grows out of the barrel of a gun was prefigured in Holmes's view that law is ultimately the force that a government will bring to bear to enforce its commands. Citizens obey the law not because they feel morally obligated to do so but because they fear the consequences if they do not. Just as a chemist tells me that gasoline will explode if I bring it too near a fire, my lawyer tells me that I must pay damages if I breach a contract, or go to jail if I steal money. Of course if I am a "good" person I may refrain from promise-breaking and theft for independent reasons, but this, according to Holmes, has nothing to do with law. Goodness has no important role in legal science, because bad as well as good persons can be compelled to obey the law.

Holmes defined law as simply "the prophecies of what the courts will do in fact." What, then, of the lawmaker? If Supreme Court justices are in doubt about whether to create or maintain a right of abortion, or legislators are in doubt about whether to allow divorce on demand, they need to be told something more than that whatever they enact will be law. They need to know how to tell the difference between good law and bad law. Should the law reflect traditional morality, or should it strike out in new directions to further social utility and personal freedom?

Holmes urged lawmakers to put aside considerations of morality and tradition and to base law squarely on rational policy, informed by scientific disciplines such as economics and psychology. In short, to Holmes the practice of law was the prediction of outcomes, the making of law was an exercise in policy science, and the law itself was basically a statement about when the state would use its overwhelming force to coerce its citizens. We can see this concept of law in the modernist framing of the abortion issue: morality becomes a matter of personal preference. The law is concerned only with the extent to which state coercion should be limited by considerations of personal freedom.

This modernist, Holmesian theory of law is inadequate and misleading. Coercion is one aspect to law, but it is far from the whole story. Apart from coercion, law provides symbolic public affirmation for some worldviews and values and implied public repudiation or denial of others. Traditional law prohibited bestiality not because the lawmakers thought the threat of criminal punishment was particularly effective in deterring this vice, but because the enactment of such a law symbolized the state's endorsement of a particular understanding of human sexuality.

Beginning the schoolday with a moment of silence for prayer or meditation is not likely to fill the children of agnostics with religious zeal, but it is not likely to do them psychological harm either. The issue is bitterly contested because adults on both sides of the culture wars rightly place great importance on the symbolism of beginning the school day with prayer. The battle is over whose values the school system will endorse.

The reason that public funding for abortions is so bitterly contested has little to do with fiscal matters on either side. It is a battle over the symbolism of implied public endorsement of the decision to abort. The "therapeutic abortion statutes,"* which were the main vehicle of abortion-law reform before the Supreme Court's decision in *Roe* v. *Wade* made them irrelevant, did not provoke a firestorm—even though perceptive opponents pointed out that these statutes came very close to endorsing abortion on demand. Symbolically, the statutes left the existing moral code intact and merely enacted some (open-ended) medical exceptions. The Supreme Court decision did provoke a firestorm, because it was perceived as a radical repudiation of traditional Judeo-Christian morality on this subject.

The political battles that followed the Supreme Court decision are as much about symbolic enforcement of competing norms as they are about coercion. Battles over whether abortions should be publicly funded have little to do on either side with the small amount of money involved, and everything to do with whether abortion should be stigmatized. Prochoice advocates even oppose any governmental measure aimed at giving the aborted fetus the kind of burial that would be routine for a dead child. This is because the logic of the prochoice position demands not merely that the expectant mother wishing to abort should be free of any physical restraint, but that she should be free of any publicly endorsed moral restraint as well.

To read morality out of the law, as Holmes aspired to do, is impossible. What this program means in practice is to enlist the law on behalf of a new morality, based on relativism.

---

*In the years immediately before the Supreme Court decision in *Roe v. Wade*, various states enacted "therapeutic abortion statutes" which allowed abortion where necessary to protect the life or health of the mother, and sometimes also where the pregnancy was caused by rape or incest, or where the fetus was greatly deformed. In retrospect, these statutes can best be understood as attempts to go as far as possible in adopting what we now call the "pro-choice" position, without explicitly challenging the prevailing social attitude that fetal life is worthy of legal protection. The basic idea was to build on the conceded point that abortion could be justified where the life of the mother was at stake, and extend this "medical treatment" logic as far as the political climate would allow.

Holmes did not actually deny that there is such a thing as morality. At one point he even wrote, "The law is the witness and external deposit of our moral life. Its history is the history of the moral development of the race." Just as modernists have a modernist understanding of God, however, they also have a modernist understanding of morality. That people have moral notions is a fact about people, and hence it is also a fact about the law and about how the law has developed over time as moral notions have changed. Morality is entirely a human creation, however, and it is based on emotions or feelings rather than knowledge.

As a convinced Darwinist who profoundly understood the philosophical implications of Darwinism, Holmes found it difficult to take morality seriously. Responding to the suggestion that a law might be so immoral that public opinion would not tolerate its enforcement, Holmes responded flippantly, "I once heard the late Professor Agassiz say that a German population would rise [in rebellion] if you added two cents to the price of a glass of beer." If morality is purely subjective, a moral principle is just as strong as the emotional force it generates. If people feel strongly enough about the price of beer (or the price of a rent-controlled apartment in New York City), their outrage at a price increase is a perfectly good example of "moral" conviction.

Law: Normative or Descriptive?
In Darwinian terms, the traditionalist concept of natural law as a normative rather than a descriptive term is simply a category mistake. An outstanding contemporary legal scholar in the tradition of Holmes, Judge Richard Posner, explained this point in his major work on jurisprudence:

Even the term "natural law" is an anachronism. The majority of educated Americans believe that nature is the amoral scene of Darwinian struggle. Occasional attempts are made to derive social norms from nature so conceived, but they are not likely to succeed. It is true that a variety of widely accepted norms, including the keeping of certain promises, the abhorrence of unjustified killing of human beings, and perhaps even the sanctity of property rights, promote the adaption of the human species to its environment. But so does genocide.

Genocide, of course, is merely a shocking name for the process of natural selection by which one gene pool replaces another. Darwin himself explained this in *The Descent of Man,* when he had to deal with the absence of "missing links" between ape and human. Such gaps were to be expected, he wrote, in view of the extinctions that necessarily accompany evolution. He coolly predicted that evolution would make the gaps wider in the future, because the most civilized (that is, European) humans would soon exterminate the rest of the human species and go on from there to kill off our nearest kin in the ape world.

Modern Darwinists do not call attention to such passages, which make vivid how easily the picture of amoral nature inherent in evolutionary naturalism can be converted into a plan of action. Darwin's foremost original disciple, T. H. Huxley, also had no sentimental illusions about the moral meaning of Darwinism. When he had taken a deep enough bath in the implications of the Darwinian worldview, Huxley emerged with the conclusion that morality consists of opposing nature rather than imitating it.

Given the scientific understanding of reality, natural law in a normative (as opposed to a descriptive) sense cannot exist. Nonetheless, it is about as easy to stop invoking natural law as it is to stop speaking in prose. Even the nihilistic position that morality is an illusion and law should therefore concern itself solely with utility is a statement about "how things really are" and therefore a proposition of natural law.

As we have seen, the right to abortion is founded on natural law doctrines, however confused: asserted facts about the human condition that human lawmakers must not overrule. At bottom, the prochoice position asserts that abortion is *not* the premeditated killing of another human being, because it *is* a choice made by a woman about her own body. Prochoice advocates do not consider a prospective justice fit to be on the Supreme Court if he cannot recognize this way of thinking as moral fact, just as prolife advocates would reject a prospective justice who could not perceive that an unborn child is really a human being possessing a right to life.

The Varieties of Marxist Natural Law

Other examples of modernist natural law involve the many versions of Marxism. What is common to all varieties of Marxist thought is the proposition that the fundamental moral fact about the human condition is that a class of victims is dominated by a class of oppressors. It follows that the cure for oppression is liberation, whether through violent revolution or by cultural transformation. In classical Marxism the oppressor class was the bourgeoisie or capitalists, while the revolutionary class was the proletariat or industrial wage-laborers. The specific cure was for the workers to seize control of the factories and establish a dictatorship of the proletariat, to be followed by the utopia of communism.

Contemporary versions of this exciting drama flourish in universities, with a new cast of characters. Now the oppressor is the heterosexual white male; the new proletariat consists of racial minorities, women, gays and lesbians; and the struggle is for control of the terms of discourse. Great victories are won, as when newspaper editorialists and judges accepted the term *homophobia* as a fair descriptive term for the state of mind that leads people to oppose gay-rights ordinances. Institutions once thought to be obviously healthy, such as motherhood and the family, become reinterpreted as means of oppression—just as the original Marxists reinterpreted employment as "wage slavery."

One important doctrine of classical Marxism illustrates how a proposition of natural law can be tested in practice and falsified.

Traditionalist natural law assumes that human beings are naturally acquisitive and have an inherent tendency to abuse power. On the basis of these assumptions, it is desirable to preserve free markets to produce general prosperity from selfish activity, and also to maintain constitutional checks and balances in government, to restrain the temptations of power. Marxists posited on the contrary that human nature is malleable and that acquisitiveness is an artifact of certain economic arrangements. Change those arrangements and you change human nature. It follows that the elimination of exploitation could produce a new kind of being, the "new Soviet man" who would labor for the communal order. Moreover, the maxim "Power corrupts" was replaced with the doctrine that government represents the interests of the ruling class. Power would not necessarily corrupt the dictatorship of the proletariat, because this kind of government would by its nature represent the progressive elements in society.

If the Marxist experiment in the Soviet Union and elsewhere had worked as advertised, the traditionalist view of human nature would have been falsified. Instead, the collapse of that experiment everywhere proved as conclusively as anything can be proved that Marxist assumptions about human nature were erroneous. That does not imply that the Marxists were wrong about everything, of course, nor does it prove that free markets and liberal constitutions are panaceas for the ills of human nature. Powerful lobbies representing private interests can make a mockery of political democracy, and the people themselves may develop the outlook that government can give the voters something for nothing. In fact, America's individualistic version of modernism incorporates a contradiction that may in time have as fatal consequences for the social order as did the Marxist mistakes about human nature.

America's Moral Deficit
Americans have been taught to expect a lot from the national

government. Government is expected to take care of the poor, to ensure the delivery of high-quality health care to rich and poor alike, to protect the natural environment, to wage a war on drugs, to make the streets and neighborhoods safe from violent criminals, and to project its power into distant lands to deal with things like famines and human-rights abuses. This same government is supposed to achieve these ambitious goals with only minimal moral authority, because modernist philosophy makes each individual sovereign over moral questions. We want our rulers to undertake ambitious programs of social reform, which require extensive coercion of others, but we grant them no authority to tell us what we ought to do.

As Yale Law School professor Arthur Leff remarked in a brilliant lecture that is frequently quoted in law-journal articles, the all-purpose response to assertions of authority in our society is "the grand sez who." By this whimsical expression Leff meant that following the death of God there remains no universally accepted source of moral authority. In consequence there is no obvious reason for any person to feel obligated to obey the commands of another—other than the threat of force which keeps the Holmesian "bad man" in line. People feel entitled to behave as they please and to have no obligations other than those they choose to recognize.

On the other hand, people also feel entitled to a lot of protection when things go wrong. Liberal political theories reinforce this belief by giving the least gifted or least productive persons important rights against the society as a whole. Education through college, medical care, and income supplements for needy and low-paid persons are increasingly viewed as rights both by the recipients and by the opinion-molders of the media. Lawsuits and liability insurance are now employed as vehicles for wealth redistribution. Liability rules have expanded enormously to allow injured persons to find a "deep pocket" to pay damages not only for medical costs and lost income but also for pain and suffering and other intangibles. Drug addicts and alcoholics are considered "disabled" and hence entitled to social security payments. Vast sums are appropriated for diseases that are largely the result of substance abuse or recklessly promiscuous sexual behavior, and government is bitterly denounced for not doing still more.

By a convergence of redistributionist laws and "the grand sez who," we are arriving at an absurd condition that might be called libertarian socialism. Everyone has a right to live exactly as he or she pleases, but if something goes wrong, some abstraction called "society" is to blame and must pay the bill for damages. The savings and loan debacle of the 1980s was not an isolated incident but a paradigmatic example of the delusionary character of American thought near the end of the twentieth century. The S&L debacle occurred because the government freed financiers to make risky investments and at the same time insured the depositors who put up the money from any loss. The same generous public policy applies to individual behavior. Everyone must be free to make risky choices, and everyone must be protected from unpleasant consequences by social insurance that is ultimately provided by government, which is to say by nobody. In consequence there is a "moral deficit" of huge and growing proportions.

In economic terms the moral deficit is the difference between what people feel morally obligated to put into society's treasury and what they feel morally entitled to take out. A rough measure of the economic moral deficit is reflected in the difference between the total of all budgetary "entitlements" (social security, welfare, medical benefits and so on) and the revenue the government can raise for such purposes without setting off a tax revolt. In the Holmesian formulation of natural law, the deficit is practically infinite, and also a matter of no concern, since the bad (irresponsible) person pays taxes anyway for fear of the consequences. Holmes forgot to take into account that in a democracy, the irresponsible people elect the government if they are in the majority.

One reflection of "the grand sez who" is the inability of legislators to stem the growth of the national debt. People are willing up to a point to pay taxes for government programs like police protection and public education, which they see as benefiting the community as a whole, but increasingly taxation is perceived as a kind of Robin Hood activity in which money is taken from productive citizens for redistribution to other persons toward whom the taxpayers feel no sense of moral obligation. The politicians are under equally great pressure to fund benefits, now legally protected from budget-cutters as entitlements, to hungry constituencies that have been taught to view the benefits as a right.

The result is that government has increasingly to finance its expenditures with borrowed money and to conceal its real costs with ever more elaborate financial gimmickry. A financial crisis is inevitable. By sometime not far into the twenty-first century, all the revenues available to the government will be consumed by entitlements and interest on the federal debt. To try to solve the budgetary crisis with economic policy measures is about as realistic as treating cancer with painkillers. The financial deficit is merely a reflection of the underlying moral deficit, which is incurable unless there is a moral renewal.

Toward Moral Renewal

To set the agenda for that renewal in any detail would be premature, especially since few people will see the need for renewal as long as we can fend off the economic consequences of the moral deficit with borrowed money. When the need for renewal becomes too obvious to ignore, though, the first step will be to change the subject of our political discussions. Instead of talking about "who gets what," we will need to talk about "who contributes what." I do not have financiers in mind when I phrase the question that way, but ordinary people who raise their children to put in more than they take out and schoolteachers who reinforce that message in the classroom. These are the kinds of people who supply the moral capital that makes social justice achievable. The law needs to stop undermining the values that make people responsible citizens and start reinforcing them.

The way to reduce a moral deficit is to reinforce the sense of duty, honor and prudence—and to discourage the impression that "the world owes me a living." Fortunately, this can be done not by lying to people or manipulating them, but by telling them the truth about the human condition. Most people at heart do not want to be irresponsible hedonists or careerists, which is why they spend so much effort on inventing moral rationalizations for their behavior. Genuine satisfaction comes from being a productive member of a community and from gaining the respect and love of other persons the old-fashioned way, by earning it. Compared to that kind of satisfaction, the cheap pleasure that comes from having a closet full of expensive clothes or an ever-changing stable of sexual partners is not really all that satisfying.

A responsible society is based first and foremost on responsible parents who fulfill their obligations to each other and to their children. Probably the most important thing that most adults do is to prepare the next generation for the joys and responsibilities of life. To do this they must ensure to the best of their ability that their children are born healthy. Following birth, children must be nurtured and educated in moral behavior by loving parents, preferably *two* parents. That is one reason it is important for lovers to regard marriage as a sacred bond, rather than as a contractual arrangement to be terminated at the convenience of either party. That is also why mothers in a rational society regard their children, born and unborn, as a sacred trust rather than primarily as an encumbrance that men impose on women in order to make them unhappy and impede their pursuit of wealth, power and pleasure. Similarly, fathers in a rational society regard their offspring from the beginning of pregnancy as their own flesh, so that they become enthusiastic providers and conurturers rather than the unwilling objects of child-support orders.

Through its educational and legal institutions, a rational government does what it can to encourage these healthy attitudes and to discourage any tendency toward self-indulgent hedonism, to the end that there may be enough productive and responsible citizens around to do the essential work and to take care of the minority of unfortunate persons who did not get a proper start in life.

In view of the importance of families to the social order, it is irrational for lawmakers to encourage people to think of themselves primarily as rights-bearing and pleasure-seeking individuals who form and sever sexual relationships with other people according to their own convenience. Yet contemporary American law does exactly that. One way it does it is by permitting easy divorce at the option of either party, so that men and women alike know that they can leave a marriage whenever they get tired of the arrangement or find a better opportunity. Another thing the law does is to foster the impression that the unborn child in the womb is the expectant mother's sole property, to dispose of as she wishes. This invites fathers who are inclined to hedonism to draw the logical conclusion that what is the mother's sole property is also her sole responsibility.

With the social stigma deliberately removed from divorce and the production of illegitimate children, and with welfare instituted to replace the absent father as wage-earner, the norm for family life in many areas may become single mothers struggling alone with the problems of raising their children. The law can promise to collect child support from irresponsible fathers, but it will not be able to keep that promise with any consistency. Children raised in a single-parent welfare culture predictably develop social pathologies, and the young males fill the jails. Mothers themselves, the natural last bastion of responsibility in a hedonistic society, may be tempted to give up on their responsibilities and pursue pleasure instead. Con-

sidering what men get away with, why should anyone be such a fool
as to sacrifice the best years of her life for a stranger that has
invaded her body and her home?

Law relating to family life is not important primarily because of
its direct effect in coercing compliance. If anything, law is more
important as a reflector of social norms than as their cause. Our
laws reflect how we—or those who govern us—see ourselves and
what kinds of behavior we value. Law is important because social
morality needs public reinforcement and because people who are
doing the right thing need to feel that they are good citizens rather
than suckers.

Holmes had it backwards. The primary focus of the lawmaker's
interest is not the bad person but the good ones who want to do
the right thing. How can the law encourage them to keep on doing
it? Of course the law also tries to coerce the irresponsible person,
such as the man who fathers children and declines to support them.
But coercion loses its effectiveness when irresponsibility becomes
the norm rather than the exception.

To say that the first business of law in a rational society is to
identify the norm for responsible family life and reinforce it is not
to sanction intolerance. In a democratic society that values freedom, there must be tolerance for those who depart from the norm.
But the question of how much tolerance there should be is different
from the question of what the norm ought to be. Unmarried and
same-sex couples, for example, are entitled to tolerance. When the
question is not what a rational society should tolerate but what it
should affirmatively encourage, however, the first priority must be
to encourage stable marriages and good parenting. Tolerance does
not mean relativism. A rational society will be generous in recognizing exceptions, but it will emphatically define the norm around
the values of the stable families that build the future.

The problem for a rational democratic social order is how to
encourage morally rational behavior so that it remains the norm

rather than the exception. In this task law is important as a reflection of community values, but the main influence on behavior is public education, including the education that adult and juvenile citizens receive from the public media. Let us see next what our educators are trying to achieve.

8

Education

YALE LAW SCHOOL PROFESSOR BRUCE ACKERMAN IS ONE OF the many scholars who have tried to provide an overall theoretical justification for liberal rationalism, the dominant political and legal philosophy of contemporary America. His book *Social Justice in the Liberal State* is not widely known except to law professors, but it does a particularly good job of articulating the mindset of contemporary agnostic liberalism, particularly on the subject of education. Ackerman's starting point is the naturalistic premise that opinions about values or morality are inherently subjective. This premise implies that every person's goals in life are intrinsically as good as every other person's. In principle every citizen of a liberal state is entitled to live as he or she pleases—up to the point where the individual's activities infringe upon the right of other citizens to a similar liberty. At that point, the law has to step in to resolve the conflict.

Because there is no way to rank competing goals or values as inherently good or bad, conflicts between citizens must be settled by a "neutral" dialogue, by which Ackerman means a debate in which no citizen claims any intrinsic superiority for his or her values. If I like to collect wild orchids and you like to hunt foxes on horseback, there is no way to rank any of our desires as superior or inferior. This neutrality-in-principle does not mean that in practice all persons will actually be able to realize their life plans, because Ackerman's liberalism contemplates an egalitarian distribution of wealth. Fox hunters will not be banned on moral grounds, but they have no right to compel their fellow citizens to finance this costly activity. The category of "citizens" who get to participate in the neutral conversation over the distribution of wealth and other issues of public policy includes all persons, including juveniles, who are capable of uttering what Arthur Leff called "the grand sez who"—that is, all persons who are capable of demanding a justification for any restraint on their freedom of action.

Ackerman's basic assumption is that what emerges from the neutral conversation is not utter chaos, but rather a set of laws very much like those generally advocated by political liberals in contemporary America. The liberal state aims to maximize personal freedom within a framework of economic equality, while maintaining a strict neutrality on differing conceptions of the good life and a firm agnosticism toward religious claims.

Goals of a Liberal Education

I will not attempt to describe how this system of government works out overall, because my focus in this chapter is limited to education. How can parents and teachers educate children without imposing a concept of the good life on them? The starting point for Ackerman is that a liberal education must *not* be authoritarian. An authoritarian education attempts to train the child in a particular direction, so that it will grow up to be the kind of person the parents or educators wish it to be. Raising Jack to take over the family business or to become a priest is authoritarian; a liberal education aims instead to maximize Jack's ability to choose among alternate futures. Raising Jill to be a mother and home-maker is probably even more objectionable; she should be encour-aged to think of careers outside the home and of possibilities for personal fulfillment other than heterosexual marriage. The goal is to produce self-defining adults who choose their own values and lifestyles from among a host of alternatives, rather than obedient children who follow a particular course laid down for them by their elders.

Ackerman concedes that a liberal society cannot begin offering alternatives all at once, because very young children need to have a coherent upbringing rather than a smorgasbord of choices. Dur-ing the first five years parents therefore have a free hand, within broad limits, to bring up their children as they think best. By the age of five, however, the normal child begins to question parental authority and to leave the home during part of the day to go to school. At around this time most children begin demanding a justification for parent-imposed limits on their freedom. By issuing that demand (sez who?) children begin to become citizens of the liberal state, and they must be answered with something more neutral than that Father or Mother knows best (sez me!). More-over, educators other than the parents become available with the onset of primary school, and they may be entitled to offer the child choices that the parents have withheld.

Ackerman illustrates his main points with hypothetical dia-logues. To illustrate the problem of the rebellious kindergartner, he imagines a "Daughter" who wants to play with trucks instead of dolls and an authoritarian "Parent" who insists that girls should play only with dolls. An adult citizen named Noble, who seems to represent the public school system, demands the right to encour-age the girl in her resistance to gender stereotyping. Parent feebly resists, but Noble has the better of the argument, because Parent cannot come up with a value-neutral justification for "his continuing effort to monopolize his daughter's moral vocabulary and perception." (It is no accident that the public official who announces his intention to undermine Parent's authority is named Noble rather than, say, Meddler.)

The practical meaning of this dialogue is that the public schools in a liberal state should actively seek to free children from parental authority, at least where that authority is based on a tradition that the educators regard as unduly restrictive. Readers may wonder what would happen if Parent were an agnostic and instead of the liberal Noble, "Evangelist" appeared at the door to introduce the child to the claims of Jesus Christ, or if "Creationist" asked to be admitted to tell children that the theory of evolution they are being taught in the schools is not true.

Ackerman does not seriously consider such possibilities, but he does say that the educational authorities will screen all would-be intervenors to ensure that they are "trustworthy." Evangelist and Creationist will undoubtedly fail that test, because Ackerman's liberal state—like our real-life public school system—implicitly excludes all claims about God from public discussion.

The hypothetical situation embodied in the dialogue thus faithfully reflects public educational policy in late-twentieth-century America. Liberal educators aim to free the children under their care from what they see as authoritarian parents, meaning parents who have traditional views of gender roles or religious morality.

Consistent with his support for this practice, Ackerman vehemently disapproves of plans to offer parents tuition vouchers that would make private schools affordable for families with modest incomes. He reasons,

> Surely, parents will refuse to spend "their" vouchers on anything but "education" that strives to reinforce whatever values they have—with so much effort—imposed on "their" children.

Thus, [voucher plans] legitimate a series of petty tyrannies in which like-minded parents club together to force-feed their children without restraint. Such an education is a mockery of the liberal ideal.

Significantly, Ackerman does not extend this condemnation to private schools that are funded by private tuition and endowments. This also is consistent with current liberal educational policy, which does not really object to parents or private education as such, but to those parents who seek to pass traditional religious and moral values on to their children. The kind of private schools to which Ivy League professors and high government officials tend to send their own children actually do provide a liberal education based on naturalistic philosophical principles, and hence they are compatible with the state's educational policies. Voucher plans would extend the privilege of private education to the lower classes, and many of the voucher schools would reflect the conservative religious values of those parents. When liberals argue that voucher plans would violate the constitutional principle of separation of church and state, what they mean is that the established religious philosophy might lose control of public education.

The Fruits of Liberal Education

The practical results of liberal educational theory in contemporary public education are described in a splendid book by education professor William Kilpatrick of Boston College, *Why Johnny Can't Tell Right from Wrong*. Kilpatrick reports on some of the more spectacular failures of our notoriously failure-prone public educational system, such as drug-abuse programs that actually encourage drug use and sex-education programs that encourage teens to experiment with sex. A common feature of the educational materials in these subjects is the repeated reminder to students that they are ultimately the only proper judges of what is right and wrong for them, and that they should not accept traditional standards of behavior merely because their parents have taught them that way. The message "Only you can judge" is reinforced by role-playing and discussion scenarios in which parents are typically overbearing and unfair, and teens do the right thing by charting their own course.

Classes in moral reasoning and values clarification present teen-agers with complex hypothetical problems, unlikely to be encountered in day-to-day adolescent life, which tend by their nature to encourage relativism. Is it right to steal money to buy medicine for a dying person? If a man will help a young woman to reach her lover (save her family, avoid some disaster) only if she sleeps with him, should she do it? Should a refugee mother suffocate her infant son if necessary to prevent his crying from reaching the ears of the Gestapo, who are searching for the refugees' hiding place? Exercises of that kind are questionable guides to real-world problems, such as whether a teenager should steal spending money from her mother's purse or sleep with her boyfriend, and tend to train the students in rationalizing whatever they are inclined to do.

Some of the problems in drug-abuse education in particular seem to stem from fads like the human potential movement of the 1960s, and these problems are probably curable without major surgery on the culture. That teenagers should be told emphatically not to use drugs is acceptable these days even in liberal circles, and on this issue law-enforcement policy is eager to help enforce the message. Other problems, particularly in the area of sex education, reflect deeper cultural trends that are not so easy to address.

One bitterly contended issue is whether sex education should encourage teenagers to have sexual intercourse only with the use of condoms or not to have sexual intercourse at all. The leading liberal response is to say that it should do both; that is, education should encourage students to postpone sex until they are more mature, but it should also encourage them to use proper protection if they are unwilling or unable to postpone. The problem with this solution is that in practice the two messages are contradictory. If the emphasis is to be on preventing disease and unwanted pregnancy by condom use, the students have to be taught how to use condoms properly and encouraged to employ them without embarrassment. To that end they must be relieved of any feelings of reticence or modesty that might make them reluctant to broach the subject of condom use with a partner before it is too late. The logical result is classroom exercises where girls practice putting condoms on cucumbers, or even on boys' fingers, and where boys and girls alike are encouraged to have condoms constantly available and ready in case of need.

As Kilpatrick puts it, education in safe sex has a tendency to make sex seem like another school body-contact sport in which the proper equipment must be worn to avoid injury. Or as a former surgeon general of the United States famously put it, sex education can be regarded as an extension of driver training: "We taught them what to do in the front seat [of a car]. Now it's time to teach them what to do in the back seat." Why not? If teenagers enjoy sex, and if technology is available to prevent disease and unwanted pregnancy, then a liberal state is hard put to find a neutral reason for telling them not to have fun.

What teenagers do as teenagers is important, but what they do for the rest of their lives is still more important. Kilpatrick notes that one thing progressive sex-education courses do *not* do is concentrate on preparing teenagers for stable and faithful marriages. In his words,

> What sort of spouse will a youngster make after years of being desensitized to sex? What sort of parent? If sex isn't special before marriage, what will make it special afterwards? If there is nothing particularly special about sex, then adultery won't seem particularly bad either. And why put devotion to your wife and children ahead of your own pleasures? Why bother about getting married at all? If you get someone pregnant, she can

have an abortion. If she doesn't want to, that's her problem. After all, everyone has to make their [sic] own decisions.

In fact, modernist liberal society does not place a high priority on encouraging stable marriages and two-parent families. The reason is that to endorse traditional marriage is implicitly to criticize other arrangements. Any public figure who argues that children benefit from being raised in a traditional, two-parent family risks being accused of insulting single parents, as Dan Quayle found out the hard way when he criticized the television show *Murphy Brown*. In progressive circles, traditional marriage is increasingly regarded as discriminatory, because it is associated with traditional gender roles and because same-sex couples are not entitled to marry. Marriage in modernist culture is viewed mainly as a contract much like any other, between sexual partners who keep their own names and terminate the relationship at will. On the basis of modernist principles, such arrangements are perfectly logical. Exactly what *is* so special about marriage, if God is really dead? Sez who?

Many people have reservations and second thoughts about these matters, and the media have paid some attention recently to studies showing that children raised in what used to be called "broken homes" are not on average as successful academically or socially as those in intact, two-parent families. Correlation studies are never conclusive evidence of cause and effect, however, and they deal with averages rather than with specific cases. In any case, modernism has no doctrine of natural duty to explain why or to what extent adults should sacrifice their own happiness for speculative advantages to "their" children, who might not be appreciative of more parental attention and discipline. Educators may think vaguely that it is beneficial to society for couples to stay married, but they have no moral authority to demand (or even to advise) that citizens should remain in unhappy marriages if they would prefer to leave.

If a school district were to announce a policy of preparing children for stable, traditional marriages and for two-parent child-rearing, and also for discouraging high schoolers from developing the kind of casual attitude toward sex described by Kilpatrick, the whole idea would be characterized in the media as a plot by the religious right and met with a mighty chorus of "the grand sez who." People who accept modernist premises see nothing wrong with a relativist approach to family and sexual morality—or at least they have considerable difficulty justifying whatever uneasiness they may feel.

Teaching Values

There are some subjects on which modernist educators are not relativists, however, and one of them is the teaching of evolution. Martin Eger, professor of physics and philosophy of science at the City University of New York, has written of the immense difference in the prevailing educational philosophy regarding the teaching of evolution as opposed to the teaching of values and ethics. In moral-reasoning or values-clarification classes, students are encouraged to reason their way to a personal moral philosophy after a critical consideration of alternatives, including alternatives of which their parents might heartily disapprove—like lying or drug use or sexual experimentation.

The inspiration for this approach to moral education comes from a superficial understanding of one of the classic texts of liberal philosophy, John Stuart Mill's "On Liberty." Mill explained that it is unsatisfactory to hold even a *correct* belief on the basis of prejudice: "Assuming that true opinion abides in the mind, but abides as a prejudice, a belief independent of, and proof against, argument—this is not the way truth ought to be held by a rational being."

Mill drew the conclusion that it is always necessary to consider alternatives to socially approved opinions, including even alternatives that seem erroneous. He reasoned that an opinion that is on the whole erroneous "may, and very commonly does, contain a portion of the truth; and since the general or prevailing opinion on any subject is rarely or never the whole truth, it is only by a collision of adverse opinions that the remainder of the truth has any chance of being supplied."

Mill's method is excellent when it is applied by mature adults who know how to make discriminating judgments, but its application to the teaching of correct behavior to children or adolescents is another matter. The basic problem is that immature minds may be all too eager to seize upon some facile idea that permits them to rationalize their disinclination to resist temptation. A value may become truly real to an individual only after it has been tested, but it does not follow that the way to teach values to children in the first place is to encourage them to exercise their immature judgment about such things as the costs and benefits of marijuana smoking, promiscuous sex and cheating on tests. Perhaps critical rationality with respect to morals is an excellent quality to develop in maturity, but no-nonsense training in good moral habits is more appropriate for children and even adolescents.

Mill himself would probably have agreed, because he said explicitly in *On Liberty* that his prescriptions were for the benefit of mature adults in a highly civilized culture, the products of a Victorian education in childhood. (Mill himself was mainly educated by his very authoritarian father, who trained his son from childhood to follow in his own footsteps as a utilitarian philosopher.)

But training children in good moral habits is possible only if there is some way to determine which habits are good. If values are so subjective that we cannot judge their goodness objectively, then the process by which the individual comes to identify and choose those values *may be* the only measure of goodness. A liberal educational system committed to value neutrality may be unable to endorse any moral habit other than the habit of making personal choices and the habit of giving everybody's value judgments equal weight. In that case, educators may have no alternative but to try to extend down into childhood a process of rational choice designed for adults.

Eger observed that the prevailing educational philosophy is entirely different when the question is whether teachers and students ought to come to grips with creationist challenges to naturalistic evolution. The educators have no doubt that on this subject, right thinking involves a total rejection of creationism and embrace of evolutionism, and they are determined that students will hear only orthodox teaching. Eger did not think this difference could be justified on the ground that scientific knowledge is objective whereas moral values are subjective and hence always fairly debatable. Our society is in fact quite definite about certain moral doctrines, such as that slavery and racial discrimination are wrong, and on these doctrines the educators are not relativists. The difference is not between science and morality, but between those doctrines that educators are really determined to induce children to believe and those that they do not care about so much. When it comes to important matters, the educators understand very well that immature minds cannot be trusted to come to correct answers.

Eger quotes Philip Kitcher, a leading Darwinist philosopher of science, who explained why it is not a good idea to expose secondary-school students to creationist arguments:

> There will be . . . much dredging up of misguided objections to evolutionary theory. The objections are spurious—but how is the teacher to reveal their errors to students who are at the beginning of their science studies? . . . What Creationists really propose is a situation in which people without scientific training—fourteen-year-old students, for example—are asked to decide a complex issue on partial evidence.

In matters of ethics and morality, fourteen-year-old students are invited to challenge the standards of their parents and make their own decisions. When it comes to evolution, however, the same pupils must be protected from spurious notions that may seem valid to their untutored judgment. Eger observes that a great many parents think it would be much wiser to do the reverse: to tell the adolescents firmly what limits on behavior they must observe and to encourage them to practice their critical thinking on more theoretical subjects like evolution, where mistakes are much less likely to cause permanent damage.

Naturalism in Education
The combination of absolutism in evolutionary science and relativism (or selective relativism) in morals perfectly reflects the established religious philosophy of late-twentieth-century America. Naturalism in science provides the foundation for liberal rationalism in morals, by keeping the possibility of divine authority effectively out of the picture. Belief in naturalistic evolution is foundational to a great deal else, and so it can hardly be presented as open to doubt. The schools accordingly teach that humans *discover* the profound truth of evolution but they *invent* moral standards and can change them as human needs change.

The principles that govern the curriculum in primary and secondary schools are developed in the universities, where teachers, administrators and textbook writers receive their training. If naturalistic thinking increasingly dominates public education at the primary and secondary levels, this triumph was possible only because similar thinking came to dominate the universities long before. George Marsden's 1994 book *The Soul of the American University* provides an illuminating account of how the universities shed their Christian heritage and moved, in the words of his subtitle, "from Protestant establishment to established nonbelief."

Today we take it for granted that secular universities, both public and private, are pervasively dominated by naturalistic thinking and pervasively unfriendly to theism. This is true, or even especially true, in universities that have religious studies departments. "Religious belief" is an acceptable subject of study, but religion is almost always studied from a naturalistic and relativistic perspective. Many university professors and administrators, and even some judges, are under the impression that it is unprofessional or even unconstitutional for a professor to advocate a religious position or to attribute human existence to a supernatural Creator. Of course, similar restrictions do not apply to the advocacy of opinions on other subjects, or even to the classroom advocacy of atheism. At the typical secular university a few professors and a fairly large number of students will be believing Christians or religiously observant Jews, but with rare exceptions theism is absent from the classroom and from the deliberations of professional societies. The prevailing attitude with respect to religion in the universities ranges from indifference to contempt.

Things were not always this way. According to Marsden, a Protestant establishment dominated American higher education until fairly recently. Even state universities were explicitly Christian a century ago, and leading private universities retained a formal Christian identification as late as the 1950s. When William F. Buckley's 1951 book *God and Man at Yale* charged Yale faculty with undermining the university's traditional commitment to Christianity (and conservative values), university authorities responded indignantly and with apparent sincerity that Yale remained Christian "in a broad sense." A generation later such a claim would have been met with a firestorm of protest—or howls of laughter.

At Duke University, famous today for basketball championships and postmodernist literary theory, a plaque at the center of the campus states, "The aims of Duke University are to assert a faith in the eternal union of knowledge and religion set forth in the teachings and character of Jesus Christ, the Son of God." That was what Duke officially stood for at its initial endowment in

1924, and many other universities would then have viewed their mission similarly. By the time Duke formulated a mission statement in 1988, however, its aims had become entirely secular in character, stressing only values like "the spirit of free inquiry" and the promotion of "diversity and mutual tolerance." The university's previous Christian identity was relegated to history with a statement that "Duke cherishes its historic ties with the United Methodist Church and the religious faith of its founders, while remaining non-sectarian." The new mission statement made clear, in Marsden's words, that today "Christianity as such is peripheral to the main business of the university."

Marsden's subtitle, *From Protestant Establishment to Established Nonbelief,* aptly summarizes the story of secularization that he tells with a wealth of detail appropriate for a fine academic historian.* The Protestant establishment that ruled the universities through the first half of the twentieth century was a *liberal* establishment. As such it made common cause with secular rationalists to marginalize liberal Protestantism's chief religious rivals, which were Roman Catholicism and the more conservative forms of Protestantism. By "Christianity" the religious liberals came to mean something not fundamentally different from Enlightenment rationalism. To them Christianity stood for free inquiry, the growth of knowledge, scientific progress, tolerance and social service. Doctrines distinctive to historical Christianity, such as original sin, salvation by faith in Christ, and the resurrection, were relegated to the background or ignored altogether.

In this sense the 1924 plaque at Duke University and the 1988

---

*George Marsden began his career as a history professor at Calvin College and was an important witness for the "evolution" side in the 1981 federal trial that ruled unconstitutional the Arkansas statute mandating "balanced treatment for creation-science." As an authority on American religious history, Marsden testified that creation-science was a religious rather than a scientific position. (For details on this trial see chapter nine of my book *Darwin on Trial* and the research notes to that chapter.) Marsden later moved to Duke University's divinity school, where he wrote *The Soul of the American University,* and he is now professor of history at Notre Dame University.

mission statement are more alike than might appear on the surface. By unifying religion with "knowledge" and hence with the rationalist spirit of the age, liberal Protestants prepared the way for a later generation that, attributing knowledge solely to human reason and experience, saw no need to retain religion.

Marsden's concluding chapter describes the present dilemma of the universities. Originally the liberal establishment had encouraged scientific naturalism because it was assumed that scientific truth would always be compatible with philosophical and religious truth. Eventually, however, naturalism and pragmatism took full command of the intellectual terrain, leaving no need or room in the academic enterprise for the religious tradition. The result has not been the expected triumph of rationalism, however, but the intellectual crisis described in chapter six of this book. According to Marsden,

> The postmodernist intellectual crisis may thus be understood as a crisis within the naturalistic community. Given a purely naturalistic evolutionary and radically historicist set of premises, finding any rational grounds for building a consensus on any significant human question becomes problematic. Consistent application of the hermeneutics of suspicion reduces everything to the interests of individuals or groups. . . . Old-style liberal opponents of such relativism have no place to stand in establishing a basis for their moral claims. Appeals to natural law have far less chance of commanding a consensus then they did in Robert Hutchins' day. Yet the alternative of liberal pragmatism has led, much as Hutchins predicted, to postmodernist relativism.*

---

*Robert Maynard Hutchins, who served as president or chancellor of the University of Chicago from 1929 to 1951, attempted to counter the trend toward scientism and pragmatism in the universities by reinvigorating the philosophical tradition of Plato, Aristotle and Aquinas. In company with the philosopher Mortimer Adler, Hutchins championed the "Great Books" approach to education and the existence of natural law. He resigned as chancellor in 1951, frustrated by faculty opposition to his educational philosophy. Marsden concludes from Hutchins's failure that "even a person of immense prestige and ability could not deflect the educational stream that was so firmly set in its course [toward scientific naturalism and pragmatism]."

In this situation, Marsden argues, the universities should recognize that metaphysical naturalism is neither a self-evident fact nor a finding of science, but merely a methodological premise that is sometimes useful. "As a claim about reality, however, naturalism is unsubstantiated and unfalsifiable." Theistic perspectives can also provide a worthy starting point for intellectual inquiry, but today "the only points of view that are allowed full academic credence are those that presuppose purely naturalistic worldviews." Universities have no justification for establishing naturalism as the exclusive orthodoxy for academic thinking, and they should allow theists as such to participate fully in academic life. Religious professors should no longer be compelled by rule or custom to suppress their religious commitments, but should be free to acknowledge them and base scholarly work on them—just as professors with personal commitments to ideologies like feminism and socialism are already doing. Of course theists, like others, should be expected to meet professional standards of rationality, but the standards should not assume that rationality and naturalism are virtually the same thing.

Marsden's argument provides not only a justification for a theistic presence in the university but also a rough agenda of issues that theists ought to consider tackling. First and foremost is the status of naturalism itself. Is naturalism really nothing more than a methodological premise that is sometimes useful, or is it "the way things really are" and thus the essential foundation of rationality itself? Possibly naturalism is not always useful, and possibly it has even led twentieth-century culture into serious errors.

If naturalists defend their philosophy on the pragmatic ground that it is useful, theists might have grounds to reply that naturalism has not apparently been fruitful as a starting point for education, at least when it is so established that it excludes other ways of thinking. There is little dispute that American public schools are in a deplorable state, with academic standards shockingly low and standards of student behavior even lower. The state of the universities is more difficult to assess, but there is a substantial literature suggesting not only that universities are in the midst of an intellectual crisis but also that campuses are centers of politicization and intolerance. The causes of such problems are likely to be complex, of course, but it is worth considering the possibility that some of our educational problems stem at least in part from the loss of moral authority that has followed from the turn to naturalism and relativism.

The philosopher Dallas Willard likes to quote the motto that appears at the entrance to California's Pomona College: "Let only the eager, thoughtful and reverent enter here." One would never expect such an admonition to be taken literally, but at one time it seemed credible as an ideal. Today it would just seem ridiculous.

9

The
Subtext
of Contempt

P HILLIP BISHOP TEACHES CLASSES IN EXERCISE PHYSIOLOGY
in the College of Education at the University of Alabama.
Like many other college teachers, he likes to tell his students
something about himself and what he values. In his case, this personal disclosure involved saying that he believes that "God came
to earth in the form of Jesus Christ and he has something to tell
us about life which is crucial to success and happiness." Because of
this belief, Bishop said, he prefers to invest his time in people rather
than in publishing "a stack of technical papers." He presented this
view as his own "bias" and told students, "If that is not your bias,
that is fine." He also urged students to keep in mind that whatever
he said might reflect his Christian bias and asked them to tell him
if his behavior fell short of his Christian ideals.

Viewpoint Discrimination or Harassment?
Courts that later reviewed his conduct agreed that Bishop was

otherwise very restrained. He never engaged in prayer, read passages from the Bible, handed out religious tracts or lectured on any religious topic during class. On the other hand, Bishop made no secret of his skepticism about the orthodox doctrine that the human body evolved by purely naturalistic and material processes such as random mutation and natural selection. He did not discourse on this subject in class, but he did invite students and others to a voluntary, after-hours meeting at which he lectured on "evidences of God in human physiology."

Bishop discussed the creation issue only outside of regular class hours because, unlike many college professors, he was scrupulous about sticking to the assigned topic and not imposing his opinions on a captive audience. To naturalists determined to exclude theism from university life altogether, however, it seemed unlikely that students would voluntarily attend a lecture on a topic so absurd as Bishop's notion that a supernatural Creator was needed to create human beings. If they really did want to attend such a lecture, what did this say about the rest of their education? That sort of thing can be tolerated at a university like Berkeley or Harvard, where deans and professors do not worry overmuch about being accused of sympathizing with "fundamentalists," but in Alabama God is not yet safely buried. Something had to be done to protect the university's good name, and something *was* done.

The head of Bishop's academic unit, Carl Westerfield, later testified that some students (whose names he could not remember) had complained about Bishop's statements. Westerfield himself worried that Bishop's statements might hurt the university's academic reputation, because "other professional colleagues around the nation consider this the 'Bible Belt' and [think] that . . . a lot of this type of activity goes on in the University." He shared his anxiety with the dean of the college, and the two went to see the university's legal counsel to decide whether Bishop's remarks amounted to an unconstitutional establishment of religion.

The university's lawyers assumed that what a state university professor says in a classroom is tantamount to an act of state government and so is governed by Supreme Court decisions that prohibit government support of religion. In the light of those decisions, the lawyers thought the university had a duty to "control this kind of activity" because Bishop's remarks were religious in their purpose and effect.

Westerfield accordingly ordered Bishop not only to cease referring to his religious beliefs during class time but also to discontinue "the optional classes where a 'Christian perspective' on an academic topic is delivered." Everyone seems to have taken for granted that it would be impermissible for Bishop to advance a "Christian" (that is, theistic) perspective on the origin of the human body during regular class hours. The university's rationale for forbidding even after-hours discussion of a dissenting opinion about this sensitive subject was that students might feel coerced to agree with Bishop's religion in hopes of gaining some favorable treatment.

Bishop challenged the restrictions in federal court, and at first he was successful. The federal district court observed that the university's restrictions were aimed not at coercive speech, irrelevant speech or offensive speech, but only at religious speech. The court cited written statements from other professors which established that it is a common practice for professors to share their personal views and biases with students, and that the university never objected to this common practice except in Bishop's case. Furthermore, there was no university policy against holding optional, after-hours classes in whatever subject the professor might want to address. In light of these conceded facts, the district court held that a policy banning only religious expression is unconstitutional viewpoint discrimination, under the legal principles reviewed in the first chapter of this book.

So far, so good; but the university appealed the district court decision and overturned it. The opinion by Judge Floyd Gibson for the federal court of appeals said that the relevant principle was not freedom of speech but the right of educational administrators to control what is said in the classroom. The judiciary should not interfere with such internal university matters, said Gibson, because "federal judges should not be ersatz deans or educators." If Bishop and other professors were dissatisfied with the restrictions placed on them by their academic superiors, their remedy was not to go to federal court but to seek employment at a different university that was more tolerant. As the court stated in this *reductio ad absurdum* of free-market ideology, "University officials are undoubtedly aware that quality faculty members will be hard to attract and retain if they are to be shackled in much of what they do."

The district court had been particularly impressed by the selectivity of the university's policy, which did not exclude the *subject* of religion but permitted only one kind of opinion on that subject to be discussed. The district court commented that the policy "would allow groups of young philosophers to meet to discuss their skepticism that a Supreme Being exists, or a group of political scientists to meet to debate the accuracy of the view that religion is the 'opium of the people.' " The district court went on to observe that the university actually offered courses in religion and theology but prohibited instructors in those courses (but not in other subjects) from stating their personal views about the subjects they taught. How could the First Amendment be read to permit, much less require, such viewpoint discrimination on the subject of religion?

Judge Gibson answered that such selectivity was entirely justified, because Bishop's viewpoint was particularly likely to cause "apprehension":

> Dr. Bishop has tried to make much of the fact that the University has no policy for limiting the speech of its professors only

to their subject areas. . . . [He] has filed numerous affidavits by other instructors at the University describing their extracurricular speech in the classroom as efforts to reach out to students. These attempts at professor-student affinity are laudable. But plainly some topics understandably produce more apprehension than comfort in students. Just as women students would find no comfort in an openly sexist instructor, an Islamic or Jewish student will not likely savor the Christian bias that Dr. Bishop professes. . . . There is no suggestion that any other professor has produced student complaints or struck constitutional chords.

Although the court of appeals insisted that it was for administrators to decide which opinions were too likely to cause "apprehension" to be uttered in the classroom, the administrators themselves were under the impression that they were obligated on legal grounds to silence Bishop. In fact, the university defended its position in court on the theory that Bishop's remarks violated the First Amendment's prohibition of an "establishment of religion."

The court of appeals did not formally decide the religious establishment question, but hinted broadly that it agreed with the university's counsel. "Dr. Bishop's optional class was particularly suspect," remarked the opinion, because the "creation/design aspect of his lecture could have lent itself to an analysis as found in Edwards v. Aguillard." The *Edwards* case, which was discussed in the first chapter of this book, held that it is unconstitutional for a state to require classes in evolution to give consideration to "the religious viewpoint that a supernatural being created mankind." By referring to that holding, the court of appeals implied that it would probably be unconstitutional for the university to allow Bishop to express in the classroom—or even in voluntary, after-hours classes—his opinion that the human body was designed. Thus the court of appeals implicitly affirmed the administrators' impression that they were legally bound to act as they did, and then justified its decision on the ground that judges should not tell administrators what to do.

I do not think that the United States Supreme Court would agree with this logic, but that is no more than a speculation, because in fact the Supreme Court refused to grant a hearing in the case and thus left the court of appeals decision standing. I am also confident that most professors would be shocked to hear that the constitution imposes no restrictions on the power of administrators to silence faculty members who challenge orthodox doctrines in their classes. Nonetheless, the American Association of University Professors, which might have been expected to jump into such a case with both feet, declined to support Professor Bishop's petition to the Supreme Court to review the decision of the court of appeals.

The academic and legal elites genuinely support academic freedom and freedom of speech, but they are divided about how those principles apply to "religion." Because representatives of the academic community can send no clear message to the Supreme Court about where they stand, the court also is ambivalent about whether academic freedom extends to religious statements.

The Selective Application of Academic Freedom

If the professors ever have to face the issue directly, however, I am sure that in the end they will agree that academic freedom applies even to religion and that critical thinking is permissible even when it is directed at evolution or naturalism. There are at least two academic precedents, neither of which led to a judicial decision, in which Christian professors who challenged orthodox opinions about evolution won their case by pursuing internal university remedies.

In chapter one I described the Dean Kenyon case at San Francisco State University, where the university's academic senate supported a biology professor who advocated intelligent design. A particularly delightful instance of the same kind involved Professor Henry F. Schaefer. Schaefer, an internationally famous quantum chemist who has won every award in his discipline short of the Nobel Prize, was recruited to the University of Georgia from Berkeley. The president of the university announced this academic coup with a level of pride approaching that with which the university might have greeted the recruitment of the best high-school quarterback in the nation.

Schaefer is not only a famous scientist but also a dedicated and effective teacher in the large undergraduate courses that other eminent professors often tend to avoid. In addition, he is an outspoken evangelical Christian who likes to explain why it is a misperception to assume (as many students are taught to do) that science is inherently antithetical to belief in God. He gives regular, voluntary after-hours classes to students in which he explains his Christian faith and approach to science, including his skepticism toward some of the claims made about evolution. These classes tend to be well attended, because Schaefer is such an impressive role model for students.

But some other professors thought that the classes violated the constitutional prohibition of an establishment of religion, and they formed a movement to ban religious advocacy from the campus. After much controversy, the university's president ruled that Schaefer was exercising his right of free speech and thus avoided the embarrassment of proceeding against Georgia's most prestigious scientist on the ground that he was violating the canons of scientific orthodoxy. If Schaefer had not ranked so high in the academic pecking order, he might well have met the fate of Phillip Bishop.

"Neutrality" and Contempt

Although the legal and academic situation is unresolved, the *Bishop* opinion is fascinating as a kind of literary text that reveals the

implicit contempt for Christian theism that often lies behind purportedly neutral judicial decisions and academic pronouncements.
It is common in departments of literature nowadays to distinguish
between the surface meaning of a text and the more subtle implications of the "subtext"—meaning the implied understandings
that lie behind the words actually used. This practice can be carried too far, but certain texts practically beg for such an analysis
because the subtext is so near to the surface. Judge Gibson made
only a token effort at maintaining the posture of judicial neutrality
that is customary in cases like *Bishop,* and he laid out for every
discerning reader his real opinion that Christianity, or at least
Phillip Bishop's kind of Christianity, deserves to be censored because it is irrational and hateful.

Take the offhand statement that Bishop's "bias" would cause
"apprehension" in the minds of non-Christian students, just as an
instructor's admission that he is a sexist might cause apprehension
in the minds of women. The implication is that such a hypothetical
student would be justified in feeling such apprehension, because
a Christian professor who takes Christian metaphysics seriously
(as opposed to a nominal Christian who adds a religious gloss to
secular ideas) really is scary. It is inconceivable that a federal court
would express comparable approval of a university order telling
a Jewish professor not to tell his class that he is religiously observant, on the ground that the professor might thereby offend some
hypothetical anti-Semite in the class. In such a case the prejudiced
student rather than the professor would be the wrongdoer and
would probably become a candidate for sensitivity training or
psychiatric care.

On the other hand, a professor who announced to his classes
that he was a Nazi or a supporter of the Ku Klux Klan might well
be deemed unsuitable for a teaching job. At the very least, student
complaints would be treated sympathetically. The difference is
that there is nothing wrong or offensive about being a religious

Jew, but there is something very wrong and offensive about being a Nazi. Gibson's subtext was that Christianity falls in the category of the genuinely offensive.

A similar subtext of contempt appeared when Gibson explained why a professor of physiology was not allowed to tell his class about his doubts concerning the orthodox theory of human evolution. As the opinion put it,

> Dr. Bishop has expressed certain personal (perhaps even professional) opinions about his work that happen to have a religious source. The University has concluded that those opinions should not be represented in the courses he teaches at the University. The University has not suggested that Dr. Bishop cannot hold his particular views; express them, on his own time, far and wide and to whomever [sic] will listen; or write and publish, no doubt authoritatively, on them; nor could it so prohibit him. The University has simply said that he may not discuss his religious beliefs or opinions under the guise of University courses.

Only a tin ear could miss the sarcasm. If Bishop really had opinions about evolution that qualified as rational (let alone authoritative!), they would be welcome in classroom discussion. Of course the university could not, and would not, prevent a professor from saying (to whoever would listen) that he had been held captive on a flying saucer or that he thought the Holocaust never happened—although the university would certainly regard such a professor as an embarrassment and would try to keep the damage to a minimum. The court even tried to imply that Bishop was somehow guilty of dishonesty—by discussing his religious beliefs "under the guise of University courses."

The opinion in the *Bishop* case is a prime example of what I call the "sham neutrality" of liberal rationalism. Because of the relativism inherent in naturalistic metaphysics, liberal rationalists are reluctant to describe a metaphysical position as "wrong," in the

strong sense of not being in accord with "how things really are."
What gives anyone, even a federal judge, the right to say how
things really are? Sez who? Nonetheless, liberal rationalists, like
other people, do make metaphysical judgments. That was plainly
true of Westerfield, of the hypothetical complaining students, of
the hypothetical Ivy League professors who might think less of the
University of Alabama if it allowed Christian speech in the classroom, and of Judge Gibson. When metaphysical statements cannot be made honestly, they have to be stated in code and enforced
with power. Thus *religion* is used as a surrogate word for *nonsense,* and toleration (which may include the right to censor the
"insensitive" speech of others) is extended to the morally worthy
and denied to the unworthy without any explanation of the difference.

The Misunderstood Conflict

The *Bishop* case illustrates a general practice that is described by
sociologist James Davison Hunter in his illuminating books on the
"culture wars." Hunter explains that the great divisive issues of
American society, such as the abortion issue, involve at root a
conflict between radically different notions about what it means
to be human and how humans fit into the rest of reality. Unfortunately, the competing understandings of reality are not precisely
identified and debated, but rather are argued in propagandistic
terms, as when abortion doctors are described as "baby killers"
and their adversaries are labeled as proposing "compulsory pregnancy." Such labeling presents conflicting claims as fundamental
rights that transcend the democratic process and thus can only be
mediated by force. As Hunter explains,

> The antidemocratic impulse in cultural conflict is implicit in the
> way activists frame their positions on issues. This is what is
> meant by the popular phrase *political correctness*—a position
> is so "obviously superior," so "obviously correct," and its op-

posite is so "obviously out of bounds" that they are beyond serious discussion and debate. Indeed, to hold the "wrong" opinion, one must be either mentally imbalanced (phobic—as in *homophobic*—irrational, codependent, or similarly afflicted) or, more likely, evil. Needless to say, in a culture war, one finds different and opposing understandings of the politically correct view of the world.

We can see how that way of conducting politics grows naturally out of what are called "postmodernist" (relativistic) ideas about truth. Relativism about truth does not lead to tolerance. Rather, it leads to the conclusion that social conflicts cannot be resolved by reason or even compromise, because there is no common reason that can unite groups that differ on fundamental questions.

In the battle between creationists and evolutionists, for example, the perception in elite intellectual circles is that there is nothing to discuss and no possibility of compromise. The creationists (supposedly) reject science and therefore reject reason and will never be content until they can impose their beliefs on everybody else. There is nothing to do but to fight a culture war, and no terms to offer short of unconditional surrender. If creationists offer moderate-sounding arguments, they are merely disguising their true purpose, and if creationist parents run for election to a school board, they are waging a "stealth campaign" and deceitfully speaking in places like churches, where they can hide from intelligent scrutiny.

When the people with the most cultural influence see society as divided between the party of rationality and goodness on one side and the party of irrationality and oppression on the other, the state is set for a culture war. Thus, as chapter six pointed out, the postmodernist relativism of Richard Rorty led him to engage in serious discussion only within his own party of progressive intellectuals and to consign much of the rest of the nation to perdition as Hitler's natural constituency. Similarly, chapter seven showed that before *Roe* v. *Wade* the political process was handling the volatile abortion issue successfully, granting greater legal freedom without launching anything remotely resembling a culture war. Then the Supreme Court abruptly withdrew the issue from normal politics by declaring abortion to be a "fundamental right," and the dominant party no longer had to persuade or negotiate. There is no point in trying to reason with people who belong to Hitler's natural constituency or who want to abrogate a woman's most fundamental rights. With the backing of the courts and the federal bureaucracies, the "good" people can simply dominate them.

Culture War or Democratic Debate?

What Hunter means by "democracy" is not simply a nation in which the most powerful offices are attained by election. A democracy in the profound sense is a community of mutual respect, where even the most divisive issues can be addressed in a debate—however aggressive—of fellow citizens who can argue with all the ferocity of brothers because they share agreement on something more fundamental than the partisan issue of the moment. Real democracy ends when citizens give up on the debate because the issues that divide them seem to be so fundamental that only force can decide who is to prevail. This is precisely the mindset that leads to "culture war" propaganda in elite newspapers and conservative talk shows alike. Hunter warns us that "culture wars always precede shooting wars"—particularly when we are talking about civil wars. We must first demonize our enemies before we can rationalize killing them.

The way out of the culture wars and back to normal democratic conflict requires that the issues that really concern people no longer be ruled out of bounds with pejorative labels like *religion* and *phobia*. What it takes to accomplish this is mainly a willingness to deal with adversaries as the complex human beings they are rather than as cardboard stereotypes. It also takes a little moral courage, because to deal with another person (and even more a group of people) on a plane of equality is to become vulnerable. It is much safer to stay within a community of belief, where potentially awkward issues are off the table by mutual agreement. Many churches are filled with people who want to do that, and so are many university departments. But there are also exceptions, and their example may suggest some ways to escape from the fruitless name-calling of the culture wars.

Steps Toward Real Dialogue

James Carper and James Sears are both professors in the College of Education at the University of South Carolina. Sears describes himself as an "agnostic progressive" and an out-of-the-closet homosexual, author of a book titled *Growing Up Gay in the South*. He attracted statewide attention by agreeing to sponsor a graduate-level summer course called "Christian Fundamentalism and Public Education." The announcement said that the course would "assist school practitioners and others in understanding the fundamentalist phenomenon, and combatting its challenge to public education in a secular democracy." That is the language of cultural warfare, of course. The subtext was that "fundamentalists"—a term broad enough to apply in practice to anyone who believes in God and accepts biblical standards of morality—are by definition enemies of democracy and public education. They should be "understood" in the sense that J. Edgar Hoover would have urged good Americans to understand communists, in order to "combat" their insidious influence more effectively. That the millions of Christian parents dissatisfied with current notions of "public education in a secular democracy" might be right about something did not seem to be on the agenda.

Some of the people to be combated understandably objected to having their tax money used for this purpose and saw the Sears course as a challenge to battle in the culture wars. The protestors approached Carper, a prominent evangelical Christian, to join a letter-writing campaign. Carper responded that he wasn't going to write to anybody. "I told them the best thing to do when there's someone with whom you have a grievance or grudge is to go to that individual personally before you start yelling at department heads, deans, trustees and the president of the university." So when Carper happened to meet Sears in a grocery store, he arranged to meet with him to discuss the content of the course.

The meeting went very differently from what might have been imagined. Sears admitted that the course announcement was poorly worded and explained to Carper that he had meant the fundamentalists should be combated only when they were trying to accomplish something unconstitutional. For anyone who has read the *Bishop* opinion, that admission may not be terribly reassuring, but Sears's partial retreat also had a subtext. It was that "when I meet a real 'fundamentalist' instead of a cardboard stereotype, I cannot in good conscience say to the man that he does not have a point of view worth considering." Moreover, Sears recognized that he had a political problem and that he needed help in solving it. To Carper's surprise, Sears asked for his help in compiling a reading list and a slate of speakers who could represent both sides of the issue. The effect was rather as if an evolutionary biology professor had requested a creationist to submit a list of respected scholars on "both sides" of the evolution-creation dispute. Because the party line is that on that dispute there is only one side, to which all rational people belong, such an invitation would be very significant.

Carper did provide the list of books and speakers, and Sears took his suggestions seriously. The result was a very successful course, at which the guest speakers represented organizations as diverse as James Dobson's Focus on the Family and Norman Lear's People for the American Way. Among the more prominent guest speakers were George Marsden, the Notre Dame professor whose history of the American university was discussed in the preceding chapter, and University of Chicago law professor Michael McConnell, an authority on religious freedom who represented Phillip Bishop in his unsuccessful petition to the U.S. Supreme Court. It must have been a great experience for the students.

When academic people think that they are doing something worthy of notice, they immediately want to produce a book. Despite their differing perspectives on Christianity and sexual morality, Sears and Carper are both sufficiently like other academics to see a book as their next step in a successful collaboration. So now there is a collection in preparation titled *Public Education and Religion,* with a subtitle that promises "conversations for an enlarging public square." It is, in a small way, a response to Hunter's diagnosis of the culture wars.

Can we really address fundamental, divisive questions in the academic world, or must educators assume a politically correct standpoint and go on from there? The second alternative involves submerging the genuine intellectual questions in labels and thus tacitly conceding that academic intellectuals operate strictly within their own ideological boundaries and have nothing much to say to outsiders. In that case the only recourse of ordinary citizens who are not willing to be ruled by self-appointed Platonic guardians is to fight power with power. Is that what the intellectuals really want?

Two of the professors who will be contributing to the Sears and Carper volume are William Provine and Phillip E. Johnson. We form another unusual combination. Provine is a prominent scholar in the history of science and the teacher of a large course in evolutionary biology at Cornell University. Among scholars of biological evolution, Provine is famous for his insistence that Darwinism implies an uncompromisingly materialist view of reality. In his article "Progress in Evolution and Meaning in Life," Provine explained how the neo-Darwinian understanding of evolution has destroyed the widespread hope that evolution and theistic religion could be reconciled by understanding evolution to be a process that is guided by some conscious or purposeful entity.

The triumph of Darwinism after the publication of *The Origin of Species* in 1859 captured biology for "evolution," but there were many different theories of how evolution worked, and Darwin's own key principle of natural selection was only one of the competitors. Many respectable scientists rejected natural selection as the primary mechanism of evolution, in part because of an absence of convincing examples and in part because they disliked the idea that such a purposeless and ruthless principle as "survival of the fittest" was responsible for our creation. Provine estimates that the majority of biologists at the end of the nineteenth century, or even as late as 1930, believed that some nonmaterial, purposeful entity played a role in evolution.

All this changed some time between 1930 and the great Darwinian centennial celebration in 1959 at the University of Chicago. By 1959 the neo-Darwinian synthesis had triumphed. But what was the synthesis, and what did it establish? According to Provine, the synthesis amounted mainly to an agreement among a new generation of evolutionary biologists to restrict their theory to a small number of purposeless mechanisms: random genetic change and natural selection. This "evolutionary constriction" was possible not because of new empirical discoveries but because mathematic models had demonstrated—if the assumptions behind the models were not questioned—that evolutionary change in populations could be explained without going beyond the key Darwinian concepts of random variation and natural selection.

Provine concluded that after the triumph of the synthesis, it is no longer possible to reconcile the scientific understanding of evolution with the theistic understanding that some purposeful entity has ruled the history of life. As Provine vividly put the point to

a liberal churchman who wanted to be both scientifically and religiously correct: "You have to check your brains at the church-
house door if you take modern evolutionary biology seriously."

One might have thought that Provine and I would be bitterly
opposed, since I am a Christian who emphatically affirms that the
world is the product of a purposeful Creator, not a blind material
mechanism. But in fact I think Provine has done a lot to clarify
the point at issue, and I agree with him about how to define the
question. I had noticed that all the modern Darwinists with any
scientific standing agreed with Provine that evolution is a purposeless and undirected process. I had also noticed that prominent
academic Christians like to talk and write as if the nineteenth-
century idea that evolution might be a purposeful process was still
acceptable in late-twentieth-century science. So while mainstream
science educators take for granted that science has discredited the
"God created by evolution" compromise, Christian educators tend
to go on presenting "evolution" as if all that agreement with the
scientific establishment requires is a certain flexibility in interpreting the details of Genesis.

Provine and I also agree that both the Christian educators and
the rulers of science have an incentive to keep the underlying
worldview conflict implicit rather than explicit. The Christians are
fearful about getting into a conflict with "science," while the evolutionary scientists are afraid of awakening a sleeping giant that
can still wield great political power. As Provine put it,

> Consider the following fantasy: the National Academy of Sci-
> ences publishes a position paper on science and religion stating
> that modern science leads directly to atheism. What would
> happen to its funding? . . . I suspect that scientific leaders tread
> very warily on the religious implications of science for fear of
> jeopardizing the funding for scientific research. And I think that
> many scientists feel some sympathy with the need for moral
> education and recognize the role that religion plays in this en-

deavor. These rationalizations are politic but intellectually dishonest.*

The concern about funding is real enough, but there is also a deeper concern at the philosophical level. As we have seen, the doctrine that only purposeless forces played a role in biological history is not an empirical finding but a metaphysical assumption built into the definition of science. This foundational assumption is protected from criticism by the "two subjects" doctrine, which identifies naturalism with science and objections to naturalism with religion. If the NAS were to declare explicitly that science favors atheism over theism, the pretense that science and religion are separate subjects would have to be abandoned. It would follow that creationists should have a fair opportunity to argue that the naturalistic conclusions presented to the public in the name of science are philosophical assumptions rather empirical findings and that there is nothing in the nature of science that requires legitimate empirical research to be based on a dogmatic adherence to metaphysical naturalism.

Provine recognizes that the implications of his stand for intellectual honesty require giving creationists a fair hearing. In consequence, he assigns his Cornell students to read and critique my book *Darwin on Trial* and invites me annually to spend as much time as I can spare at Cornell, arguing my point of view to his class. Provine and I have become the friendliest of adversaries, because we recognize each other as fellow honest critics of the

---

*When the National Academy of Sciences actually did issue a position paper on the relationship of science and religion, it prevaricated. The pamphlet *Science and Creationism: A View from the National Academy of Sciences* assured the nation that it is "false . . . to think that the theory of evolution represents an irreconcilable conflict between religion and science." The statement explained, "A great many religious leaders accept evolution on scientific grounds without relinquishing their belief in religious principles." The statement did not say whether those religious leaders achieved this reconciliation by overlooking a logical contradiction, by misunderstanding evolution as a purposeful process or by conforming their religious principles to naturalistic metaphysics. This classic of Orwellian doublespeak was published, appropriately, in 1984.

mendacity that rules the academic world on this subject. We both scoff at such noble lies as the National Academy of Science's 1981 pronouncement that "religion and science are separate and mutually exclusive realms of human thought whose presentation in the same context leads to a misunderstanding of both scientific theory and religious belief." On the contrary, cosmologists and evolutionary biologists write and speak constantly about the implications of their work for religion, and it is right that they should do so rather than pretend that they are unconcerned with the subject in order to avoid controversy.

The Christmas-week cover story of *Time* magazine in 1992 posed the question "What does science tell us about God?" and the editors had no difficulty finding eminent scientists willing to offer answers. *Time*'s reporter Robert Wright observed that those answers are eagerly received by the many people who "believe in a deity but wouldn't mind seeing some hard evidence; or they believe strongly in some kind of deity, but it's vague in form, open to any tailoring that scientific measurement may dictate." And as the title of Nancey Murphy's book correctly implies, even theology recognizes that we live in an age dominated by scientific reasoning.

The value of Provine's candor is that it points to a way to turn the central issue of the culture wars into an intellectual topic that can be honestly addressed. Does science prove naturalism, or does it merely assume it? Does the scientific community, represented by the National Academy of Sciences, see it as part of its mission to convince the public that naturalism is true? Has the metaphysical basis for traditional biblical morality been destroyed by scientific discoveries? An enormous effort has gone into evading and burying those questions; it is time they be honestly addressed.

Addressing the metaphysical questions honestly will not heat up the culture wars, but rather tend to make them a part of the normal political and intellectual debate that characterizes a free and pluralistic society. What infuriates people is not disagreement

but the subtext of contempt that necessarily accompanies the pronouncements of a ruling intellectual establishment whose power is
based on a secret it is unwilling to disclose. If science now teaches
that naturalism is true, and if science is unimpeachable, then theists ought to face the consequences instead of pretending that they
can go on as if nothing had happened. But maybe naturalism is
false. It seems that the rulers of science are terrified at the prospect
of having to address that possibility.

10

The Beginning of Reason

I N LATE 1994 I LECTURED ON THE CAMPUS OF THE OHIO
State University under the auspices of an organization previously unfamiliar to me, the Veritas Forum. This group brings
prominent Christian speakers to university campuses on an annual
basis, to engage students and faculty in discussion of religious
issues that tend to be neglected in modern education. My schedule
called for six lectures or colloquia in two days. These included a
public lecture before a huge audience (followed by a panel discussion with faculty members), a colloquium with law professors on
a paper that became the first chapter of this book, a colloquium
with science faculty on the issues discussed in chapters three and
four, and a special evening with foreign students.

In the course of this hectic visit I became acquainted with Jerry
Mercer, an Ohio businessman who is the driving spirit behind the
Veritas Forum, which is expanding its annual programs to dozens
of universities. I was impressed with Jerry's vision and especially

by the Forum's four-point mission statement:

> To begin to answer these perplexing questions: "What is Truth?" and "Are the truth claims of Jesus Christ credible and meaningful in today's modern world?"
>
> To provide a forum for dialogue that continues to test the question, "Is there truth that brings unity to the diversity of the university and society?"
>
> To exercise critical thinking skills of logic and reason to discover first principles and premises that will help us to base our lives, worldviews and communities on truth and not error.
>
> To encourage a pragmatic demonstration of love, undergirded by the truth, within our spheres of influence, moving from logos and ethos to pathos, from word to deed.

What appealed to me about that agenda was that it places the emphasis on *truth* rather than on what makes people feel good or works for social utility. The third item best describes my own part in the project: to encourage critical thinking about first principles so that we base our thinking on truth and not error.

First Principles

But what is the truth about first principles? If it is that the universe was created by God for a purpose, the truth claims of Jesus Christ may well be credible and meaningful. Those claims are not even conceivably credible or meaningful if the universe is a meaningless chain of material causes. Evolutionary naturalism of this sort is the orthodox belief in our universities, and it is seldom discussed because it is so foundational to other beliefs. For those of us who care about what is true and what is not, naturalism is the great forbidding taboo of modernist society, the illusion that makes a bankrupt way of thinking seem forever beyond challenge.

Any list of the thinkers who most profoundly influenced the twentieth century mind would contain four names: Darwin, Marx, Freud and Nietzsche. The purported death of God, proclaimed explicitly by Nietzsche, was the foundational event of modernism. The most widely used college evolutionary biology textbook, by Douglas Futuyma, matter-of-factly (and accurately) informs biology majors about what made Darwin so important to the modernist metaphysical program:

> By coupling undirected, purposeless variation to the blind, uncaring process of natural selection, Darwin made theological or spiritual explanations of the life processes superfluous. Together with Marx's materialistic theory of history and society and Freud's attribution of human behavior to influences over which we have little control, Darwin's theory of evolution was a crucial plank in the platform of mechanism and materialism—of much of science, in short—that has since been the stage of most Western thought.

That platform of mechanism and materialism is now so firmly established in the world of higher education that it is very difficult for most professors even to imagine that the platform might be shaky. When a few years ago I began pressing in university circles the question whether evolutionary naturalism is true, I was met mainly with blank incomprehension. Ask a group of intellectuals whether neo-Darwinism is really true, I learned, and you can hear the sound of minds snapping shut all around the room.

When I did get a reply, it usually was that "evolution" is the best naturalistic theory and that naturalism is the philosophical basis of science and thus equivalent to rationality. Hence naturalism is "the way we think today." To ask modernists whether science is true is like asking them whether rationality is rational or truth is truthful. Science is, by modernist definition, our only truly objective way of knowing anything.

Alfred North Whitehead was among the greatest of twentieth-century philosophers of science. In his classic work *Science and the Modern World* Whitehead wrote that to understand the philosophy of an age, the important thing to concentrate on is not the ideas that people are explicitly debating. More important by far are the presuppositions that practically everybody with any influence takes for granted, presuppositions that are rarely defended or even articulated because they seem so obviously true. These constitute the cultural definition of rationality, the beginning of reason.

In the late twentieth century, the most important presuppositions in intellectual circles are that science has preeminent authority to describe reality and that science is based on naturalism—or methodological atheism, as it is sometimes called. This starting point necessarily implies, whether everyone understands the implication or not, that room for God exists only in the world of the imagination, or perhaps somewhere back in a "big bang singularity" at the ultimate beginning of time.

Belief in God may persist, particularly in people who have only a shallow understanding of science, but the believers can never have more than a tenuous standing in the world of the mind. Science can step forward at any time and employ its prestige to take control of any subject, even subjects inaccessible to empirical investigation like the ultimate beginning itself. Metaphysical statements by prominent scientists are accepted in the press and throughout public education as advances in scientific knowledge; contrary statements by theologians or religious leaders are dismissed as "fundamentalism." The naturalists hold the cultural power; theists in academic life have to accommodate as best they can.

Questions of Truth

The Veritas Forum approach is to direct attention away from questions of power and toward questions of truth. This emphasis on truth as an absolute seems almost quaint in an era dominated by naturalism and hence by pragmatism. Pragmatism is less concerned with what is absolutely true than with what is useful for some specific professional agenda (the scientific outlook) or for some worthy social program (empowering the victims, saving the environment). The very idea of an absolute truth, independent of and superior to the consensus of opinion among the most educated people, is fundamentally a theistic concept that makes little sense in terms of modernist metaphysics.

If humans are animals whose mental capacities evolved solely for their effectiveness in leaving viable offspring in a hunter-gatherer environment, it is difficult to see how we could have access to an absolute truth that transcends our common sensory experience. For modernists the important concept is not truth but knowledge, and knowledge comes from the interpretation of data accessible to our senses by the standards of an authoritative community such as the scientific establishment. Modernists do not often ask whether theism is *true;* they prefer to ask whether a supernatural Creator is consistent with scientific knowledge. And of course it is not—because science is defined to exclude the supernatural.

To ask whether theism or naturalism is true is therefore to move the discussion onto ground where theists are more comfortable than naturalists. In fact, one way to define theism is that it is a story about the universe that proclaims the reality of the true, the good and the beautiful. It is these things, and not the unified physical theory envisaged by the "theory of everything" physicists, that are the starting point for those who want to know the mind of God.

Scientific naturalism is a story that reduces reality to physical particles and impersonal laws, portrays life as a meaningless competition among organisms that exist only to survive and reproduce, and sees the mind as no more than an emergent property of biochemical reactions. In consequence, a merely scientific concept of rationality prepares the way for the irrationalist and tribalist reaction that is so visible all around us. Theism tells us that we should by nature want whatever is true, good and beautiful; naturalism implies that such a unifying vision is fantasy and that the real business of life is to find the knowledge that can supply whatever it is that we happen to want.

The Veritas Forum's emphasis on truth is reinforced by its motto, taken from a quotation attributed to Thomas Jefferson: "We are not afraid to follow truth wherever it may lead, nor to tolerate any error so long as reason is left free to combat it." To modernists that must seem like a very strange motto for an organization of theists to adopt, especially an organization of theists dedicated to the proposition that the truth claims of Jesus Christ really do make sense in the conditions of the late twentieth century. Doesn't "everybody know" that those truth claims were disposed of long ago by such sages as Hume and Voltaire, and that Nietzsche merely executed a death sentence on God that had been pronounced even before Darwin supplied the essential mechanism of naturalistic creation? One of the most important stereotypes in naturalistic thinking is that "religion" is based on faith rather than reason, and that persons who believe in God are inherently unwilling to follow the truth wherever it may lead because that path leads to naturalism.

Challenging the Priesthood

In all the world there is no greater dogmatist than "everybody knows." Dogmatism is a human characteristic that grows out of insecurity. It is particularly pronounced in the case of individuals or groups that hold power positions which are threatened by criticism. Religious priesthoods have sometimes tried to protect their power by forbidding the translation of the Bible into vernacular languages or by taking a know-nothing attitude toward scientific observations that threatened traditional ways of viewing the world. In our own day the ruling priesthood consists of authoritative bodies like the National Academy of Sciences, the academic and legal elites, and the managers of the national media.

The new priesthood, like the old ones, has a vested interest in safeguarding its cultural authority by making it as difficult as possible for critics to be heard. The modern equivalent of excommunication is marginalization, which is much more humane than physical punishment but just as effective in protecting the ruling philosophy. Those who try to challenge naturalism are confined not in a prison cell but in a stereotype, and the terms in which the media and the textbooks report any controversy are defined in a manner designed to prevent dangerous ideas from getting serious consideration. Whatever the critics of naturalism say is mere "religious belief," in opposition to "scientific knowledge"; hence it is, by definition, fantasy as opposed to solid fact.

Seeking Unity in Diversity

The Veritas approach, then, is to advance truth rather than social usefulness as the first item on the intellectual agenda and to define terms so as to open up truth questions to intellectual inquiry rather than settle them by verbal manipulation. One benefit of the truth, as the mission statement recognizes, is that it "brings unity to the diversity" of a society. The unity and the diversity deserve equal emphasis. Dogmatic doctrines, backed by coercion, can bring unity of a sort, but they deny diversity and eventually perish of their own inflexibility. Relativistic philosophies endorse diversity, but they fail to unify. The kind of truth that brings unity to diversity is therefore not a set of fixed propositions but a common sense of rationality that permits the inevitable differences of outlook to be understood, debated and respected.

From this standpoint it is easy to see why many persons have wanted scientific naturalism to have the role of a unifying public philosophy. Revelations from God come only to some persons, and telling the difference between true and false prophets is notoriously difficult. The difficulty in finding common ground to reason about conflicting claims of supernatural revelation has led to many wars and persecutions. Sense experience, in contrast, is common to everyone whose senses are in order, and the scientific method—meaning the specific requirement that factual statements be verified by observation or by repeatable experiments—commands universal respect. In that sense science truly is a unifying element in modern society, on matters that are subject to experimental verification. No one, regardless of religion or politics, wants to fly in an airplane that was not built and maintained according to generally accepted scientific principles. It was only natural that rationalists fed up with religious conflict would seek to extend the scientific method to all human problems as the common rationality capable of bringing unity to diversity.

The error was understandable, but it was nonetheless an error. The experimental method that guarantees the reliability of scientific claims is available only to solve certain kinds of problems, particularly those dealing with material causation under observable conditions. By its very nature, the scientific method has no power to resolve disputes about value or teleology (the purpose for which things like living organisms were created). Moreover, when it is trying to describe events in the remote past, such as the origin of life, or complex matters like human behavior, science has to rely heavily on philosophical presuppositions. Experiments are employed mainly to test minor aspects of some grand synthesis like behaviorism or social Darwinism, thus providing the illusion that the grand theory itself has been experimentally tested.

Because science is practiced by individuals who can be just as ambitious in their way as television evangelists or political candidates, there are always persons eager to underwrite value-laden philosophies by borrowing against the deserved prestige of experimental science. Marxism and Freudianism are only two notorious examples.

The Choice We Face

The theologians of the nineteenth and twentieth centuries mostly went along with naturalism in science because they failed to understand how all-encompassing the ambitions of scientific metaphysicians tend to become. Theologians assumed that science would observe its natural limits and that Christian theism (or some other theism) would still be left to decide the important spiritual questions, such as what life really is about and how we are to know the difference between good and evil. Things turned out differently, because modernist science is just as imperialistic as it is naturalistic. When science gained the authority to tell the culture "how things really are," it told the culture that reality excludes God, because God is inconvenient to a science that aspires to tell a grand metaphysical story of a naturalistic universe. The result was that theology became the theory of nothing and lost almost all its prestige among intellectuals.

Now that the consequences of a purely scientific understanding of reality have become unmistakably clear, Christian theists need to consider whether a policy of following truth wherever it may lead truly does end in naturalism. If so, they should accept the inevitable. Accepting naturalism does not necessarily mean discarding "religion," because many naturalists acknowledge that evolution has endowed humans with spiritual yearnings that must be satisfied one way or another. What it requires is simply that honest theologians acknowledge (as many effectively have) that God is a subjective experience in certain human minds, not an objective reality for everyone. It follows that theologians have no resources for deciding moral questions other than those available to secular philosophers and anthropologists— namely human experience, logic and subjective intuitions. In that case it is both inevitable and appropriate that churches should take their cue from the best available secular thought and center their ministry on this-worldly causes like feminism, patriotism or environmentalism. And so they do.

Equivocation with respect to naturalism makes religion look like fraud to many secular observers. The skeptic Martin Gardner put the dilemma of contemporary theism particularly well, writing that modernist clergy face a choice between being "loyal liars" and "truthful traitors." The loyal liar reassures the simple folk by pretending to believe that the universe was created by a supernatural being called God who had a Son who really did rise from the dead; the truthful traitor betrays the faithful by admitting that the supernatural elements in religion are all fantasy. Of course Gardner's "liars" see themselves as merely tactful, and his "traitors" usually see themselves as saving the faith rather than betraying it.

In fact, it is perfectly possible to continue Christianity for a time on a naturalistic basis. People do have religious feelings, even if those feelings are anachronistic byproducts of evolution rather than signposts pointing to an ultimate reality. Naturalistic Christianity exists in plenty, but it is a hollow shell sustained mainly by nostalgia. Once Christian institutions have accepted naturalistic metaphysics, they inevitably repeat the process of secularization that the formerly Christian universities completed years ago.

The other road for those willing to follow truth to the end is to assert that God is real and that the evidence reflects the truth that nature was created by God. Challenging naturalism this way takes a certain amount of nerve, because it is possible that the grand metaphysical story of science could turn out to be true, even if particular theories like neo-Darwinism are not. If Christian theists stake their case on evidence from nature, they may only spur scientists on to produce far better and more complete naturalistic theories—and then what will happen to Christianity? Better to accept the existing state of affairs, some argue, than to fight a hopeless war against advancing scientific knowledge. That is the thinking of theistic naturalists who argue that to challenge naturalism is to invoke a "God of the gaps," who will gradually disappear from reality like a Cheshire cat as science steadily advances. If the grand metaphysical story is true, then the best strategy for preserving theistic religion is to retreat to the sanctuary of "religion," where perhaps the naturalists will leave us alone.

But of course the naturalists do not leave theistic enclaves alone, nor should they. A naturalistic government that regulates everything else does not hesitate to reward theistic educational institutions with their own tax money if they agree to accept "diversity" standards. Secular academic societies understandably withhold their approval from faculties that do not meet secular standards of rationality. Seminarians trained in naturalistic thinking enter the ministry in droves with the mission of saving Christianity by leading it into an accommodation with modernism.

Granted the metaphysical assumptions, none of this is in any way reprehensible. People who think they have truth on their side naturally want to share the truth with others and to bring enlightenment to private enclaves of superstition. People who believe in what they are saying tend to be persuasive in arguments with people who suspect deep down that what they have been taught to believe is only a comforting fantasy. A religion that no longer believes it is founded on objective truth is thus condemned to a lingering death, and the death sentence is just.

What the times call for is not a strategy to preserve a dying Christianity as long as possible, but a dedication to discover the first principles and premises that will help us to base our lives, worldviews and communities on truth and not error. When the issue is put that way, it is the naturalists who soon feel a need to retreat into a sanctuary, the sanctuary called "science." At this point we begin to hear that the naturalists have merely been defining the rules of a particular game called "science," that science never claims to have absolute truth, that naturalists have never claimed that creationism is *false* but merely that it is not "science," that "evolution" is a modest doctrine of biological change that says nothing about ultimate origins, and even that science itself is neutral about "the existence of God" and is therefore fully compatible with "religion."

I encounter these evasions constantly in debates, but I know that the moment my opponents think the coast is clear, they will go back to proclaiming absolute truths. Of course the scientific naturalists claim to have absolute truth, and of course they reject theistic religion as false. That they retreat so quickly when firmly challenged shows that their truth is built on a foundation of sand.

Christianity makes sense only if its factual premises are true and if it is providing meaningful answers to questions that people ought to be asking. The essential factual premise is that God created us for a purpose, and our destiny is a glorious one in eternity. The right question is how, granted the premise, things got to be in such a state of confusion. The answer is that humans saw the glory of God in the things that were created but chose to turn their own way and fashion idols of their own making—the latest fashion in idols being the grand metaphysical story of science.

The way out? The good news is so simple a child can understand it at once, and so subtle that the greatest intellects never quite get to the bottom of it. "In the beginning was the Word, and the Word was with God, and the Word was God. . . . For God so loved the world that he gave his only Son, so that everyone who believes in him may not perish but may have eternal life."

That's the way things really are, and recognizing how things really are is the beginning of reason.

APPENDIX

Naturalism, Methodological & Otherwise

D URING THE YEARS FOLLOWING THE ORIGINAL PUBLICA-
tion of *Darwin on Trial* in 1991, I have been engaged in
intensive discussion about evolution and creation on university campuses, in churches, in the media and especially on the
Internet. Naturally, all this discussion and debate has helped me
to refine my own position and to frame the issues in dispute more
precisely. One thing that surprised me at first, until I grew accus-
tomed to it, was that many Christian professors, both at religious
institutions and at secular universities, were staunch defenders of
the evolutionary orthodoxy that I was attacking as a product of
metaphysical naturalism.

It was easy for me to understand why atheists and agnostics
defended naturalistic evolution, because the existence of an unintelligent material mechanism of biological creation (verified by
unimpeachable "science") provides essential support to their pre-
ferred worldview. But why were so many Christian academics re-

luctant to encourage anyone to challenge the scientific claims of
the metaphysical naturalists who dominated evolutionary science?
Why did they constantly warn me that to suggest the possibility
of divine action in the history of life was merely to invoke a futile
"God of the gaps"?

These Christian professors insisted that their belief in "evolution" was based on evidence. I told them that they were deceiving
themselves and that they accepted the current scientific orthodoxy
only because they were looking at the evidence through naturalistic spectacles. They understandably resented this, and much debate ensued. Sometimes it was acrimonious, but in my opinion
that was because the issues under debate are fundamental and
everyone has a lot at stake in their resolution, not because the
debaters really disliked each other.

One of the central issues was an asserted difference between
"metaphysical" and "methodological" naturalism. There was
general agreement that Christian theism and *metaphysical* naturalism are contradictory, but some of the Christian professors argued
that a *methodological* naturalism in science is appropriate even for
metaphysical theists.

The immediate occasion for this paper was a remark by a Christian college professor who had argued that my "creationist bias"
was affecting my assessment of the scientific evidence for evolution. I include the paper here as an appendix instead of trying to
fit it into the text, because the issues that fascinate persons who
devote a professional interest to this subject may be overly complex for general readers who have other matters to occupy their
attention. On the other hand, I want to preserve this statement as
a starting point for further discussion among professional academics in particular.

Memorandum on Evolution and Naturalism
William Hasker is publishing a second book review of *Darwin on*

Trial in a forthcoming special issue on evolution of the *Christian Scholar's Review* (1995). In it Hasker, a supporter of methodological naturalism in science who is critical of my book in many respects, applauds my efforts to force the scientific establishment to clarify its position on naturalism and theism. He says,

> Whether or not Darwinian evolution is incompatible with a meaningful theism in general and orthodox Christianity in particular, it is beyond dispute that many leading evolutionists maintain that it is, and viewed in that light their advocacy of Darwinism as "established scientific truth" amounts to discrediting Christianity as scientifically untenable. Surely, as Johnson remarks, "a bit of clarification is in order, and also a bit of discussion about whether it is appropriate to enlist science education in the job of selling a worldview."

I appreciate Hasker's support, but I would add that to say that "many" leading evolutionists advocate or assume metaphysical naturalism is an understatement. The list of the promoters of scientific naturalism would include such prominent voices of official science as Hawking, Weinberg, Davies, Crick, Sagan, Dawkins, Johanson, Richard Leakey, Suzuki, Gould and Futuyma, as well as countless others who promote naturalistic philosophy in the name of science on television, in textbooks and in classes. As far as the public is concerned, these people all speak in the name of SCIENCE. The most aggressive naturalists—Dawkins and Sagan—have received top awards for their services to public education from the British Royal Society and the National Academy of Sciences, respectively. What they say thus has at least the apparent backing of the most prestigious scientific organizations.

Why do the leading voices of official science teach that science and naturalism are inseparable? The reason is that they assume that the scientific method is inherently characterized by a thoroughgoing methodological naturalism (hereafter MN), and MN strictly limits the alternatives that may be taken seriously. MN is by far the dominant position in contemporary science, endorsed almost without exception by atheist materialists, agnostic naturalists *and* theistic evolutionists. MN in science is only superficially reconcilable with theism in religion. When MN is understood profoundly, theism becomes intellectually untenable.

Part 1: Philosophy
First, here is a definition of MN, followed by a contrasting definition of my own position, which I label "theistic realism" (TR). Following that are some illustrations and commentary.

1. A methodological naturalist defines science as the search for the best naturalistic theories. A theory would not be naturalistic if it left something (such as the existence of genetic information or consciousness) to be explained by a supernatural cause. Hence all events in evolution (before the evolution of intelligence) are assumed to be attributable to unintelligent causes. The question is not *whether* life (genetic information) arose by some combination of chance and chemical laws, to pick one example, but merely *how* it did so.

Methodological naturalists concede that some problems are not yet solved, but they are confident that science will solve them by proposing natural mechanisms because science has so often been successful in the past. Bringing God or intelligent design into the picture is giving up on science by turning to religion (miracle) and invoking a "God of the gaps." The Creator belongs to the realm of religion, not scientific investigation. Some methodological naturalists are theists. Their theism affects how they interpret the overall results of science (whatever happened was under God's governance), but it has no effect on how they reason to scientific conclusions.

2. A theistic realist assumes that the universe and all its creatures were brought into existence for a purpose by God. Theistic realists expect this "fact" of creation to have empirical, observable con-

sequences that are different from the consequences one would observe if the universe were the product of nonrational causes (such as Jacques Monod's "chance and necessity"). Since God is rational and created our minds in his image, we would expect the universe to be on the whole orderly, and therefore the success of science in determining many regular processes and mechanisms is entirely consistent with TR. God always has the option of working through regular secondary mechanisms, and we observe such mechanisms frequently. On the other hand, many important questions—including the origin of genetic information and human consciousness—may not be explicable in terms of unintelligent causes, just as a computer or a book cannot be explained that way.

A naturalistic science that assumes it can explain everything is likely to offer explanations that are not true. It may imagine a nonexistent reducing atmosphere and prebiotic soup, for example, and a nonexistent process of complexity building through random mutation and natural selection. It may assume falsely that the mind can be completely understood as the product of material mechanisms produced by naturalistic evolution.

3. Here are concrete illustrations of the difference between MN and TR. First, Richard Dawkins begins *The Blind Watchmaker* with the statement "Biology is the study of complicated things that give the appearance of having been designed for a purpose." A theistic realist finds the appearance of design unsurprising, because living things really are the product of a designer. This does *not* mean that organisms were necessarily created by instantaneous fiat as opposed to gradual development (although they might have been), and it emphatically *does* contemplate that organisms employ regular mechanisms amenable to scientific study, just like other products of intelligence such as airplanes and computers. Dawkins, like other methodological naturalists, takes for granted that the appearance of design is actually the product of unintelligent causes. TR insists that this claim be demonstrated, not as-

sumed. MN responds that this demand is unfair, since the process takes too long to duplicate in ecological time, the fossil record is incomplete, and so on.

Second illustration: A prominent Christian professor of science, reporting on a debate between some chemical evolutionists and some scientists who attributed life to intelligent design, remarked that although he is a theist, he felt much more on the side of the chemical evolutionists, because at least they were not "giving up on the problem." TR considers that recognizing the irreducibility of genetic intelligence may be facing reality; MN views it as "giving up." Methodological naturalists have no comparable reluctance to "give up" on the investigation of mind-reading or the search for the Loch Ness monster. The difference is that a naturalistic origin of life is indispensable to the naturalistic worldview, and so no amount of experimental discouragement destroys the faith that a valid naturalistic theory can someday be found.

4. Some may wonder if there is a compromise position somewhere between MN and TR. I doubt it, because experience leads me to predict that any compromise position will turn out to be MN whenever the chips are down. For example, some methodological naturalists express an abstract willingness to consider a supernatural origin of life or the existence of irreducible genetic information only at some time in the indefinite future, after all naturalistic possibilities have been exhausted. Others put the issue in a vocabulary that settles the outcome a priori. To cite a recent example, an evolutionary biologist who recently debated me repeatedly denied that his position was founded upon an a priori commitment to naturalism, but just as repeatedly characterized any alternative to naturalistic evolution as equivalent to belief in a "flat earth."

Leaving MN requires giving truly serious consideration to other possibilities, not merely waving at them in passing. Even explicit disavowals of MN cannot always be taken at face value. I often encounter theists whose thinking is perfect MN, but who dislike the term. Theistic evolutionists' standard use of the phrase "God of the gaps" to discourage consideration of nonnaturalistic possibilities, for example, comes straight out of their implicit MN.

5. A *theistic naturalist* is a theist who thinks MN is the correct approach to scientific inquiry and hence to understanding (for example) how living things came into existence. Some resent my use of that term, but it is precisely descriptive and the position is widely held. What is resented is that the term directs critical attention to a serious problem that many would prefer to overlook.

The problem, very briefly stated, is this: if employing MN is the only way to reach true conclusions about the history of the universe, and if the attempt to provide a naturalistic history of the universe has continually gone from success to success, and if even theists concede that trying to do science on theistic premises always leads nowhere or into error (the embarrassing "God of the gaps"), then the likely explanation for this state of affairs is that naturalism is true and theism is false.

Persons who are sufficiently motivated to do so can find ways to resist the easy pathway from MN to atheism, agnosticism or deism. For example, perhaps God actively directs the evolutionary process but (for some inscrutable reason) does so in a way that is empirically imperceptible. No one can disprove that sort of possibility, but not many people regard it as intellectually impressive either. That they seem to rely on "faith"—in the sense of belief without evidence—is why theists are a marginalized minority in the academic world and always on the defensive. Usually they protect their reputation for good judgment by restricting their theism to private life and assuming for professional purposes a position that is indistinguishable from naturalism.

MN is widespread even among persons who are theologically conservative, by the way. At heart many fundamentalists are methodological naturalists who just want to reconcile Scripture (the Genesis chronology and/or Noah's flood) with a science that is otherwise as naturalistic in methodology as possible. The same can be said of other nondeistic Christians who allow a very small number of supernatural interventions (the resurrection, the implanting of the image of God into a hominid) but try otherwise to stick to MN. If MN is so sound in general, why make arbitrary exceptions? Makeshift compromises between supernaturalism in religion and naturalism in science may satisfy individuals, but they have little standing in the intellectual world because they are recognized as a forced accommodation of conflicting lines of thought.*

Part 2: Scientific Alternatives

Here is how MN and TR address four differing scientific positions.

Position A: The orthodox neo-Darwinian theory—that microevolution extrapolates to macroevolution—is a satisfactory explanation of the history of life from the first living organism to the

---

*In a March 1992 lecture in Dallas I made the following observation:

The statement defining the agenda for this Symposium asserts that an *a priori* commitment to metaphysical naturalism is necessary to support Darwinism. . . . *Methodological* naturalism—the principle that science can study only the things that are accessible to its instruments and techniques—is not in question. Of course science can study only what science can study. Methodological naturalism becomes metaphysical naturalism only when the limitations of science are taken to be limitations upon reality. (From "Darwinism's Rules of Reasoning," in *Darwinism: Science or Philosophy?* ed. Jon Buell and Virginia Hearn [Foundation for Thought and Ethics, 1994], pp. 6, 15)

I would not express the point that way today, but any seeming inconsistency with the views stated in this paper is semantic rather than substantive. The key question raised by the qualifier *methodological* is this: What is being limited—science or reality? When "methodological naturalism" is combined with a very strong a priori confidence that materialistic theories invoking only unintelligent causes can account for such phenomena as genetic information and human intelligence, the distinction between methodological and metaphysical naturalism tends to collapse. (Example: "Science can study only naturalistic mechanisms; therefore we can be confident that life must have arisen by a naturalistic mechanism, since science continually advances and solves problems of this kind.") That science has its limitations is not in doubt; the question is whether unsound assumptions about reality have been made to permit science to escape those limitations.

emergence of humans. There are some unsolved problems and many details to fill in, but the theory itself is in good shape and needs no major alterations or additions. This is the position of people like Dawkins, Futuyma, Simpson, J. Huxley and the author of *The Beak of the Finch*. It is taught as "scientific knowledge" or even "fact" in schools, museums and other institutions.

Position B: The orthodox neo-Darwinian theory is satisfactory only at the "micro" level and does not explain the appearance of new body plans or other major evolutionary innovations. Something really new, perhaps a macromutational mechanism or even a new physical law, is needed to produce a satisfactory macroevolutionary theory. Science will no doubt come up with this new mechanism eventually, but science hasn't found it yet. This is roughly the position of Goldschmidt, Grassé, Schindewolf, Gould (sometimes) and Stuart Kauffmann (sometimes). The reason it is hard to be sure where many methodological naturalists stand on this position will be explained later.

Position C: Organisms contain irreducible information, meaning information not explainable in terms of physical laws and/or chance. Hence the neo-Darwinian theory is inadequate (except at the micro level) in a way that probably cannot be fixed. This is the position of Wilder-Smith, Michael Behe's forthcoming book, and those who endorse "intelligent design." Support for it comes also from the writings of antireductionists like Polanyi and Yockey (who do not explore or welcome the theistic implications).

Position D: Common ancestry, although initially appealing as a hypothesis, is not the true explanation for the pattern of classification (at least at higher taxonomic levels). The supposed common ancestors for the animal phyla, for example, never existed. The evidence from developmental biology, supposedly a major support for the common ancestry thesis, actually undermines it. This is not noticed in mainstream science because common ancestry is axiomatic and hence never in question. If one treats common ancestry as a hypothesis and not as an inescapable deduction from the existence of natural groups, there is plenty of reason to doubt that the hypothesis is true. Paul Nelson and Jonathan Wells are developing materials concerning this subject. Their research deserves to be funded, but of course it is difficult to get people to understand why a hypothesis that has become axiomatic should be investigated.

The purpose of this paper is not to argue the ultimate merits of these positions, but to note how a methodological naturalist and a theistic realist tend to approach them.

First, the TR approach. To a theistic realist, position B is very different from position A, because it is impressive to have actually solved a problem and much less impressive to promise to solve it in the future. If the scientific establishment were explicitly to abandon A and move over to B, this would constitute a major recantation. Theistic realists would compare the claim of evolutionary biologists that "we have the problem well in hand" with the claim of a defaulting debtor that "the check is in the mail."

To a theistic realist, position C is plausible and falsifiable—and also supported by considerable positive evidence. Theistic realists are not impressed by arguments from methodological naturalists that "intelligent cause" is somehow outside of science. Theistic realists know that science does regularly distinguish between intelligent and unintelligent causes. It pretends to be unable to do so only when the intelligent cause would be something unacceptable to MN, like God.

Position D is a legitimate possibility to a theistic realist. Common ancestry is not axiomatic but rather a plausible hypothesis that is already in question due to the general failure to identify specific fossil ancestors for the major groups. If the evidence from developmental biology really does create major problems, then something much weirder than common ancestry may be the true answer. Why not, even from an agnostic perspective? After the success of quantum mechanics, we should be used to a nature that is much odder than nineteenth-century science could conceive.

Here, from my personal experience in debate, is how a typical methodological naturalist (including those who are theists in religion) approaches these same alternatives.

A and B are not really very different. The scientists in both groups all accept "evolution," and that is the main point. All they are doing is arguing about the mechanism. Maybe additional mechanisms are needed, maybe not. If new mechanisms are needed, we will know that when we find them. The only difference between the two positions is that A emphasizes more what is known and B places more emphasis on what remains to be known. That is why Stephen Jay Gould and Stuart Kauffmann sometimes sound like A and sometimes like B; it is mainly a matter of what they are emphasizing at the time.

To methodological naturalists, C is not really a positive position but an argument that there are "gaps" in our understanding of evolution. Even if it is correct that the origin of genetic information is unexplained (and that is disputed), all C is saying is that we haven't found an adequate information-generating mechanism yet. Moreover, C doesn't say anything about common ancestry and so doesn't deny "the fact of evolution."

C is thus basically the same as B, which in turn is basically the same as A. All three positions come down to saying that there is general agreement in science in favor of "evolution," which is what really matters, but there are healthy debates over the precise mechanism, and more work needs to be done. Many methodological naturalists don't even acknowledge that accounting for complexity is a problem, since they focus on diversity. Evolution produces plenty of diversity (finch beaks one-quarter of the way to speciation in a few years), and there was plenty of time for the process to produce all the diversity we see today. Besides, Dawkins and others have modeled the whole process on their computers.

D to a typical methodological naturalist is like arguing for a flat earth. Methodological naturalists find it hard to believe that an otherwise sane and well-informed individual could be serious in denying common ancestry. The pattern of classification proves common ancestry regardless of the state of the fossil record, because there is no other rational possibility.

Thus for methodological naturalists A, B and C are fundamentally similar, and D is absurd. That means that there is not a great deal to discuss, other than the details of the evolutionary picture. When theistic methodological naturalists talk to persons who reject "evolution" (that is, reject MN), they are primarily engaged in damage control: "How can we persuade these people not to cause trouble by, for example, dragging religion into an unnecessary and futile conflict with science?" See for example the opening paragraph of Howard Van Till's response to one of my articles:

> Although the rhetoric Phillip E. Johnson employs in his article "Creator or Blind Watchmaker" differs in some details from that of the "scientific creationists" of North American Christian fundamentalism, the effect of his pronouncements is the same. That is, it perpetuates the association of Christian belief with the rejection of scientific theorizing, thereby ensuring that the gulf between the academy and the sanctuary will only grow wider.

Anyone who rejects MN invites conflict with the all-powerful rulers of science, whose approval is indispensable to Christian professors who want to be in the academic mainstream. The point of theistic MN is to allow theists to survive in a naturalistic academy. But if the academy is committed to naturalism, then the gulf between the academy and the sanctuary can be narrowed only to the extent that naturalism also dominates the sanctuary.

Conclusion: Evidence and Bias
Bias is a negative word for viewpoint. I have a rational viewpoint;

you have a bias; he is hopelessly prejudiced. Consider this statement (from a Christian college science professor):

Just as Phil is concerned with "naturalistic" biases which cause me to find the data convincing, theistic critics of Phil are concerned with his biases which cause him to find the data unconvincing. The line from the talk.origins FAQ on Phil Johnson . . . says it nicely: "His argument about the a priori doesn't seem half-bad, but I think he is wrong about the state of the empirical evidence—and that his *own* presuppositions are biasing his own examination of it."*

Whether my evaluation of the evidence is "biased" depends on whether TR as defined above is a "bias." For example, as a theistic realist I do not think that the pattern of nature (Darwin's argument from classification) "proves" common ancestry. Common ancestry was a most reasonable hypothesis in 1859, but there is reason to suspect that the seemingly "obvious" explanation for the pattern may not be the true one. I do not think that the Cambrian explosion illustrates anything I would call "evolution." I do not think that the variation illustrated by the peppered moth and finch-beak examples convincingly demonstrates a process that either could or did produce new body plans or complex organs. Each of these judgments is based on evidence—evaluated from the TR perspective.

Everybody has a viewpoint. The negative word *bias* is appropriate for viewpoints that unduly constrict the possibilities that the mind may consider. Thus racial or religious bias may lead an employer to reject the most qualified employee.

Science always has to fight the prevalent bias of the age if it is to be free to follow the evidence where it leads. In the past geology

---

*Internet "talk.origins" is an e-mail discussion group devoted to origins and is dominated by some very aggressive defenders of scientific orthodoxy. "FAQ" (frequently asked questions) is a sort of treatise provided for newcomers to the group, who will naturally tend to ask questions that have been answered many times in previous discussions.

had to free itself from religious bias so that it could consider possibilities like an old earth or the occurrence of ice ages rather than a worldwide flood. That job was accomplished long ago, and now scientific thought is restricted by naturalistic bias. Methodological naturalism is a bias in the sense that it constricts the mind, by limiting the possibilities open to serious consideration. Theistic realism opens the mind to additional possibilities, without preventing the acceptance of anything that really is convincingly demonstrated by empirical evidence.

Research Notes

Introduction
George Gaylord Simpson's words are from his book *The Meaning of Evolution* (rev. ed., Yale University Press, 1967), pp. 344-45. The quotation by Douglas Futuyma is from his book *Science on Trial: The Case for Evolution* (Pantheon, 1983), pp. 12-13.

Chapter 1: Is God Unconstitutional?
The citation for the Lamb's Chapel case is *Lamb's Chapel* v. *Center Moriches School District,* 113 S.Ct. 2141 (1993; hereafter *Lamb's Chapel*). The Dobson film series is described in footnote 3 of that opinion. The Supreme Court reversed a judgment in favor of the school administrators and the state, the legal citation of which is *Lamb's Chapel* v. *Center Moriches Union Free School District,* 959 F.2d 381 (2d cir. 1992), affirming 770 F.Supp. 91 (E.D.N.Y. 1991). Justice White's opinion for the majority quotes from the Supreme Court's opinion in *Cornelius* v. *NAACP Legal Defense and Educational Fund,* 473 U.S. 788, 806 (1985). Footnote 2 of Justice White's opinion, 113 S.Ct. at 2146-47, lists a sampling of groups that were considered acceptably nonreligious by the school authorities. The list includes "a New Age religious group known as the Mind Center," which claimed that its lecture on parapsychology was "scientific." The quotation from the school district's brief about the undesirability of allowing a "radical" church to "proselytize" on school property is paraphrased in Justice White's opinion, 113 S.Ct. at p. 2148. The "friend of the court" brief quoted in the text is from the brief filed by the New York State School Boards' Association, p. 4.

Although the judgment of the Supreme Court in *Lamb's Chapel* was unanimous, there were separate concurring opinions by Justice Anthony Kennedy and by Justice Antonin Scalia (joined by Justice Clarence Thomas). These justices objected to White's implicit approval of the standard test for interpreting the First Amendment's religious establishment clause set out in the opinion in *Lemon v. Kurtzman,* 403 U.S. 602 (1971). The *Lemon* test says that a challenged statute comports with the First Amendment's establishment clause only if (1) the legislature had a secular purpose, (2) the statute's principal effect is not to advance or inhibit religion and (3) the statute does not excessively entangle government with religion. The test has been applied to a wide range of government activities other than statutes and has led many judges to conclude that allowing any expression of religious opinion in a school building is unconstitutional. Justice Scalia in particular has been urging the Supreme Court to overrule the *Lemon* decision, which has been cited by the Supreme Court and lower federal courts to justify extensive judicial interference with attempts by other branches of government to arrive at sensible ways of accommodating religious and secular values in public life.

The argument of the New York attorney general that religious speech is valuable only to those who already believe is from the state's brief in the *Lamb's Chapel* case. It is quoted in Justice Scalia's opinion, 113 S.Ct. at p. 2151. See also the reference to it in the majority opinion, 113 S.Ct. at 2148-49. Justices focused on this argument in their questions at oral argument and their opinions, because it seemed to concede that the state's policy was in no way "neutral" toward religion.

The citation for the Supreme Court's decision in the Louisiana "balanced time for creationism" case is *Edwards* v. *Aguillard,* 482 U.S. 578 (1987). Justice William Brennan's opinion holds on page 591 that the statute was unconstitutional because "the preeminent purpose of the Louisiana Legislature was clearly to advance the religious viewpoint that a supernatural being created humankind." The opinion assumes throughout the "official caricature" of the creation-evolution controversy as discussed at the beginning of chapter four of this book. Further details on that case and my analysis of the constitutional issues may be found in the research notes to chapter one of *Darwin on Trial* (rev. ed., InterVarsity Press, 1993).

The Dean Kenyon story is reliably told in Stephen C. Meyer's article "A Scopes Trial for the '90's," in *The Wall Street Journal,* December 6, 1993, p. A14. I have personal knowledge of the facts as a participant in the controversy.

Stephen Jay Gould's review of *Darwin on Trial* was published in the July 1992 issue of *Scientific American,* pp. 118-20, with the title "Impeaching a Self-Appointed Judge." The editor of *Scientific American* predictably refused to print my rebuttal or even any letters (many were submitted) exposing the distortions in this classic hatchet job. My response to Gould and other critics may be found in the epilogue (and attached research notes) of *Darwin on Trial* (rev. ed., InterVarsity Press, 1993). Despite his intentions, Gould helped to further the success of *Darwin on Trial* by publishing an attack that was so easily recognized as unfair.

Chapter 2: The Established Religious Philosophy of America

The prevailing mythology in legal circles is that the interpretation of the First Amendment's religious establishment clause by the Supreme Court in the second half of the twentieth century continues a constitutional tradition established by Thomas Jefferson's reference to a "wall of separation" between church and state. Any attempt to change these recent decisions is therefore reported in the press as if it were an attack on the Constitution itself. To get a flavor of how things really were when memory of the Constitution was still fresh, one can do no better than to read the relevant passages of Alexis de Tocqueville's classic *Democracy in America* (trans. Lawrence; Harper & Row, 1988), pp. 290-301. Here are excerpts:

> There is an innumerable multitude of sects in the United States. They are all different in the worship they offer to the Creator, but all agree concerning the duties of men to one another. Each sect worships God in its own fashion, but all preach the same morality in the name of God. Though it is very important for man as an individual that his religion should be true, that is not the case for society. Society has nothing to fear or hope from another life; what is most important for it is not that all citizens should profess the true religion but that they should profess religion. Moreover, all the sects in the United States belong to the great unity of Christendom, and Christian morality is everywhere the same. . . .

> I do not doubt for an instant that the great severity of mores which one notices in the United States has its primary origin in beliefs. There religion is often powerless to restrain men in the midst of innumerable temptations which fortune offers. It cannot moderate their eagerness to enrich themselves, which everything contributes to arouse, but it reigns supreme in the souls of the women, and it is women who shape mores. Certainly of all countries in the world America is the one in which the marriage tie is most respected and where the highest and truest conception of conjugal happiness has been conceived.

> In Europe almost all the disorders of society are born around the domestic hearth and not far from the nuptial bed. It is there that men come to feel scorn for natural ties and legitimate pleasures and develop a taste for disorder, restlessness of spirit, and instability of desires. Shaken by the tumultuous passions which have often troubled his own house, the European finds it hard to submit to the authority of the state's legislators. When the American returns from the turmoil of politics to the bosom of the family, he immediately finds a perfect picture of order and peace. There all his pleasures are simple and natural and his joys innocent and quiet, and as the regularity of life brings him happiness, he easily forms the habit of regulating his opinions as well as his tastes.

> Whereas the European tries to escape his sorrows at home by troubling society, the American derives from his home that love of order which he carries over into affairs of state.

> In the United States it is not only mores that are controlled by religion, but

its sway extends even over reason.

Among the Anglo-Americans there are some who profess Christian dogmas because they believe them and others who do so because they are afraid to look as though they did not believe in them. So Christianity reigns without obstacles, by universal consent; consequently, as I have said elsewhere, everything in the moral field is certain and fixed, although the world of politics seems given over to argument and experiment. So the human spirit never sees an unlimited field before itself; however bold it is, from time to time it feels that it must halt before insurmountable barriers. Before innovating, it is forced to accept certain primary assumptions and to submit its boldest conceptions to certain formalities which retard and check it. . . .

While I was in America, a witness called at assizes of the county of Chester (state of New York) declared that he did not believe in the existence of God and the immortality of the soul. The judge refused to allow him to be sworn in, on the ground that the witness had destroyed beforehand all possible confidence in his testimony. Newspapers reported the fact without comment.

For the Americans the ideas of Christianity and liberty are so completely mingled that it is almost impossible to get them to conceive of the one without the other; it is not a question with them of sterile beliefs bequeathed by the past and vegetating rather than living in the depths of the soul.

Today, references to the religious heritage described by de Tocqueville are systematically excluded from textbooks.

A representative *Los Angeles Times* article about the Vista, California, school board controversy is Michael Granberg, "Vista Board OKs Teaching of Creationism," August 14, 1993, p. A1. Here are the opening paragraphs from that story:

The embattled but resilient Christian right majority of the Vista school board early Friday achieved what its three members had been promising for months: It formally opened the door to the teaching of creationism in the city's public schools.

It did so in defiance of state educational guidelines and its own vehement teachers association, and over the complaints of many parents and students of the San Diego County district at an emotional public meeting Thursday night that dragged on past midnight.

By a 3-2 vote, the board ordered that "discussions of divine creation, ultimate purposes, or ultimate causes (the 'why') shall be included at appropriate times in the history-social sciences and/or English-language arts curricula."

The new policy mandates "exploration and dialogue" of "scientific evidence that challenges any theory in science" and states that "no student shall be compelled to believe or accept any theory presented in the curriculum."

Board President Deidre Holliday, who heads the majority, said the change came at the urging of her constituency. "People kept asking: 'Why can't we have creationism? Why is evolution being taught as fact?' Those questions kept coming up, so we decided to do something. We now have creationism on an equal footing with evolution."

The policy, which takes effect immediately, threatens to further divide this city of 76,000 that voted in the conservative majority on a fundamentalist ticket in November.

"Make no mistake—teaching creationism is illegal. We are going to get sued," said Trustee Linda Rhoades, who, with board member Sandee Carter, forms the two-member minority that has consistently—but futilely—opposed the wishes of the other three.

But support was evident Friday afternoon among students gathered at the Vista Recreation Center, the local bowling alley. Tom Turner, 14, who will enter Vista High School this fall, said: "I think that if they are able to teach evolution, they should also be giving opinions about the Bible." Tom described his family as Christian and members of a Baptist church.

Tim Hickey, 14, a student at Roosevelt Middle School, was in agreement. "It's true—so they should be able to teach it," he said of the Bible's story of Genesis in which God created the world in seven days. "Without question, without doubt, it's true."

In the wake of the vote, American Civil Liberties Union representatives said they are considering a lawsuit and will sue immediately should any Vista teacher begin teaching biblical creationism in the classroom.

Some of the city's outraged citizenry were saying for the first time Friday that a recall drive to remove the three-member majority is an imminent possibility.

Susie Lange, spokeswoman for the State Department of Education in Sacramento, expressed concern that what the board has done is mandate the teaching of biblical creation through the "back door" method of bringing it up in discussion of history and the humanities—just not in science classes.

She added that this is the first time any California school board has taken such a step.

Lange said state education officials will "watch the situation closely" and monitor whether the board introduces textbooks that promote Christian teachings rather than offer scholarly views about all religions.

"The law they're in danger of breaking is the constitutional protection against promoting a single religion," Lange said. "But they will also be in violation of the framework guide set forth by the State Board of Education if they try to promote only one religious view."

Lange said the courts "would be the ultimate enforcement" but that, if state education officials turn up evidence of Vista schools "promoting Christianity, we would notify them of our intention to stop it."

She said the State Board of Education has no enforcement powers but could petition the Legislature to cut off the district's funding. The more likely response would be a lawsuit brought by the state board. If the implementation of the policy has the broader effect of fostering a discussion of all religious viewpoints—rather than promoting one over another—Lange said neither the State Board of Education nor the courts could object.

Tom Conry, president of the Vista Teachers Assn., which bitterly opposed the policy, said teachers "will just go on teaching what we always have anyway"—in open defiance of the three-member majority.

"We are not happy with the board majority, by any means whatsoever," Conry said.

A very well informed reader would know from that story that the Vista board had done nothing illegal or educationally indefensible. The California State Board of Education Policy Statement on the Teaching of Natural Sciences, which the *Los Angeles Times* repeatedly accused the board of violating, contains the following specific provisions:

2. Discussions of any scientific fact, hypothesis, or theory related to the origins of the Universe, the Earth, and of life [the "how"] are appropriate to the science curriculum. Discussions of divine creation, ultimate purposes, or ultimate causes [the "why"] are appropriate to the History/Social Science and English/Language Arts Curriculum.

3. Nothing in science or any other field shall be taught dogmatically. A dogma is a system of beliefs that is not subject to scientific test and refutation. Compelling beliefs is inconsistent with the goal of education; the goal is to increase understanding.

The fault of the Vista school board members was that they read the text of the policy statement rather than the subtext. (See chapter nine of this book for a discussion of the "subtext of contempt" employed by modernists toward creationism.) The coalition of science educators and journalists represented by the *Los Angeles Times* understood the policy statement to mean that naturalistic evolution is to be taught as fact, no dissent is to be permitted in the schools, and compelling belief on this subject is what science education is all about. They understood the paragraph numbered 2 above to mean that "creationism"—that is, the concept that God created—could be taught in literature and social science classes as a discredited prescientific myth, not as a tenable intellectual concept. To modernists, "science"—that is, metaphysical naturalism—is not a "dogma" but the foundation of rationality itself.

Egged on by such "news stories" and by the teachers' unions, crowds attended the school board meetings to keep the board majority on the defensive, defending itself from accusations based mostly on speculation about their intentions. Media reports of the controversy consistently repeated a stock list of accusations, inciting conflict and then blaming the board majority for dividing the community. The media campaign was successful in the end, as the offending members lost their seats at the next election. The distortions in the press coverage of the Vista school board controversy are reviewed by a reporter with local knowledge in Randy Dotinga, "Wronging the Right," *Columbia Journalism Review,* March/ April 1995, p. 17.

Roy A. Clouser's *The Myth of Religious Neutrality: An Essay on the Hidden Role of Religious Belief in Theories* (Notre Dame, 1991) is an important companion piece for the themes of this chapter and the remainder of the book. Clouser's book is addressed to a professional academic audience and mine is addressed to general readers, and Clouser uses the word *religious* where I tend to say *metaphysical*. He also applies his analysis to a different range of problems.

In general, my impression is that we are profoundly in agreement.

Chapter 3: The Grand Metaphysical Story of Science

The full title of Stephen Hawking's bestseller is *A Brief History of Time: From the Big Bang to Black Holes* (Bantam, 1988). Quotations used in this chapter are from pages 175, 49, 136 and 12-13. The quotation from Carl Sagan's introduction appears on page x.

Hawking dedicated the book to "Jane," the heroic wife who nursed him through his disabling illness and raised his children. Jane Hawking does not appear in the excellent made-for-television movie of the book, because by that time their marriage had ended. London *Sunday Times* reporter Bryan Appleyard interviewed the Hawkings in 1988, and anyone reading Jane's candid comments about Stephen's philosophy could have guessed that trouble was brewing.

"There's one aspect of [Stephen's] thought that I find increasingly upsetting and difficult to live with," Jane told Appleyard. "It's the feeling that, because everything is reduced to a rational, mathematical formula, that must be the truth. There doesn't seem to be room in the minds of people who are working on these things for other sorts of inspiration."

When Jane tried to ask Stephen whether his theory of a cosmos with no beginning and no need for God was advanced merely as a mathematical model or as the truth itself, she could get no reply other than the famous Hawking grin. Appleyard commented, "For Mrs. Hawking, a devout Anglican, it seems like an agnostic door slamming in her face." At another point in the interview, commenting on Stephen's growing fame, Jane remarked that her role was no longer to care for a sick man but "simply to tell him he is not God." (From Bryan Appleyard, "A Master of the Universe: Will Stephen Hawking Live to Find the Secret?" *Sunday Times* [London], July 3, 1988.)

I mention Jane Hawking's opinion not because it involves marital difficulties, which can happen to anyone, but because her criticism is extremely perceptive. Hawking, like other scientific metaphysicians discussed in this book, has an evident need to wrap reality up into a package that can be fully understood by the kind of logic that his science can employ. Whatever cannot be understood that way is pushed out of reality—however important it may be to the business of living. Who is better qualified to criticize a man's simplistic rationalism and hubris than his wife?

John Polkinghorne, a physicist, Anglican priest and president of Queens' College of Cambridge University, provides valuable reflections on science and theology in his 1993 Gifford Lectures, published as *The Faith of a Physicist* (Princeton University Press, 1994). Polkinghorne characterizes Hawking's "no beginning point" hypothesis as "scientifically interesting but theologically insignificant," because "the idea of creation has no special stake in a datable start to the universe. . . . God is not a God of the edges, with a vested interest in boundaries. Creation is not something he did fifteen billion years ago, but it is something he is doing now" (p. 73).

This fails to take account of the role the mathematical elimination of a beginning point plays in shoring up the confidence of the scientific naturalists, a confidence that was clearly disturbed by the prospect of having to acknowledge a scientifically ascertainable moment of creation. The "no beginning point" concept is *not* scientifically interesting: it is a mathematical construct that has no empirical basis, makes no predictions and generates no research agenda. Its sole purpose is to support the metaphysical principle that nature is self-contained and effectively eternal.

It is true that theologians can adjust to even the most complete naturalistic system by responding, as Polkinghorne does, that God is "the sustainer of the self-contained spacetime egg and the ordainer of its quantum laws," but naturalists perceive such reasoning as defensive and indicating merely that theism is unfalsifiable. Scientific naturalists do not think it necessary or possible to prove the nonexistence of an undetectable sustainer and lawgiver. All they aspire to do is to complete the naturalistic agenda as far as observable reality is concerned and leave everything beyond that to the subjective imagination. The Bible's opening words—"in the beginning God created the heavens and the earth"—state a proposition very different from a modernist theologian's concept of an undetectable sustainer of a self-contained space-time egg that has no beginning. When naturalists have forced theologians to retreat from the former to the latter, they have accomplished their purpose.

David Lindley's *The End of Physics: The Myth of a Unified Theory* (BasicBooks, 1993) is an excellent corrective to the expansive scientism of the "theory of everything" school of particle physicists and cosmologists. Lindley predicts that the "end of physics" will come not because physicists will have discovered the coveted grand unified physical theory but because, long before that point, their theories will have gone so far beyond experimental testing that physics will be a branch of aesthetics more than of experimental science. The theories will seem "beautiful" in the eyes of the physicists, but they will not be testable.

Paul Davies's *The Mind of God: The Scientific Basis for a Rational World* (Simon & Schuster, 1992) unabashedly presents physics as metaphysics and seems to end in pantheistic mysticism. The quotation in the text is from page 40.

Francis Crick explains his materialist starting point on page 3 of *The Astonishing Hypothesis: The Scientific Search for the Soul* (Scribner's, 1994). His dismissal of religion and philosophy occurs on page 258. Crick wears his materialism on his sleeve and is refreshingly candid in expressing his contempt for the alternatives.

The quotation attributed to Arthur Kornberg is from his lecture "The Two Cultures: Chemistry and Biology," delivered at the annual meeting of the American Association for the Advancement of Science in Chicago in 1987. It was published in *Biochemistry* 26 (1987): 6888-91.

The quotation attributed to Donald Johanson is from Maitland A. Edey and Donald C. Johanson, *Blueprints: Solving the Mystery of Evolution* (Little, Brown, 1989), p. 2.

Chapter 4: Is There a Blind Watchmaker?
Jonathan Weiner's summary of the argument of *The Beak of the Finch* appeared

in *The New York Times Magazine* for Sunday, May 8, 1994, p. 40. The laudatory review of the book by Douglas H. Chadwick (in substance practically identical to Weiner's summary) appeared in the *New York Times* Sunday book review section for May 22, 1994, p. 7. The book itself was published by Alfred A. Knopf in 1994.

Stephen Jay Gould wrote on page 267 of his collection *Ever Since Darwin* (Pelican, 1977), "Before Darwin, we thought that a benevolent God had created us." The longer quotation that immediately follows is from his essay "In Praise of Charles Darwin," in *Darwin's Legacy,* ed. Charles L. Hamrum (Harper & Row, 1983), pp. 6-7. This essay appeared originally in *Discover* magazine, February 1982.

I need to emphasize at every opportunity that I am not taking advantage of any offhand statements by individual Darwinists when I make the point that *Darwinism implies a naturalistic understanding of the development of life, with no room for a supernatural Creator.* Every prominent neo-Darwinist authority has said this at one time or another, and they mean what they say. The most aggressive naturalistic metaphysicians of science, including Dawkins, Sagan and all the others, promote naturalism with the backing of the organized scientific enterprise—whatever reservations and qualifications individual scientists may express in private. When Carl Sagan received the National Academy of Science's "Public Welfare Medal" in 1994, the accompanying citations left no doubt that he was being honored for the *Cosmos* television series in particular, where he supposedly communicated "the wonder and importance of science." What he communicated was the metaphysics of the naturalistic worldview, dressed up in the robes of science.

Richard Dawkins's *The Blind Watchmaker* (Longman, 1986) is brilliantly argued, but Jane Hawking's criticism of Stephen Hawking's thinking is equally applicable to Dawkins: whatever does not fit into his narrow logical system is expelled from reality. Francis Crick's effusive praise of Dawkins is from his autobiography, *What Mad Pursuit: A Personal View of Scientific Discovery* (BasicBooks, 1988), p. 29. Quotations from *The Blind Watchmaker* (original ed.) are from pages 1, 5-6, 89-90. The "Replicator" story of the origin of life is taken from Dawkins's other famous book, *The Selfish Gene* (Oxford University Press, 1976, 1989).

The second part of chapter four relies mainly on Stephen Jay Gould's review article "The Confusion About Evolution," in *The New York Review of Books,* November 19, 1992. Gould was reviewing Helena Cronin's *The Ant and the Peacock: Altruism and Sexual Selection from Darwin to Today* (Cambridge University Press, 1991). The review was so overheated that it drew indignant protests from John Maynard Smith and Daniel Dennett, to which Gould replied with his usual dexterity in *The New York Review of Books,* January 14, 1993. My opinion is that Cronin's book was very good in its way (as an application of Dawkins's logic to certain important problems of evolutionary biology) and that Gould's review came very close to repudiating Darwinism in favor of a concept of "evolution" that resembles the pre-Darwinian catastrophism of Georges Cuvier. I wrote to Gould after this review to suggest that he is no more a Darwinist than I am, and that he refuses to acknowledge this only because he fears the metaphysical consequences. He did not answer. I understand that Gould's long-anticipated theoretical work on macroevolution will appear soon. I hope that in it he will attempt to say precisely how he understands complex organs to have evolved.

I also refer to Gould's popular book *Wonderful Life* (Norton, 1989). The description of the Burgess Shale fossil issues in this book is excellent. The philosophy (if you rewind a hypothetical videotape of the history of life and replay it, evolution won't necessarily produce humans again) reflects Gould's determination to attribute our existence to chance rather than either divine purpose or predictable natural laws. For further discussion on the issues raised by the "Cambrian explosion," see chapter 4 of *Darwin on Trial* (rev. ed., InterVarsity Press, 1993) and the research notes to that chapter.

Chapter 5: Theistic Naturalism and Theistic Realism

Steven Jay Gould's essay "The Panda's Thumb" is found in the collection by the same title (Norton, 1980). An update of Gould's basic argument was published by Kenneth R. Miller in *Technology Review* 97 (February 1994): 24. Miller cites the panda's thumb example, along with asserted deficiencies in the construction of the eye, "pseudogenes" that do not perform evident useful functions, and so-called hen's teeth that have allegedly been produced by putting mouse tissue in contact with chicken epithelial cells. It would require an additional chapter to address these examples here, and the effort would distract readers from the main philosophical themes, so I will merely say that I look forward to discussing these examples before scientific audiences with the support of my very capable associates who have investigated them all.

In any case, the use of theological arguments—"God wouldn't have done it this way"—is a very questionable way of proving that Darwinian evolution was capable of creating complex biological organs. This issue is thoroughly explored in Paul Nelson's article "The Role of Theology in Current Evolutionary Reasoning," in *Facets of Faith and Science,* vol. 3, ed. J. M. van der Meer (University Press of America, 1995).

Steven Weinberg's book *Dreams of a Final Theory* is valuable as a clear-headed statement of the scientific reductionist perspective on reality. I am favorably impressed that he sent the pages criticizing my position (246-50) to me for comment before publishing them. In his writings and in his conversations with me, Weinberg has made no secret of his dislike for Christian theism and his hope that discovery of the "final theory" will convince Americans to give up their belief that a conscious supernatural entity rules the universe. I don't agree with Weinberg's answers, but I do respect his determination to state clearly what is at stake.

I reviewed *Dreams of a Final Theory* in *The Wall Street Journal,* May 10, 1993, p. A12. For a longer and much better review, see Roger Penrose, "Nature's Biggest Secret," *The New York Review of Books,* October 21, 1993. Weinberg has been the most important proponent among scientists of the ill-fated Texas Superconducting Supercollider, a $10-billion-plus project that would certainly have provided employment for many particle physicists and might possibly have found the famous Higgs particle—called "the God particle" by some theoretical physicists. Among other fascinating insights, Penrose explains that the God particle was originally proposed by Peter Higgs as "an ingenious theoretical device, and not necessarily appearing as an actual particle. As a device, it allowed *other* particles to acquire mass, where all particles were described according to a theoretical scheme in which everything was initially massless. . . . The Higgs mechanism, in its specific new role, is still the giver of mass to other particles, but it also provides a new, real, observable particle with a finite intrinsic mass of its own. Its complete role is not just as a God in Heaven, but as a God who also deigns to live among His mortal subjects."

The reference in the text to the "molecular Eve" controversy simplifies a complex story. The molecular Eve hypothesis asserted that the ancestors of modern humans evolved in Africa about 200,000 years ago, thereafter spreading through the world and replacing (that is, exterminating) all preexisting hominid species. Opposition to this hypothesis was stated most forcefully by University of Michigan paleoanthropologist Milford Wolpoff, who championed the contrary view that various groups of humans evolved to their modern status separately in the locations where they are found today. Wolpoff also insisted that fossils, rather than molecular theories, are the final authority when one is deciding among rival theories of human evolution. See Alan G. Thorne and Milford Wolpoff, "The Multiregional Evolution of Humans," *Scientific American* 266 (April 1992): 76.

The multiregionalists won a great victory when errors were exposed in the calculations of the molecular Eve theorists, but the controversy continues. See Ann Gibbons, "Molecular Eve Refuses to Die," *Science* 259 (February 26, 1993): 1249. While all parties to such a controversy are truth-seekers, they also have professional status at stake. If newly available molecular evidence alone can tell an accurate story of evolution, then the importance of fossil experts is greatly reduced.

Nancey Murphy's review essay "Phillip Johnson on Trial: A Critique of His Critique of Darwin," was published in the American Scientific Affiliation's journal, *Perspectives on Science and Christian Faith* 45 (March 1993): 26-36. Murphy's general approach is to relate her theological concerns to the philosophy of science of Imre Lakatos. Her major book is *Theology in the Age of Scientific Reasoning* (Cornell University Press, 1990).

John Polkinghorne provides a good brief description of Lakatos's philosophy and Murphy's use of it in *The Faith of a Physicist* (Princeton University Press, 1994), pp. 47-48. Lakatos aimed to improve on Karl Popper's idea that to be scientific a theory must be falsifiable. The falsifiability criterion applies fairly well to low-level hypotheses (such as "it will rain tomorrow") but not to more general theories like relativity, which scientists do not abandon merely because of some unfavorable data. As Stephen Weinberg pointed out, it is usual for theories that are generally considered successful to coexist with a variety of anomalies.

Lakatos proposed that science proceeds by adopting a central research program, the central core of which is dogmatically held and protected by a belt of auxiliary hypotheses that can be adjusted as necessary to improve the program's fit with the empirical data. The program is successful—"progressive" in Lakatos's terminology—if pursuing it leads to "stunning" new discoveries. For example, anomalies in the observed orbit of Uranus did not lead scientists to abandon Newton's theory of gravity, but to postulate the existence of an outer planet (Neptune), which was subsequently discovered. A program is unsuccessful ("degenerating") when the difficulties multiply to the extent that the cost of generating unproductive auxiliary hypotheses exceeds the value of protecting the central core.

Polkinghorne observes that this model of science appeals to some theologians, because it seems to allow them to be dogmatic in protecting a core set of fundamental commitments (such as the existence of God) while employing a certain flexibility of interpretation with subsidiary ideas to deal with difficulties. Polkinghorne wryly exclaims that, with a boost from Lakatos, "theology is a scientific research program!" He goes on to comment, "Perhaps the most enthusiastic and extensive use of Lakatosian ideas in theology has been attempted recently by Nancey Murphy. The difficulty will always be to substantiate the claim to the generation of stunning new results. Murphy uses Catholic Modernism as a test case, characterizing it as 'progressive' on the basis of George Tyrrell's 'predictions' that scientific history would not contradict Biblical history on fundamental points, and that papal absolutism would prove a passing phase. The case looks a little thin" (p. 48).

In her review of *Darwin on Trial* Murphy faults me for failing to evaluate Darwinism on Lakatosian criteria. She concedes that it is difficult to determine whether a program is progressive or degenerative. (If Catholic modernism is an example of a progressive program, I certainly see the difficulty.) Even specific examples are hard to classify. Is the neutral theory of molecular evolution a stunning discovery of the Darwinian research program or an auxiliary hypothesis invented to protect the core concept of evolution by natural selection from falsification? Murphy eventually decides that the Lakatosian criteria are inapplicable to this case, because they are designed for relative rather than absolute assessment of theories. She concludes that it is futile to attack Darwinism, because no replacement is available, and she asks, "What would evolutionary biologists *do* if there is no conception of the field to guide their research?"

The answer is that evolutionary biologists would still have a theory of microevolution to explicate, and they could spend the rest of their time looking for a valid theory of biological innovation rather than pretending that they already have one. (That evolutionary biologists fear unemployment tends more to call their objectivity into question than to establish that the theory they cherish is true.) Moreover, the reason Darwinism is the only game in town is that Darwinism (that is, blind watchmaker evolution) actually is the best biological creation story that the scientific naturalists who make the rules have been able to come up with. The true core idea that all the auxiliary hypotheses of Darwinism are protecting is *naturalism*.

The story of Stephen Hawking's meeting with the pope is from pages 46-47 and

116 of *A Brief History of Time: From the Big Bang to Black Holes* (Bantam, 1988). Few people have understood the meaning of this story, in which Hawking pretends to be afraid of persecution, while the pope is merely trying (without success) to persuade the scientists that humility is a virtue. Why be humble when you are about to discover a theory of everything?

For scholarly discussions of the relationship of science and Christian theism from a more conservative Christian viewpoint, see Nancy R. Pearcey and Charles B. Thaxton, *The Soul of Science: Christian Faith and Natural Philosophy* (Crossway, 1994), and J. P. Moreland, *Christianity and the Nature of Science* (Baker Book House, 1989).

Chapter 6: Realism and Rationality
John Searle's article "Is There a Crisis in American Higher Education?" was published in the *Bulletin of the American Academy of Arts and Sciences* 46, no. 4, pp. 24-47. Quotations attributed to Searle regarding the university crisis are from this article, which was originally presented as a lecture at the University of California, Berkeley, on April 10, 1992. Quotations regarding Searle's philosophy of mind are from his book *The Rediscovery of the Mind* (Bradford/MIT Press, 1992), pp. 14, 24, 28.

Francis Crick provides a concise explanation of the two, very different meanings of *emergent* on page 11 of *The Astonishing Hypothesis: The Scientific Search for the Soul* (Scribner's, 1994):

> There are two meanings of the term emergent. The first has mystical overtones. It implies that the emergent behavior cannot in any way, even in principle, be understood as the combined behavior of its separate parts. I find it difficult to relate to this type of thinking. The scientific meaning of emergent, or at least the one I use, assumes that, while the whole may be more than the simple sum of the separate parts, its behavior can, at least in principle, be understood from the nature and behavior of its parts plus the knowledge of how all these parts interact.
>
> A simple example, from elementary chemistry, would be an organic compound, such as benzene. A benzene molecule is made of six carbon atoms, arranged symmetrically in a ring with a hydrogen atom attached, on the outside of the ring, to each carbon atom. Apart from its mass, the properties of a benzene molecule are not in any sense the simple arithmetical sum of the properties of its twelve constituent atoms. Nevertheless, the behavior of benzene, such as its chemical reactivity and its absorption of light, can be calculated if we know how these parts interact, although we need quantum mechanics to tell us how to do this. It is curious that nobody derives some kind of mystical satisfaction by saying "the benzene molecule is more than the sum of its parts," whereas too many people are happy to make such statements about the brain and nod their heads wisely as they do so.

In *The Rediscovery of the Mind* (pp. 111-26) Searle also emphatically rejects the meaning of *emergent* that has unacceptable mystical overtones. He nonetheless argues that consciousness is "irreducible" for philosophical reasons having to do with the nature of subjective experience. In the simplest terms, the argument is that there is a difference in kind between the subjective experience of (say) pain and the neural mechanism that produces that experience. The objective pattern of neuron firings does not convey the experience, because the subjective experience and the objective, observable cause are different phenomena. Searle complains that metaphysical dualists treat the irreducibility of consciousness as a proof that dualism is true, whereas Searle insists it is "a trivial consequence of the pragmatics of our definitional practices" which has no important metaphysical implications (p. 122). I do not understand how something can be both an impenetrable barrier to reduction and a mere definitional practice having only trivial consequences.

Richard Rorty's beautifully written essay "Wild Orchids and Trotsky" may be found in the collection *Messages from American Universities* (Edmundson ed., Viking, 1993). I first read it when it was reprinted in the April 1994 issue of the *University of Chicago Alumni Magazine*. Rorty credits the "juvenile neurotics" quip to A. J. Liebling. Rorty's essay "The Priority of Democracy to Philosophy" appears in the collection of his philosophical papers titled *Objectivity, Relativism and Truth* (Cambridge University Press, 1991).

Chapter 7: Natural Law
Senator Joseph Biden's natural law position tracks closely the path taken by Laurence Tribe of the Harvard Law School in an article in *The New York Times*. Tribe warned readers that Clarence Thomas might employ natural law theory to hold that "abortion is murder and [therefore] its practice or counseling cannot be permitted by any state" (Laurence Tribe, "Clarence Thomas and 'Natural Law,' " *The New York Times*, July 15, 1991, sec. A, p. 15). Tribe is a frequent spokesman for liberal Democrats on legal issues, and he took a leading role in the battle to defeat Judge Robert Bork's nomination to the Supreme Court. Biden's criticism of Bork is taken from his opening statement as chair of the Senate Judiciary Committee in *Hearings on the Nomination of Robert Bork to Be Associate Justice of the Supreme Court of the United States* (U.S. Government Printing Office, 1989), p. 97. For a published version of Biden's views on natural law at the time, see Joseph R. Biden Jr., "Law and Natural Law: Questions for Judge Thomas," *The Washington Post*, September 8, 1991, p. C1. This article actually lists four major points, which I have condensed to three. Biden's third point was that natural law should be viewed as an evolving body of ideals rather than as a set of static "timeless truths," and his fourth point was that natural law should not "limit government's ability to respond to changing circumstances." I interpreted these as two ways of saying essentially the same thing: natural law is not fixed for all times but evolves as society's needs change.

In *People* v. *Davis*, 7 Cal. 4th 797 (1994), the California Supreme Court held that a killing of a fetus is murder regardless of whether the fetus was "viable" (capable of surviving outside the womb), provided that the fetus has passed beyond the embryonic stage of seven or eight weeks. The dissenting opinion in the *Davis* case by Justice Stanley Mosk states that twenty-four states punish the killing of a fetus or unborn child as homicide; the states differ widely on whether the fetus has to have reached viability or some earlier stage. Mosk reckons that at least six states apply criminal penalties to the killing of "both viable and nonviable fetuses and to embryos—even to zygotes" (7 Cal. 4th at p. 843).

Oliver Wendell Holmes Jr.'s essay "The Path of the Law," stating his famous "bad man" theory, was published in the *Harvard Law Review* 10 (March 25, 1897). It was originally delivered as a lecture at the dedication of the new hall of the Boston University School of Law on January 8, 1897.

Darwin's prediction that the civilized races would soon exterminate not only the "lesser" races but also the higher apes is quoted from *The Descent of Man* (Princeton University Press ed., 1981), p. 201. Darwin was not a bloodthirsty imperialist but a scientist explaining that extinction by natural selection was responsible for the absence of intermediate forms and that the process could be expected to continue. Carl Degler's *In Search of Human Nature: The Decline and Revival of Darwinism in American Social Thought* (Oxford University Press, 1991) explains how the racism and materialistic determinism inherent in the original version of Darwinism led social scientists to abandon the theory (except insofar as it was useful to get God out of the picture) and pursue culture-based methodologies. My review of Degler's revealing book may be found in *First Things,* May 1993, p. 38.

The Richard Posner quote is from his book *The Problems of Jurisprudence* (Harvard University Press, 1990), pp. 235-36. Posner, a judge of the U.S. Court of Appeals for the Seventh Circuit, was formerly a professor at the University of Chicago Law School. He is renowned in legal circles as the leading figure in the "law and economics" movement, which advocates extensive use of economic concepts in legal reasoning.

Arthur Allen Leff's brilliant lecture was delivered at the Duke University Law School on April 2, 1979. It is published as "Unspeakable Ethics, Unnatural Law," *Duke Law Journal,* 1979, p. 1229.

Chapter 8: Education

The first part of this chapter is based on Yale law professor Bruce A. Ackerman's book *Social Justice in the Liberal State* (Yale University Press, 1980). All references and quotations are from chapter 5, "Liberal Education," especially pages 154-61.

William Kilpatrick's *Why Johnny Can't Tell Right From Wrong: Moral Illiteracy and the Case for Character Education* (Simon & Schuster, 1992) is admirable for combining a very practical approach to moral education with a solid understanding of the philosophical roots of current educational practices. The quotation about preparation for marriage is from page 68. For an example of how even the popular press has begun to recognize that current sex education practices need to be restrained, see Barbara Dafoe Whitehead, "The Failure of Sex Education," *The Atlantic Monthly,* October 1994, p. 55.

Martin Eger's article "A Tale of Two Controversies: Dissonance in the Theory and Practice of Rationality" appears as the lead article in a symposium titled

"Controversy" in *Zygon* 23 (1988): 291-368. The quotations from Mill are from chapter 2 of *On Liberty,* which deals with liberty of thought and discussion. The quotation from Philip Kitcher is from his book *Abusing Science* (MIT Press, 1982), pp. 175-76.

Zygon is a journal of religion and science that normally takes a strongly accommodationist line, and so publication of Eger's provocative article raised many eyebrows. The editors followed it with responses by six critics, and then a response to the critics by Eger. The spirit of Eger's article is illustrated by his response to a critic who wrote that creationists "reject the whole enterprise and vision of science."

Perceptions of the situation have been distorted by an indiscriminate use of the term "creationists" for millions of very different sorts of people, of whom only a tiny fraction are the "creation scientists" or creation activists (as I prefer to call them) responsible for most of the news stories.

Within that larger population of creationists, active if at all only on the local level, I found—contrary to media impressions—that the prevailing attitude is surprisingly respectful of science, despite the fact that it is also suspicious of science. In this there is no contradiction. As American political conservatives are suspicious of government, but consider it a good thing when kept in bounds, so creationist parents suspect that when it comes to evolution something is being pressed on them in the name of science that actually goes beyond science. It is at this point that the question of the rationality of teaching enters. For many people, it becomes especially important to know what one ought to believe as a rational person, and what reason does not demand. These people do not wish their own views to be in conflict with science.

No doubt, as a maximum demand, most creation activists would like to see their beliefs studied in schools on equal footing. However, many parents would be content if, in their own district school, evolution were taught in what they regard as a "less dogmatic" manner. . . . For another large group of parents and students, creationism is a starting point, a preconception; evolution appears improbable, but there is room for discussion. Finally, there is also a small number of scientifically trained people among the creationists, who have tried to offer serious, technical critiques of theories of pre-biotic evolution (see Thaxton and Bradley, *The Mystery of Life's Origins,* 1984). Because creationism does come in many varieties, I would caution against the kind of language that needlessly places large populations "out of court"— including intelligent, educated men and women who are open to dialogue. The sorts of people I describe, not members of the creation institutes, are the ones who actually interact with schools. (pp. 364-365)

The quotations from George M. Marsden's *The Soul of the American University: From Protestant Establishment to Established Nonbelief* (Oxford University Press, 1994) are from pages 422, 430-41. My review of Marsden's book, combined with a review of Douglas Sloan's *Faith and Knowledge: Mainline Protestantism and American Higher Education* (Westminster/John Knox, 1995), appears in *First Things,* March 1995. Sloan recounts the failed attempt of a group he calls the "theological reformers"—Reinhold Niebuhr, his less famous but equally esteemed brother H. Richard Niebuhr, and Paul Tillich—to reinvigorate Christianity in the intellectual world. Marsden's book contains a wealth of valuable historical information, but Sloan's makes the essential analytical point most acutely:

> In the end the theologians pulled back from affirming unambiguously the real possibility of knowledge of God and of the spiritual world. They again and again resisted seeking or talking about knowledge of God for fear of the danger of applying objectifying and manipulative modes of thought where they did not belong. At the same time, however, they wanted to affirm fully and without question, lest they be thought religious fundamentalists, the same objective, analytic modes of modern science and historical analysis in every other domain besides faith. The result was a split that forced the theological reformers back onto faith presuppositions whenever they spoke about religion, and onto an increasing reliance on naturalistic approaches to the sensible world whenever they wanted to speak about ethics, science, or knowledge in general. (p. 120)

In my opinion, Sloan has it absolutely right. Theists who accept a naturalistic understanding of knowledge fatally undercut their own intellectual position.

Chapter 9: The Subtext of Contempt
The legal citation for the court of appeals opinion in the Phillip Bishop case is *Bishop* v. *Aronov,* 926 F.2d 1066 (11th Cir. 1991), *cert. denied,* 112 S.Ct. 3026 (1992). The court of appeals reversed the trial court's judgment in favor of Bishop but accepted the trial judge's findings of fact, which were based on undisputed evidence. The trial court opinion is *Bishop* v. *Aronov,* 732 F. Supp. 1562 (N.D. Ala. 1990). Michael McConnell of the University of Chicago Law School represented Bishop in his unsuccessful petition for *"certiorari,"* that is, review in the U.S. Supreme Court. The facts related in this chapter are taken from the trial court record. I previously wrote about the *Bishop* case in my article "The Creationist and the Sociobiologist: Two Stories About Illiberal Education," *California Law Review* 80 (July 1992): 1071-90. I know about the Henry F. Schaefer incident at the University of Georgia because Schaefer, a former Berkeley professor, is a personal friend of mine.

William Provine's seminal essay is "Progress in Evolution and Meaning in Life," in *Evolutionary Progress,* ed. M. H. Nitecki (University of Chicago Press, 1988). Provine has independently published brief popular versions of his central thesis, notably in "Evolution and the Foundation of Ethics," *MBL Science* 3, no. 1, p. 25. In my opinion, these simplified essays that leave out the historical detail have done Provine a disservice, by making it appear that his atheistic materialism is a mere prejudice. The longer essay is actually a thoughtful piece that shows how a theistic understanding of evolutionary mechanisms became untenable when the founders of the neo-Darwinian synthesis achieved what Provine calls the "evolutionary constriction." At the turn of the century it was relatively easy to be a Darwinist and also a theist, because "evolution" allowed room for God to act in nature, for example by providing the needed variation. Provine reckons that the majority of evolutionists at that time were theists who thought of evolution as divinely guided or inherently progressive. With the coming of the synthesis, biological evolution became wedded to physicalist theories of nature which absolutely barred consideration of purposeful forces in evolution. Neo-Darwinists found no need or place for purposeful forces in their theory and hence concluded that evolution is unguided and purposeless.

The story of James Sears and James Carper is taken from *The Real Issue,* December 1993, p. 1. Their book, to be published by Teachers College Press, containing essays by William Provine and me, bears the title *Public Education and Religion: Conversations for an Enlarging Public Square.*

The contempt for Christian theism that is always just below the surface among scientific naturalists came out in abundance when the novelist Susan Howatch donated one million pounds to Cambridge University to found the Starbridge Lectureship in Theology and Natural Science. Successful from an early age as a novelist, Howatch converted to Christianity in her middle years and became still more successful as the author of a series of novels about the lives of clergymen involved with "Starbridge" (Salisbury) Cathedral. She is fascinated with the idea that scientists and theologians or mystics are talking about the same phenomena from different frames of reference, and so is understandably interested in getting these two groups to understand each other better.

Her generous bequest drew sneers from influential quarters of the scientific community. John Maddox, editor of *Nature,* was disgusted that Cambridge would stoop so low as to accept the money of an "airport-bookstand" novelist to create an "empty" academic post. Richard Dawkins (see chapter four) wrote a letter to the London *Independent,* taking his usual line that theology is vacuous and that the only knowledge of any value we can have comes from science. Heated newspaper correspondence on the subject followed. The best letter was from another evolutionary biologist, Gabriel Dover, who wrote, "There are two classes of questions, natural and unnatural. Can science answer both of them? No, science cannot answer the question why Dr. Dawkins is unnaturally drawn to theology like a moth to the flame. Only theology can answer that, and it has a lot to answer for."

The inaugural Starbridge lecture was given by Fraser Watts, a cognitive psychologist, about the bigotry with which the scientific community tends to regard the religious side of human life.

I recommend Susan Howatch's Church of England novels to anyone who can find them, whether in an airport bookstand or elsewhere.

Chapter 10: The Beginning of Reason
The quotation by Douglas Futuyma is from his college textbook *Evolutionary Biology,* 2nd ed. (Sunderland, 1986) p. 3.

Martin Gardner's novel of ideas *The Flight of Peter Fromm* (William Kaufmann, 1973) is happily back in print (Prometheus, 1994). I reviewed it in 1993 for a newsletter for theology students. Since the newsletter medium is perishable in the extreme, I include here my brief review of this neglected masterpiece by America's greatest living skeptic:

In 1992 I accepted an invitation to speak about Darwinism at Pacific Union College and Preparatory School, a Seventh-Day Adventist institution in the beautiful wine country of Northern California. As so often happens on these speaking trips, my wife Kathie and I met a number of fascinating people and learned something about a denomination with which we had previously had little contact. The most important legacy of the visit, however, was a book recommended to me by Eric Anderson, a Professor of History. Eric told me about Martin Gardner, a famous science writer and skeptic with a gift for explaining theology, and about Gardner's metaphysical novel *The Flight of Peter Fromm*. As soon as I got home, I ordered the book from the Berkeley library.

The book tells the story of a young Christian Pentecostal fundamentalist, Peter Fromm, who enrolls in the University of Chicago Divinity School because he plans to convert the world and wants to start with the toughest audience. At Chicago Peter falls under the influence of a divinity school professor and Unitarian minister named Homer Wilson, who sets out to convert Peter step-by-step to his own agnostic liberalism. Homer's arguments are smoothly persuasive, and as Peter succumbs to them he goes through one phase after another: a flirtation with Roman Catholicism, close encounters with Marx and Freud, intellectual immersion in the theologies of Barth, Bultmann, Niebuhr and Tillich, and finally a disastrous apprenticeship with a worldly minister whose character is based upon Norman Vincent Peale. In the end Homer does not get Peter's soul, however; Peter somehow hangs on to a corner of his faith and asserts his own spiritual integrity at the cost of a mental breakdown in hilarious circumstances.

The Flight of Peter Fromm has believable characters and dialogue, and a plot that contains enough drama and farce to be thoroughly enjoyable. The book's greatest distinction, however, is its brilliant portrayal of the theological issues as seen through the eyes of both the sophisticated Homer and the initially innocent and increasingly confused Peter. Both men agree with each other and with Paul (not to mention me) that the critical issue is whether Christ really rose from the dead, and both share a determination not to put up with the efforts of so many modern theologians and clergy to avoid committing themselves on whether the Resurrection really happened.

I happened to have Martin Gardner's address because he had dealings with a mutual friend, and I wrote to Gardner to congratulate him on the book and particularly on the character of Homer Wilson, whom I described as a "plausible Mephistopheles." Gardner was naturally pleased at the praise of his unjustly neglected novel, and impressed that I had not made the (apparently common) mistake of thinking Homer to be the hero. Gardner identifies more with Peter than with Homer, although he is very different from either of his characters. He is a professional skeptic with a naturalistic worldview who classifies himself as a "theist outside all traditional religions," and who half-believes in petitionary prayer and personal immortality. You figure it out.

I ended up buying the dozen or so copies of the book that Gardner still had in his possession, so that Kathie and I could give copies to our seminary student friends. Gardner was puzzled that I wanted the books for that purpose, but I wrote him that I consider it a matter of "spiritual inoculation," to make sure that our future ministers know every step on the well-worn theological path that leads by degrees from faith to unbelief. We do not fear that those who see where that path leads will want to set out that way. Whatever intellectual deficiencies there may have been in Peter's childhood faith, Gardner's Mephistopheles can offer only fraudulent substitutes: Marxism, Freudianism, or a liberal religion that rests upon a deceptive use of words. Even the sophistication is bogus, because it rests upon an unexamined belief that scientific investigation has validated a naturalistic worldview that makes the Resurrection an absurdity. If Peter and Homer had really understood science, and had understood how the evidence has been distorted in the service of naturalistic philosophy, it would have been Homer Wilson who would have had to take flight.

Appendix: Naturalism, Methodological and Otherwise

William Hasker is a philosophy professor at Huntington College, a former editor of the *Christian Scholar's Review (CSR)* and a leading defender in Christian academic circles of theistic evolution and methodological naturalism in science. His first review of *Darwin on Trial,* "Mr. Johnson for the Prosecution," appeared in the December 1992 issue of the *CSR* (vol. 22, p. 177); my response and his reply to the response appeared in the same volume at p. 297. His second review, in 1995, was in press (with my further response) when this footnote was written. The second review took up certain matters raised by the epilogue that I added to *Darwin on Trial* in the softcover edition (InterVarsity Press, 1993) to reply to various critics, including Hasker. Hasker is not a participant in my e-mail discussion group and was not the professor who sparked this paper by attributing a "bias" to me. I quoted him because at the time I had just written my response to his second book review, and his words were fresh in my mind.

The Van Till quotation is from "God and Evolution: An Exchange," in *Man and Creation: Perspectives on Science and Theology,* ed. Michael Bauman (Hillsdale, 1993), p. 269. Van Till was responding to an article by me that appeared in the January 1993 issue of *First Things.* His rebuttal and my reply appeared originally in the June/July 1993 issue of *First Things* and were reprinted in the Hillsdale collection.

My evolution e-mail discussion group no longer exists, but persons interested in the kind of thinking it encouraged can read books written by several participants.

Darwin's Black Box, by Michael Behe, professor of biochemistry at Lehigh University, has been accepted for publication by Free Press and should appear during 1996. The "black box" is the incredible complexity of biological structures at the molecular level. Behe explains why Darwinian selection is not a convincing explanation for the mechanisms of the cell, and he sets out the scientific grounds for concluding that the cell was intelligently designed.

The Biotic Message, by Walter ReMine, is available from St. Paul Science, P.O. Box 28006, St. Paul, MN 55128. Price is $44.95, plus applicable sales tax, which includes shipping within the United States. ReMine puts forward the daring theory that life was designed not only for survival but to convey the "biotic message" that living organisms are "the product of a single designer and not of any naturalistic evolutionary process." Whether or not readers are convinced by ReMine's theory, they will find that the book contains fascinating and revealing discussions of the major problems of evolutionary theory.

The Darwin Conspiracy, by James Scott Bell (Vision House, 1995), is a hilarious satirical novel about how a fiendishly devious Sir Max Busby promoted Darwinism as the new world religion. Darwinists will be outraged.

The Creation Hypothesis (InterVarsity Press, 1994) is a collection of essays edited by J. P. Moreland. Among the contributors are several persons who participated in the e-mail discussion group, including Moreland himself, Stephen C. Meyer, William A. Dembski, Walter L. Bradley and Kurt Wise. Meyer and Dembski, along with Paul Nelson, have a book in progress on the legitimacy of considering intelligent design in biology. *The Creation Hypothesis* received a remarkably respectful review in *Creation/Evolution,* a strongly anticreationist journal. Reviewer Arthur Shapiro, professor of zoology at the Davis campus of the University of California, concluded with this paragraph:

I can see *Science* in the year 2000 running a major feature article on the spread of theistic science as a parallel scientific culture. I can see interviews with the leading figures in history and philosophy of science about how and why this happened. For the moment, the authors of *The Creation Hypothesis* are realistically defensive. They know their way of looking at the world will not be generally accepted and that they will be restricted for a while to their own journals. They also know that they will be under intense pressure to demonstrate respectability by weeding out crackpots, kooks and purveyors of young-earth snake oil. If they are successful, the day will come when the editorial board of *Science* will convene in emergency session to decide what to do about a paper which is of the highest quality and utterly unexceptionable, of great and broad interest, and which proceeds from the prior assumption of intelligent design. For a preview of that crisis, you should read this book. Of course, if you are smug enough to think "theistic science" is an oxymoron, you won't.

Index

A
abortion *20, 22, 41, 135-45, 162, 182, 184, 232*
Ackerman, Bruce *155-59, 233*
American Civil Liberties Union *99, 223*
Anderson, Eric *237*
Appleyard, Brian *225*

B
Barbour, Ian *97*
Behe, Michael *213, 238*
Bell, James Scott *239*
Biden, Joseph *133-36, 232*
big bang *53-59, 94, 102-4, 111, 196, 225*
Bishop, Phillip *173-82, 186, 187, 235*
Bishop v. *Aronov 180-82, 186, 235*
Blackstone, William *138*
blind watchmaker thesis *14-15, 75-88;* definition *15*
Bloom, Allan *113*
Bork, Robert *133, 134, 232*

Bradley, Walter A. *239*
Brennan, Justice William *25, 27, 220*
Buckley, William F. *167*
Buell, Jon *212*
Bush, George *133*

C
California State Board of Education *43, 224*
Cambrian explosion *87, 217, 228*
Carper, James *185-87, 236*
Chadwick, Douglas H. *227*
Clouser, Roy A. *224*
Constitution, U.S. *9, 33, 34, 99, 100, 133, 134, 140, 177, 178, 221*
Cornelius v. *NAACP Legal Defense and Education Fund 219*
creation: definition as used in book *12-15*
Crick, Francis *63-67, 76, 96, 125-27, 207, 226, 227, 231*
Cronin, Helena *84, 227*
culture war *13, 112, 116, 183, 184*

Cuvier, Georges *228*

D

D'Souza, Dinesh *113*

Darwin, Charles *14, 71, 72, 85, 144, 188, 194, 195, 198, 217, 233*

Darwin on Trial 11, 15, 31, 74, 97, 168, 190, 205, 220, 228, 230, 238

Darwinian selection *16, 61, 62, 64, 107*

Darwinism *11-16, 83-88, 105-7*

Darwin's finches *71-75*

Davies, Paul *58, 207, 226*

Dawkins, Richard *14, 75-88, 90, 96, 207, 209, 213, 215, 227, 236*

Degler, Carl *233*

Dembski, William A. *239*

Dennett, Daniel *227*

Derrida, Jacques *115*

Dewey, John *117-19, 123*

Dobson, James, and the Dobson film series *19-23, 28, 30, 32, 42, 186, 219*

Dobson, Shirley *20, 32*

Dobzhansky, Theodosius *75*

Dover, Gabriel *236*

Duke University *167-69*

E

education, public *22, 36, 42-44, 149, 153, 155-71, 185-16, 233, 234*

Edwards v. *Aguillard 25-27, 30, 32, 177, 220*

Eger, Martin *163, 165, 166, 233, 234*

Einstein, Albert *59, 60, 94*

Eliot, T. S. *118*

evolution: *see* especially introduction, chaps. 1, 2, 4, 10 and appendix; empirical *86, 87;* meaning of evolution *8-17;* neutral *87*

F

final theory. *See* Grand Unified Theory

First Amendment *20, 27, 33, 34, 176, 177, 220, 221*

fossil record *82, 83, 86-88, 106, 210, 216*

Freud, Sigmund *63, 118, 194, 195, 237*

Futuyma, Douglas *9, 75, 195, 207, 213, 219, 239*

G

Gardner, Martin *202, 236-38*

General Theory of Relativity *53, 54*

Gibbons, Ann *229*

Gibson, Floyd *176, 180-82*

God of the gaps *70, 98, 105, 202, 206, 208, 211*

Goldschmidt, Richard *213*

Gould, Stephen Jay *11, 31, 75, 84-88, 90, 96, 127, 207, 213, 215, 220, 227, 228*

Granberg, Michael *222*

Grand Unified Theory (final theory, theory of everything) *38, 52-59, 66-70*

Grant, Peter and Rosemary *71-73*

Grassé, Pierre *213*

H

Hasker, William *206, 207, 238*

Hawking, Jane *225, 227*

Hawking, Stephen *51-63, 66, 96, 102, 207, 225, 227, 230, 231*

Hearn, Virginia *212*

Hegel, G. W. F. *119, 123*

Heidegger, Martin *119, 123*

Higgs, Peter (and Higgs particle) *55, 104, 229*

Hobbes, Thomas *40*
Holmes, Oliver Wendell, Jr. *139-43,
   147, 148, 152, 233*
Howatch, Susan *236*
Hull, David *11*
Hume, David *40, 123, 198*
Hunter, James Davison *182-84,
   187*
Hutchins, Robert *169*
Huxley, Julian *71, 75, 213*
Huxley, T. H. *144*

I
intelligent design *29, 30, 82, 90-92,
   99, 178, 208-10, 213, 238-39*

J
Jefferson, Thomas *198, 221*
Johanson, Donald *68, 207*
John Paul II, Pope *122*

K
Kauffmann, Stuart *213, 215*
Kennedy, John F. *41*
Kennedy, Justice Anthony *220*
Kenyon, Dean *29, 30, 178, 220*
Kilpatrick, William *159-61, 163,
   233*
Kitcher, Philip *165, 234*
Kornberg, Arthur *65, 226*
Kuhn, Thomas *116*

L
Lakatos, Imre *229, 230*
Lamb's Chapel v. *Center Moriches
   School District 21-30, 100, 219*
Leff, Arthur *147, 156, 233*
Lemon v. *Kurtzman* (and the Lemon
   test) *220*
liberal rationalism *37, 38, 40-42, 155,
   166, 181*

Liebling, A. J. *232*
Lindley, David *55, 58, 226*
Locke, John *40*
Los Angeles Times 44, 222, 224

M
McConnell, Michael *187, 235*
Maddox, John *236*
marginalization *21-29, 43, 44, 199*
Marsden, George *166-70, 186, 234,
   235*
Marxism *145, 146, 200, 238*
Mayr, Ernst *75*
Mercer, Jerry *193*
metaphysical naturalism *76, 90, 96,
   109, 122, 170, 190, 205-7, 212, 224;*
   definition *16-17*
metaphysical realism *114-16, 122,
   124, 128, 129*
methodological naturalism *17, 206,
   207, 212, 218, 238*
Meyer, Stephen C. *220, 239*
microevolution *15, 74, 213, 230*
Mill, John Stuart *40, 163, 164*
Miller, Kenneth R. *228*
modernism *42, 44-48, 70, 146,
   162, 195, 203, 230;* definition *37*
Monod, Jacques *75, 209*
Moreland, J. P. *231, 239*
Mosk, Justice Stanley *232, 233*
Murphy, Nancey *97-102, 109, 191,
   229, 230*

N
National Academy of Sciences *27,
   33, 76, 106, 189-91, 198, 207*
natural law *17, 92, 133-48, 169, 232*
natural selection *11, 13-15, 61, 69,
   72, 76-89, 106, 144, 174, 188, 195,
   209, 230, 233*
naturalism/naturalist: definitions *7-*

10, 16, 37, 38
Nelson, Paul *214, 228, 239*
Newton, Isaac *60, 75, 230*
Niebuhr, H. Richard *235*
Niebuhr, Reinhold *235, 237*
Nietzsche, Friedrich *194, 195, 198*
Numbers, Ronald *44*

O
origin of life *29, 68-70, 93, 106, 107, 200, 210, 227*
origins (including human, biological, ultimate) *9, 16, 26, 67, 204, 224*

P
particle physics *55, 66, 101*
Payne, Robert *122*
Peacocke, Arthur *97, 101, 109*
Pearcey, Nancy R. *231*
Penrose, Roger *53, 54, 56, 228, 229*
People v. *Davis 232*
peppered moth *73, 217*
philosophy: *see* especially chap. 2
physics *51-61, 91, 101, 104, 105, 126, 127, 226*
Planned Parenthood v. *Casey 136*
Polanyi, Michael *231*
Polkinghorne, John *225, 226, 229, 230*
Popper, Karl *229*
Posner, Richard *143, 233*
postmodernism/postmodernist *112, 119, 124, 167, 169, 183*
pragmatism *115, 117, 128-30, 169, 170, 196*
Provine, William *187-91, 235, 236*

R
rationality *8, 10, 32, 33, 39, 46, 65, 88, 111-31, 164, 170, 183, 195-97, 199, 200, 203, 224, 231, 233, 234*

reductionism *64, 65, 125-29*
relativism *17, 36, 114-16, 120, 121, 121, 123, 130, 142, 152, 160, 166, 169, 171, 181, 183, 232*
religion: *see* especially *19-39;* definition *35*
ReMine, Walter *239*
Roe v. *Wade 136, 137, 142, 184*
Rorty, Richard *17, 116-25, 130, 183, 232*
Ruse, Michael *11*

S
Sagan, Carl *59, 76, 96, 207, 225, 227*
Scalia, Justice Antonin *220*
Schaefer, Henry F. *179, 235*
Schindewolf, Otto *213*
Searle, John *17, 112-17, 122, 125, 127-29, 231, 232*
Sears, James *185-87, 236*
sexual morality *22, 23, 31, 36, 123, 139, 152, 163, 187*
Shapiro, Arthur *239*
Simpson, George Gaylord *8, 75, 213, 219*
Sloan, Douglas *234, 235*
Smith, Adam *40, 227*
Smith, John Maynard *227*
Supreme Court *20, 21, 23-28, 32-34, 42, 133-45, 175, 178, 184, 187, 219-21, 232, 235;* cases, *see Cornelius* v. *NAACP Legal Defense and Education Fund; Bishop* v. *Arnov; Edwards* v. *Aguillard; Lamb's Chapel* v. *Center Moriches School District; Lemon* v. *Kurtzman; People* v. *Davis; Planned Parenthood* v. *Casey; Roe* v. *Wade*

T
Thaxton, Charles B. *231, 234*

theism/theists 9, 10, 16, 17, 33, 40,
    45, 47-49, 90, 97-101, 105-10, 128,
    170, 192, 194-98, 201-6, 208-16,
    236; definition 7
theistic naturalism 97-101
theistic realism 48-50, 107
theology 14, 36, 90, 97-105, 109, 111,
    176, 191, 201, 225, 228-30, 236, 238
theory of everything. See Grand
    Unified Theory
Thomas, Clarence 133-36, 220, 232
Thorne, Alan G. 229
Tillich, Paul 235, 237
Tocqueville, Alexis de 42, 221, 222
Tribe, Laurence 134, 232
Trotsky, Leon 117, 118, 120-22, 129,
    232
truth 62, 73, 77, 98, 110, 112-16, 119,
    129, 131, 150, 163, 164, 166, 169,
    183, 194-204, 207, 225, 229
Tyrrell, George 230

U
University of Chicago 118, 169, 188

V
van der Meer, J. M. 228

Van Till, Howard 216, 238
Veritas Forum 193, 194, 196, 198
Vista District School Board 43, 44,
    222-24

W
Watts, Fraser 236
Weinberg, Stephen 11, 91-96, 99,
    126, 207, 228, 229
Weiner, Jonathan 71-73, 226, 227
Wells, Jonathan 214
Westerfield, Carl 174, 175, 182
White, Justice Byron 21, 219, 220
Whitehead, Alfred North 195
Whitehead, Barbara Dafoe 233
Wilder-Smith, A. E. 213
Willard, Dallas 171
Wise, Kurt 239
Wolpoff, Milford 229
Wright, Robert 191

Y
Yockey, Hubert 213